Excerpts from The Grea

"Jesus had an unerring ability for the recognition of truth, and truth he never hesitated to embrace, no matter from what source it appeared to emanate."

"Jesus chose to establish the kingdom of heaven in the hearts of mankind by natural, ordinary, difficult, and trying methods, just such procedures as his earth children must subsequently follow in their work of enlarging and extending that heavenly kingdom."

"One purpose which Jesus had in mind, when he sought to segregate certain features of his earthly experience, was to prevent the building up of such a versatile and spectacular career as would cause subsequent generations to venerate the teacher in place of obeying the truth which he had lived and taught. Jesus did not want to build up such a human record of achievement as would attract attention *from his teaching*. Very early he recognized that his followers would be tempted to formulate a religion *about* him that might become a competitor of the gospel of the kingdom that he intended to proclaim to the world. Accordingly, he consistently sought to suppress everything during his eventful career that he thought might be made to serve this natural human tendency to exalt the teacher in place of proclaiming his teachings. Even when he permitted the manifestation of numerous time-shortening ministrations of mercy, he almost invariably admonished the recipients of his healing ministry to tell no man about the benefits they had received. And always did he refuse the taunting challenge of his enemies to "show us a sign" in proof and demonstration of his divinity."

"Man tends to crystallize science, formulate philosophy, and dogmatize truth because he is mentally lazy in adjusting to the progressive struggles of living, while he is also terribly afraid of the unknown. Natural man is slow to initiate changes in his habits of thinking and in his techniques of living."

Please turn page for more excerpts...

More excerpts

"If you are spiritually indolent and morally unprogressive, you may take as your standards of good the religious practices and traditions of your contemporaries." But, "The spiritually blind individual who logically follows scientific dictation, social usage, and religious dogma stands in grave danger of sacrificing his moral freedom and losing his spiritual liberty. Such a soul is destined to become an intellectual parrot, a social automaton, and a slave to religious authority."

"The Father in heaven treats the Spirit Mother of the children of the universe as one equal to Himself. It is Godlike to share your life and all that relates thereto on equal terms with the mother partner who so fully shares with you that divine experience of reproducing yourselves in the lives of your children. If you can only love your children as God loves you, you will love and cherish your wife as the Father in heaven honors and exalts the Infinite Spirit, the mother of all the spirit children of a vast universe."

"If different religions recognize the spirit sovereignty of God the Father, then will all such religions remain at peace. Only when one religion assumes that it is in some way superior to all others, and that it possesses exclusive authority over other religions, will such a religion presume to be intolerant of other religions or dare to persecute other religious believers."

"Religious peace; brotherhood, can never exist unless all religions are willing to completely divest themselves of all ecclesiastical authority and fully surrender all concept of spiritual sovereignty. God alone is spirit sovereign."

"You cannot have equality among religions (religious liberty) without having religious wars unless all religions consent to the transfer of all religious sovereignty to some superhuman level, to God Himself."

THE GREATEST STORY EVER REVEALED;

THE GOSPEL ACCORDING TO ANDREW

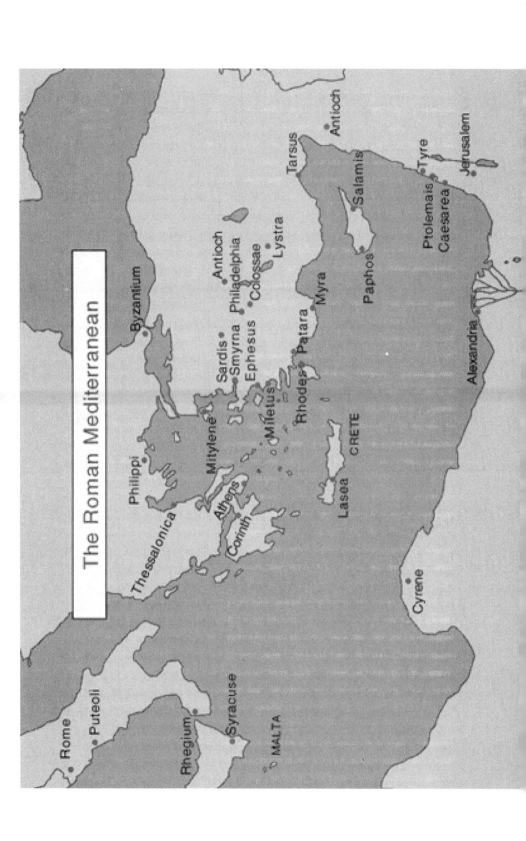

The Roman Mediterranean

THE GREATEST STORY EVER REVEALED;

THE GOSPEL ACCORDING TO ANDREW

Edited by Steve Hart

Hart-Burn Press, Inc
PO Box 99
Newton Jct, New Hampshire 03859

First Hart-Burn Press Edition, January 2004
FIRST EDITION

10 9 8 7 6 5 4 3 2 1

Published in 2004 in the United States by
Hart-Burn Press, Inc., PO Box 99,
Newton Jct., New Hampshire 03859

www.stevehartbooks.com

Hart-Burn ISBN 0-9740318-2-8

Cataloging in Publication Data:
    Hart, Steve
    The Greatest Story Ever Revealed;
    The Gospel According to Andrew-1st ed. p.224 cm.
    1-Christianity
    2- Christianity- origin
    3-Bible N.T.- criticism, interpretation, etc.

ATTENTION CORPORATIONS, UNIVERSITIES, COLLEGES,
AND PROFESSIONAL ORGANIZATIONS:

Quantity discounts are available on bulk purchases of this book for educational, gift purposes, or as
premiums for increasing magazine subscriptions or renewals.

For information contact info@stevehartbooks.com

For all of us

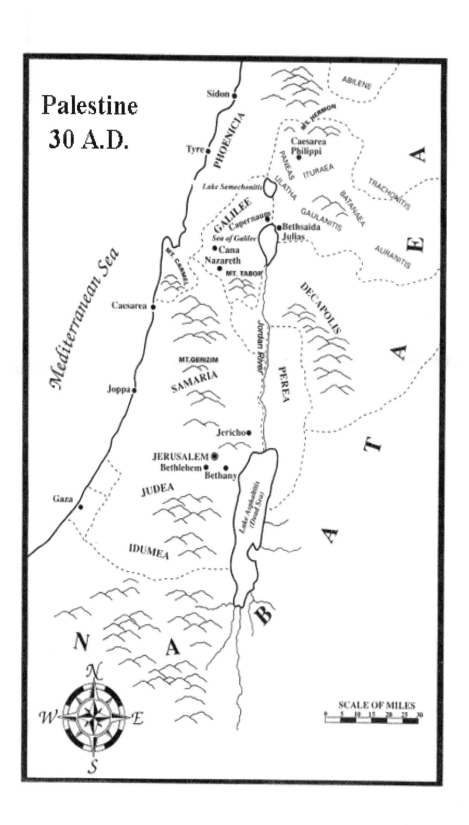

"The Father does not limit the revelation of truth to any one generation or to any one people."

-- Jesus to Nathaniel.

Note From the Editor

The time is ripe for a figurative resurrection of the human Jesus from his burial tomb amidst the theological traditions and religious dogmas of two thousand years. Jesus of Nazareth must no longer be sacrificed to even the splendid concept of the glorified Christ.

What a transcendent service if, through this revelation, the Son of Man should be recovered from the tomb of traditional theology and be presented as the living Jesus of the church that bears his name, and to all other religions!

Indeed, the social readjustments, the economic transformations, the moral rejuvenations, and the religious revisions of Christian civilization would be drastic and revolutionary if the living religion of Jesus should suddenly supplant the theologic religion about Jesus.

Do not be afraid of the religion of Jesus. As you read the story of his life you will find him to be the most understanding, compassionate, wise, and practical of men. If his followers had but the understanding to see his life as the truly wonderful inspiration it is and had not become so fixated upon his death, resurrection, and time miracles, what a different world we would find ourselves in today.

Do not be afraid of the religion of Jesus because you feel you are not ready to be as good as some day you want to be, or because you believe it will make too great demands upon you. Do not think you will be led to unhappy sacrifice and unacceptable asceticism. The religion of Jesus- the Fatherhood of God/the brotherhood of all mankind - will provide you with the most joyous and rewarding life possible. The teachings of the Master will make of you a better man or woman, a better companion, a more faithful and better friend, husband, wife, parent, son or daughter, and a more loyal and courageous citizen of earth. This I promise you.

You will find in this revelation of the life of Jesus new and deeper understanding of his mission, his challenges, his humanity, and his ultimate glorious success. Given the condition of the world as we find it today, some would think that his mission of bringing all under the protective umbrella of brotherhood has failed. But such unthinking individuals must understand that significant changes take time. Two thousand years is but an eyeblink in eternity. The religion of Jesus, buried these past centuries beneath the theologic stones of the religion about Jesus will some day arise from the grave and shine forth with radiance to embrace every individual on the planet. The challenge for us is to begin removing these burial stones, to help the process, and to so live our lives as to inspire our brothers and sisters to do likewise. My fervent hope is that by bringing this revelation to fuller light, I have helped in some small way.

Sincerely,

Steve Hart

CONTENTS

PART ONE

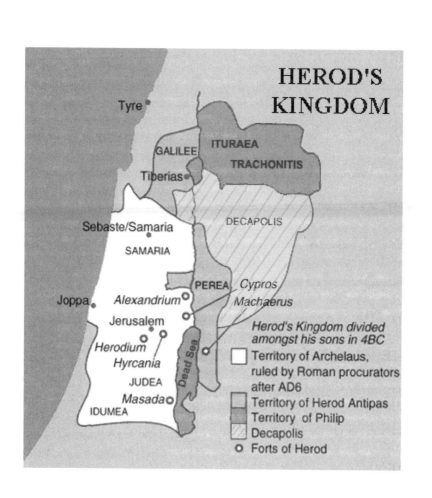

HEROD'S KINGDOM

Tyre

GALILEE
ITURAEA
TRACHONITIS
Tiberias

Sebaste/Samaria
SAMARIA

DECAPOLIS

PEREA Cypros
Machaerus

Joppa
Alexandrium

Jerusalem
Herodium
Hyrcania
JUDEA
Masada
IDUMEA

Dead Sea

Herod's Kingdom divided
amongst his sons in 4BC
☐ Territory of Archelaus,
ruled by Roman procurators
after AD6
Territory of Herod Antipas
Territory of Philip
Decapolis
o Forts of Herod

FOREWORD

WHILE THEIR Master still walked the earth, the disciples wrote little, mirroring the actions of Jesus, who wrote only upon sand after the time of his baptism by John. After he left this world they resisted the temptation to distill his life into written words. Only in later years did it seem wise to create such gospels for the enlightenment of future generations. The Gospels by young Mark and Luke, and the Gospel's of Matthew and John are four honest efforts to portray his life.

These New Testament records had their origin in the following circumstances:

1. *The Gospel by Mark*. John Mark wrote the earliest (excepting a set of notes written by Andrew), briefest, and most simple record of Jesus' life. The young camp follower presented the Master as a minister, as man among men. Although Mark was a lad lingering about many of the scenes which he depicts, his record is in reality the Gospel according to Simon Peter. He was early associated with Peter; later with Paul. Mark wrote this record at the instigation of Peter and on the earnest petition of the church at Rome. Knowing how consistently the Master refused to write out his teachings when on earth and in the flesh, Mark, like the apostles and other leading disciples, was hesitant to put them in writing. But Peter felt the church at Rome required the assistance of such a written narrative, and Mark consented to undertake its preparation. He made many notes before Peter died in A.D. 67, and in accordance with the outline approved by Peter and for the church at Rome, he began his writing soon after Peter's death. The Gospel was completed near the end of A.D. 68. Mark wrote entirely from his own memory and Peter's memory. The record has since been considerably changed, numerous passages having been taken out and some later matter added at the end

to replace the latter one fifth of the original Gospel, which was lost from the first manuscript before it was ever copied. This record by Mark, in conjunction with Andrew's and Matthew's notes, was the written basis of all subsequent Gospel narratives which sought to portray the life and teachings of Jesus.

2. *The Gospel of Matthew.* The so-called Gospel according to Matthew is the record of the Master's life which was written for the edification of Jewish Christians. The author of this record constantly seeks to show in Jesus' life that much of which he did was that "it might be fulfilled which was spoken by the prophet." Matthew's Gospel portrays Jesus as a son of David, picturing him as showing great respect for the law and the prophets.

The Apostle Matthew did not write this Gospel. It was written by Isador, one of his disciples, who had as a help in his work not only Matthew's personal remembrance of these events but also a certain record which the latter had made of the sayings of Jesus directly after the crucifixion. This record by Matthew was written in Aramaic; Isador wrote in Greek. There was no intent to deceive in accrediting the production to Matthew. It was the custom in those days for pupils thus to honor their teachers.

Matthew's original record was edited and added to in A.D. 40 just before he left Jerusalem to engage in evangelistic preaching. It was a private record, the last copy having been destroyed in the burning of a Syrian monastery in A.D. 416.

Isador escaped from Jerusalem in A.D. 70 after the investment of the city by the armies of Titus, taking with him to Pella a copy of Matthew's notes. In the year 71, while living at Pella, Isador wrote the Gospel according to Matthew. He also had with him the first four fifths of Mark's narrative.

3. *The Gospel by Luke.* Luke, the physician of Antioch in Pisidia, was a gentile convert of Paul, and he wrote quite a different story of the Master's life. He began to follow Paul and learn of the life and teachings of Jesus in A.D. 47. Luke preserves much of the "grace of the Lord Jesus Christ" in his record as he gathered up these facts from Paul and others. Luke presents the Master as "the friend of publicans and sinners." He did not formulate his many notes into the Gospel until after Paul's death. Luke wrote in the year 82 in Achaia. He planned three books dealing with the history of Christ and Christianity but died in A.D. 90 just before he finished the second of these works, the "Acts of the Apostles."

As material for the compilation of his Gospel, Luke first depended upon the story of Jesus' life as Paul had related it to him. Luke's Gospel is, therefore, in some ways the Gospel according to Paul. But Luke had other sources of information. He not only interviewed scores of eyewitnesses to the numerous episodes of Jesus' life which he records, but he also had with him a copy of Mark's Gospel, that is, the first four fifths, Isador's narrative, and a brief record made in the year A.D. 78 at Antioch by a believer named Cedes. Luke also had a mutilated and much edited copy of some notes purported to have been made by the Apostle Andrew.

4. The Gospel of John. The Gospel according to John relates much of Jesus' work in Judea and around Jerusalem which is not contained in the other records. This is the so-called Gospel according to John the son of Zebedee, and though John did not write it, he did inspire it. Since its first writing it has several times been edited to make it appear to have beenwritten by John himself. When this record was made, John had the other Gospels, and he saw that much had been omitted; accordingly, in the year A.D. 101 he encouraged his associate, Nathan, a Greek Jew from Caesarea, to begin the writing. John supplied his material from memory and by reference to the three records already in existence. He had no written records of his own. The Epistle known as "First John" was written by John himself as a covering letter for the work which Nathan ex ecutedunderhisdirection.

All these writers presented honest pictures of Jesus as they saw, remembered, or had learned of him, and as their concepts of these distant events were affected by their subsequent espousal of Paul's theology of Christianity. And these records, imperfect as they are, have been sufficient to change the course of the history of Earth for almost two thousand years.

The group of papers comprising the following revelation was sponsored by a commission of twelve acting under the supervision of a Melchizedek revelatory director. The basis of this narrative was supplied by a member of the angelic corps who was once assigned to the superhuman watchcare of the Apostle Andrew. This narrative shall be presented in English and in the common idiom of the twenty-first century. We shall start at the beginning.

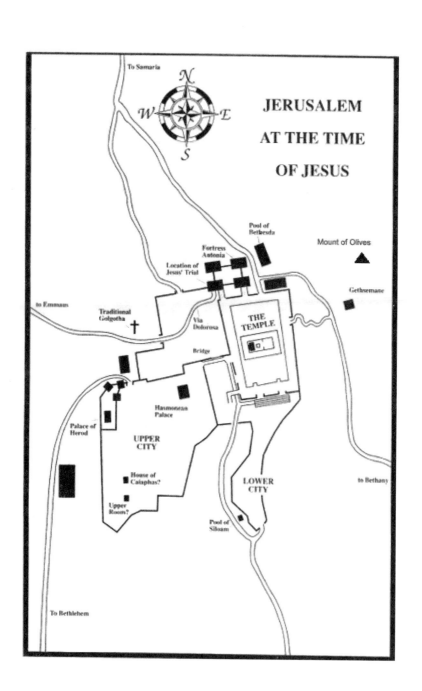

To Samaria

N
W E
S

JERUSALEM

AT THE TIME

OF JESUS

Pool of
Bethesda

Mount of Olives

Fortress
Antonia

Location of
Jesus' Trial

to Emmaus

Gethsemane

Traditional
Golgotha

Via
Dolorosa

THE
TEMPLE

Bridge

Hasmonean
Palace

Palace of
Herod

UPPER
CITY

to Bethany

House of
Caiaphas?

LOWER
CITY

Upper
Room?

Pool of
Siloam

To Bethlehem

THE GREATEST STORY EVER REVEALED;

THE GOSPEL ACCORDING TO ANDREW

"Pure religion and undefiled before God is this, To visit the fatherless and wodiws in their affliction, and to keep himself unspotted from the world"

-- James, 1, 27

★ ★ ★

PART ONE
THE EARLY YEARS

Welcome, all wonders in one sight!

Eternity shut in a span!

Summer in Winter, Day in Night!

Heaven in earth, and God in man!

Great little one! whose all-embracing birth

Lifts Earth to Heaven, and stoops Heaven to Earth.

-Richard Crashaw

BIRTH AND INFANCY OF JESUS

IT WILL hardly be possible fully to explain the many reasons which led to the selection of Palestine as the land for Michael's bestowal, and especially as to just why the family of Joseph and Mary should have been chosen as the immediate setting for the appearance of this Son of God on Earth.

After a study of the special report on the status of segregated worlds prepared by the Melchizedeks, in counsel with Gabriel, Michael finally chose Earth as the planet whereon to enact his final bestowal. Subsequent to this decision Gabriel made a personal visit to your world, and, as a result of his study of human groups and his survey of the spiritual, intellectual, racial, and geographic features of the world and its peoples, he decided that the Hebrews possessed those relative advantages which warranted their selection as the bestowal race. Upon Michael's approval of this decision, Gabriel appointed and dispatched to Earth the Family Commission of Twelve - selected from among the higher orders of universe personalities - which was intrusted with the task of making an investigation of Jewish family life. When this commission ended its labors, Gabriel was present on Earth and received the report nominating three prospective unions as being, in the opinion of the commission, equally favorable as bestowal families for Michael's projected incarnation.

From the three couples nominated, Gabriel made the personal choice of Joseph and Mary, subsequently making his personal appearance to Mary, at which time he imparted to her the glad tidings that she had been selected to become the earth mother of the bestowal child.

Joseph the human father of Jesus (Joshua ben Joseph), was a Hebrew of the Hebrews, albeit he carried many non-Jewish racial strains which had been added to his ancestral tree from time to time by the female lines of his progenitors. The ancestry of the father of Jesus went back to the days of Abraham and through this venerable patriarch to the earlier lines of inheritance leading to the Sumerians and Nodites and, through the southern tribes of the ancient blue man, to Andon and Fonta, the first humans. David and Solomon were not in the direct line of Joseph's ancestry, neither did Joseph's lineage go directly back to the planetary Adam. Joseph's immediate ancestors were mechanics - builders, carpenters, masons, and smiths. Joseph himself was a carpenter and later a contractor. His family belonged to a long and illustrious line of the nobility of the common people, accentuated in some generations by the appearance of unusual individuals who had distinguished themselves in connection with the evolution of religion on Earth.

Mary, the earth mother of Jesus, was a descendant of a long line of unique ancestors embracing many of the most remarkable women in the racial history of Earth. Although Mary was an average woman of her day and generation, possessing a fairly normal temperament, she reckoned among her ancestors such well-known women as Annon, Tamar, Ruth, Bathsheba, Ansie, Cloa, Eve, Enta, and Ratta. No Jewish woman of that day had a more illustrious lineage of common progenitors or one extending back to more auspicious beginnings. Mary's ancestry, like Joseph's, was characterized by the predominance of strong but average individuals, relieved now and then by numerous outstanding personalities in the march of civilization and the progressive evolution of religion. Racially considered, it is hardly proper to regard Mary as a Jewess. In culture and belief she was a Jew, but in hereditary endowment she was more a composite of Syrian, Hittite, Phoenician, Greek, and Egyptian stocks, her racial inheritance being more general than that of Joseph.

Of all couples living in Palestine at about the time of Michael's projected bestowal, Joseph and Mary possessed the most ideal combination of widespread racial connections and superior average of personality endowments. It was the plan of Michael to appear on earth as an *average* man, that the common people might understand him and receive him; wherefore Gabriel selected just such persons as Joseph and Mary to become the bestowal parents.

Jesus' lifework on Earth was really begun by John the Baptist. Zacharias, John's father, belonged to the Jewish priesthood, while his mother, Elizabeth, was a member of the more prosperous branch of the same large family group to which Mary the mother of Jesus also belonged. Zacharias and Elizabeth, though they had been married many years, were childless.

It was late in the month of June, 8 B.C., about three months after the marriage of Joseph and Mary, that Gabriel appeared to Elizabeth at noontide one day, just as he later made his presence known to Mary.

Said Gabriel, "While your husband, Zacharias, stands before the altar in Jerusalem, and while the assembled people pray for the coming of a deliverer, I,

Gabriel, have come to announce that you will shortly bear a son who shall be the forerunner of this divine teacher, and you shall call your son John. He will grow up dedicated to the Lord your God, and when he has come to full years, he will gladden your heart because he will turn many souls to God, and he will also proclaim the coming of the soul-healer of your people and the spirit-liberator of all mankind. Your kinswoman Mary shall be the mother of this child of promise, and I will also appear to her."

This vision greatly frightened Elizabeth. After Gabriel's departure she turned this experience over in her mind, long pondering the sayings of the majestic visitor, but did not speak of the revelation to anyone save her husband until her subsequent visit with Mary in early February of the following year.

For five months, however, Elizabeth withheld her secret even from her husband. Upon her disclosure of the story of Gabriel's visit, Zacharias was very skeptical and for weeks doubted the entire experience, only consenting halfheartedly to believe in Gabriel's visit to his wife when he could no longer question that she was expectant with child. Zacharias was very much perplexed regarding the prospective motherhood of Elizabeth, but he did not doubt the integrity of his wife, notwithstanding his own advanced age. It was not until about six weeks before John's birth that Zacharias, as the result of an impressive dream, became fully convinced that Elizabeth was to become the mother of a son of destiny, one who was to prepare the way for the coming of the Messiah.

Gabriel appeared to Mary about the middle of November, 8 B.C., while she was at work in her Nazareth home. Later on, after Mary knew without doubt that she was to become a mother, she persuaded Joseph to let her journey to the City of Judah, four miles west of Jerusalem, in the hills, to visit Elizabeth. Gabriel had informed each of these mothers-to-be of his appearance to the other. Naturally they were anxious to get together, compare experiences, and talk over the probable futures of their sons. Mary remained with her distant cousin for three weeks. Elizabeth did much to strengthen Mary's faith in the vision of Gabriel, so that she returned home more fully dedicated to the call to mother the child of destiny whom she was so soon to present to the world as a helpless babe, an average and normal infant of the realm.

John was born in the City of Judah, March 25, 7 B.C. Zacharias and Elizabeth rejoiced greatly in the realization that a son had come to them as Gabriel had promised, and when on the eighth day they presented the child for circumcision, they formally christened him John, as they had been directed aforetime. Already had a nephew of Zacharias departed for Nazareth, carrying the message of Elizabeth to Mary proclaiming that a son had been born to her and that his name was to be John.

From his earliest infancy John was judiciously impressed by his parents with the idea that he was to grow up to become a spiritual leader and religious teacher. And the soil of John's heart was ever responsive to the sowing of such suggestive seeds. Even as a child he was found frequently at the temple during the seasons of his father's service, and he was tremendously impressed with the significance of all that he saw.

One evening about sundown, before Joseph had returned home, Gabriel appeared to Mary by the side of a low stone table and, after she had recovered her composure, said, "I come at the bidding of one who is my Master and whom you shall love and nurture. To you, Mary, I bring glad tidings when I announce that the conception within you is ordained by heaven, and that in due time you will become the mother of a son; you shall call him Joshua, and he shall inaugurate the kingdom of heaven on earth and among men. Speak not of this matter save to Joseph and to Elizabeth, your kinswoman, to whom I have also appeared, and who shall presently also bear a son, whose name shall be John, and who will prepare the way for the message of deliverance which your son shall proclaim to men with great power and deep conviction. And doubt not my word, Mary, for this home has been chosen as the mortal habitat of the child of destiny. My benediction rests upon you, the power of the Most Highs will strengthen you, and the Lord of all the earth shall overshadow you."

Mary pondered this visitation secretly in her heart for many weeks until of a certainty she knew she was with child, before she dared to disclose these unusual events to her husband. When Joseph heard all about this, although he had great confidence in Mary, he was much troubled and could not sleep for many nights. At first Joseph had doubts about the Gabriel visitation. Then when he became near to persuaded that Mary had really heard the voice and beheld the form of the divine messenger, he was torn in mind as he pondered how such things could be. How could the offspring of human beings be a child of divine destiny? Never could Joseph reconcile these conflicting ideas until, after several weeks of thought, both he and Mary reached the conclusion that they had been chosen to become the parents of the Messiah, though it had hardly been the Jewish concept that the expected deliverer was to be of divine nature. Upon arriving at this momentous conclusion, Mary hastened to depart for a visit with Elizabeth.

Upon her return, Mary went to visit her parents, Joachim and Hannah. Her two brothers and two sisters, as well as her parents, were always very sceptical about the divine mission of Jesus, though of course, they knew nothing of the Gabriel visitation. But Mary did confide to her sister Salome that she thought her son was destined to become a great teacher.

Gabriel's announcement to Mary was made the day following the conception of Jesus and was the only event of supernatural occurrence connected with her entire experience of carrying and bearing the child of promise.

✶ ✶ ✶

Joseph did not become reconciled to the idea that Mary was to become the mother of an extraordinary child until after he had experienced a very impressive dream. In this dream a brilliant celestial messenger appeared to him and, among other things, said, "Joseph, I appear by command of him who now reigns on high, and I am directed to instruct you concerning the son whom Mary shall bear, and who shall become a great light in the world. In him will be life, and his life shall become the light of mankind. He shall first come to his own people, but they will hardly receive him; but to as many as shall receive him to them will he reveal that they are the children of God." After this experience Joseph never again wholly doubted Mary's story of Gabriel's visit and of the promise that the unborn child was to become a divine messenger to the world.

In all these visitations nothing was said about the house of David. Nothing was ever intimated about Jesus' becoming a "deliverer of the Jews," not even that he was to be the long-expected Messiah. Jesus was not such a Messiah as the Jews had anticipated, but he was the *world's deliverer.* His mission was to all races and peoples, not to any one group.

Joseph was not of the line of King David. Mary had more of the Davidic ancestry than Joseph. True, Joseph did go to the City of David, Bethlehem, to be registered for the Roman census, but that was because, six generations previously, Joseph's paternal ancestor of that generation, being an orphan, was adopted by one Zadoc, who was a direct descendant of David; hence was Joseph also accounted as of the "house of David."

Most of the so-called Messianic prophecies of the Old Testament were made to apply to Jesus long after his life had been lived on earth. For centuries the Hebrew prophets had proclaimed the coming of a deliverer, and these promises had been construed by successive generations as referring to a new Jewish ruler who would sit upon the throne of David and, by the reputed miraculuos methods of Moses, proceed to establish the Jews in Palestine as a powerful nation, free from all foreign domination. Again, many figurative passages found throughout the Hebrew scriptures were subsequently misapplied to the life mission of Jesus. Many Old Testament sayings were so distorted as to appear to fit some episode of the Master's earth life. Jesus himself onetime publicly denied any connection with the royal house of David. Even the passage, "a maiden shall bear a son," was made to read, "a virgin shall bear a son." This was also true of the many genealogies of both Joseph and Mary which were constructed subsequent to Michael's career on Earth. The followers of Jesus all too often succumbed to the temptation to make all the olden prophetic utterances appear to find fulfillment in the life of their Lord and Master.

✶ ✶ ✶

Joseph was a mild-mannered man, extremely conscientious, and in every way faithful to the religious conventions and practices of his people. He talked little but thought much. The sorry plight of the Jewish people caused Joseph much sadness. As a youth, among his eight brothers and sisters, he had been more cheerful, but in the earlier years of married life (during Jesus' childhood) he was subject to periods of mild spiritual discouragement. These temperamental manifestations were greatly improved just before his untimely death and after the economic condition of his family had been enhanced by his advancement from the rank of carpenter to the role of a prosperous contractor.

Mary's temperament was quite opposite to that of her husband. She was usually cheerful, was very rarely downcast, and possessed an ever-sunny disposition. Mary indulged in free and frequent expression of her emotional feelings and was never observed to be sorrowful until after the sudden death of Joseph. And she had hardly recovered from this shock when she had thrust upon her the anxieties and questionings aroused by the extraordinary career of her eldest son, which was so rapidly unfolding before her astonished gaze. But throughout all this unusual experience Mary was composed, courageous, and fairly wise in her relationship with her strange and little-understood first-born son and his surviving brothers and sisters.

Jesus derived much of his unusual gentleness and marvelous sympathetic understanding of human nature from his father; he inherited his gift as a great teacher and his tremendous capacity for righteous indignation from his mother. In emotional reactions to his adult-life environment, Jesus was at one time like his father, meditative and worshipful, sometimes characterized by apparent sadness; but more often he drove forward in the manner of his mother's optimistic and determined disposition. All in all, Mary's temperament tended to dominate the career of the divine Son as he grew up and swung into the momentous strides of his adult life. In some particulars Jesus was a blending of his parents' traits; in other respects he exhibited the traits of one in contrast with those of the other.

From Joseph Jesus secured his strict training in the usages of the Jewish ceremonials and his unusual acquaintance with the Hebrew scriptures; from Mary he derived a broader viewpoint of religious life and a more liberal concept of personal spiritual freedom.

The families of both Joseph and Mary were well educated for their time. Joseph and Mary were educated far above the average for their day and station in life. He was a thinker; she was a planner, expert in adaptation and practical in immediate execution. Joseph was a black-eyed brunet; Mary, a brown-eyed well-nigh blond type.

Had Joseph lived, he undoubtedly would have become a firm believer in the divine mission of his eldest son. Mary alternated between believing and doubting, being greatly influenced by the position taken by her other children and by her friends and relatives, but always was she steadied in her final attitude by the memory of Gabriel's appearance to her immediately after the child was conceived.

Mary was an expert weaver and more than averagely skilled in most of the household arts of that day; she was a good housekeeper and a superior home-maker. Both Joseph and Mary were good teachers, and they saw to it that their children were well versed in the learning of that day.

When Joseph was a young man, he was employed by Mary's father in the work of building an addition to his house, and it was when Mary brought Joseph a cup of water, during a noontime meal, that the courtship of the pair who were destined to become the parents of Jesus really began.

Joseph and Mary were married, in accordance with Jewish custom, at Mary's home in the environs of Nazareth when Joseph was twenty-one years old. This marriage concluded a normal courtship of almost two years' duration. Shortly thereafter they moved into their new home in Nazareth, which had been built by Joseph with the assistance of two of his brothers. The house was located near the foot of the near-by elevated land which so charmingly overlooked the surrounding countryside. In this home, especially prepared, these young and expectant parents had thought to welcome the child of promise, little realizing that this momentous event of a universe was to transpire while they would be absent from home in Bethlehem of Judea.

The larger part of Joseph's family became believers in the teachings of Jesus, but very few of Mary's people ever believed in him until after he departed from this world. Joseph leaned more toward the spiritual concept of the expected Messiah, but Mary and her family, especially her father, held to the idea of the Messiah as a temporal deliverer and political ruler. Mary's ancestors had been prominently identified with the Maccabean activities of the then but recent times.

Joseph held vigorously to the Eastern, or Babylonian, views of the Jewish religion; Mary leaned strongly toward the more liberal and broader Western, or Hellenistic, interpretation of the law and the prophets.

The home of Jesus was not far from the high hill in the northerly part of Nazareth, some distance from the village spring, which was in the eastern section of the town. Jesus' family dwelt in the outskirts of the city, and this made it all the easier for him subsequently to enjoy frequent strolls in the country and to make trips up to the top of this near-by highland, the highest of all the hills of southern Galilee save the Mount Tabor range to the east and the hill of Nain, which was about the same height. Their home was located a little to the south and east of the southern promontory of this hill and about midway between the base of this elevation and the road leading out of Nazareth toward Cana. Aside from climbing the hill, Jesus' favorite stroll was to follow a narrow trail winding about the base of the hill in a northeastrly direction to a point where it joined the road to Sepphoris.

The home of Joseph and Mary was a one-room stone structure with a flat roof and an adjoining building for housing the animals. The furniture consisted of a low stone table, earthenware and stone dishes and pots, a loom, a lampstand, several small stools, and mats for sleeping on the stone floor. In the back yard, near the animal annex, was the shelter that covered the oven and the mill for grinding grain. It required two persons to operate this type of mill, one to grind and another to feed the grain. As a small boy Jesus often fed grain to this mill while his mother turned the grinder.

In later years, as the family grew in size, they would all squat about the enlarged stone table to enjoy their meals, helping themselves from a common dish, or pot, of food. During the winter, at the evening meal the table would be lighted by a small, flat clay lamp, which was filled with olive oil. After the birth of Martha, Joseph built an addition to this house, a large room, which was used as a carpenter shop during the day and as a sleeping room at night.

In the month of March, 8 B.C. (the month Joseph and Mary were married), Caesar Augustus decreed that all inhabitants of the Roman Empire should be numbered, that a census should be made which could be used for effecting better taxation. The Jews had always been greatly prejudiced against any attempt to "number the people," and this, in connection with the serious domestic difficulties of Herod, King of Judea, had conspired to cause the postponement of the taking of this census in the Jewish kingdom for one year. Throughout all the Roman Empire this census was registered in the year 8 B.C., except in the Palestinian kingdom of Herod, where it was taken in 7 B.C., one year later.

It was not necessary that Mary should go to Bethlehem for enrollment - Joseph was authorized to register for his family - but Mary, being an adventurous and aggressive person, insisted on accompanying him. She feared being left alone lest the child be born while Joseph was away, and also, Bethlehem being not far from the City of Judah, Mary foresaw a possible pleasurable visit with her kinswoman Elizabeth, the bearer of the coming herald John.

Joseph virtually forbade Mary to accompany him, but it was of no avail; when the food was packed for the trip of three or four days, she prepared double rations and made ready for the journey. But before they actually set forth, Joseph was reconciled to Mary's going along, and they cheerfully departed from Nazareth at the break of day.

Joseph and Mary were poor, and as they had only one beast of burden, Mary, being large with child, rode on the animal with the provisions while Joseph walked, leading the beast. The building and furnishing of a home had been a great drain on Joseph since he had also to contribute to the support of his parents, as his father had been recently disabled. And so this Jewish couple went forth from their home early on the morning of August 18, 7 B.C., on their journey to Bethlehem.

Their first day of travel carried them around the foothills of Mount Gilboa, where they camped for the night by the river Jordan and engaged in many speculations as to what sort of a son would be born to them, Joseph adhering to the concept of a spiritual teacher and Mary holding to the idea of a Jewish Messiah, a deliverer of the Hebrew nation.

Bright and early the morning of August 19, Joseph and Mary were again on their way. They partook of their noontide meal at the foot of Mount Sartaba, overlooking the Jordan valley, and journeyed on, making Jericho for the night, where they stopped at an inn on the highway in the outskirts of the city. Following the evening meal and after much discussion concerning the oppressiveness of Roman rule, Herod, the census enrollment, and the comparative influence of Jerusalem and Alexandria as centers of Jewish learning and culture, the Nazareth travelers retired for the night's rest. Early in the morning of August 20 they resumed their journey, reaching Jerusalem before noon, visiting the temple, and going on to their destination, arriving at Bethlehem in midafternoon.

The inn was overcrowded. Joseph accordingly sought lodgings with distant relatives, but every room in Bethlehem was filled to overflowing. On returning to the courtyard of the inn, he was informed that the caravan stables, hewn out of the side of the rock and situated just below the inn, had been cleared of animals and cleaned up for the reception of lodgers. Leaving the donkey in the courtyard, Joseph shouldered their bags of clothing and provisions and with Mary descended the stone steps to their lodgings below. They found themselves located in what had been a grain storage room to the front of the stalls and mangers. Tent curtains had been hung, and they counted themselves fortunate to have such comfortable quarters.

Joseph had thought to go out at once and enroll, but Mary was weary; she was considerably distressed and besought him to remain by her side, which he did.

All that night Mary was restless so that neither of them slept much. By the break of day the pangs of childbirth were well in evidence, and at noon, August 21, 7 B.C., with the help and kind ministrations of women fellow travelers, Mary was delivered of a male child. Jesus of Nazareth was born into the world, was wrapped in the clothes which Mary had brought along for such a possible contingency, and laid in a near-by manger.

In just the same manner as all babies before that day and since have come into the world, the promised child was born; and on the eigth day, according to the Jewish practice, he was circumcised and formally named Joshua (Jesus).

The next day after the birth of Jesus, Joseph made his enrollment. Meeting a man they had talked with two nights previously at Jericho, Joseph was taken by him to a well-to-do friend who had a room at the inn, and who said he would gladly exchange quarters with the Nazareth couple. That afternoon they moved up to the inn, where they lived for almost three weeks until they found lodgings in the home of a distant relative of Joseph.

The second day after the birth of Jesus, Mary sent word to Elizabeth that her child had come and received word in return inviting Joseph up to Jerusalem to talk over all their affairs with Zacharias. The following week Joseph went to Jerusalem to confer with Zacharias. Both Zacharias and Elizabeth had become possessed with the sincere conviction that Jesus was indeed to become the Jewish deliverer, the Messiah, and that their son John was to be his chief of aides, his right-hand man of destiny. And since Mary held these same ideas, it was not difficult to prevail upon Joseph to remain in Bethlehem, the City of David, so that Jesus might grow up to become the successor of David on the throne of all Israel. Accordingly, they remained in Bethlehem more than a year, Joseph meantime working some at his carpenter's trade.

At the noontide birth of Jesus the seraphim of Earth, assembled under their directors, did sing anthems of glory over the Bethlehem manger, but human ears did not hear these utterances of praise. No shepherds nor any other mortal creatures came to pay homage to the babe of Bethlehem until the day of the arrival of certain priests from Ur, who were sent down from Jerusalem by Zacharias.

A strange religious teacher of their country had told these priests from Mesopotamia sometime before that he'd had a dream in which he was informed that "the light of life" was about to appear on earth as a babe and among the Jews. And thither went these three teachers looking for this "light of life." After many weeks of futile search in Jerusalem, they were about to return to Ur when Zacharias met them and disclosed his belief that Jesus was the object of their quest and sent them on to Bethlehem, where they found the babe and left their gifts with Mary, his earth mother. The babe was almost three weeks old at the time of their visit.

These wise men saw no star to guide them to Bethlehem. The beautiful legend of the star of Bethlehem originated in this way: Jesus was born August 21 at noon, 7 B.C. On May 29, 7 B.C., there occurred an extraordinary conjunction of Jupiter and Saturn in the constellation of Pisces. And it is a remarkable astronomic fact that similar conjunctions occurred on September 29 and December 5 of the same year. Upon the basis of these extraordinary but wholly natural events the well-meaning zealots of the succeeding generation constructed the appealing legend of the star of Bethlehem and the adoring Magi led thereby to the manger, where they beheld and worshiped the newborn babe. Oriental and near-Oriental minds delight in fairy stories, and they are continually spinning such beautiful myths about the lives of their religious leaders and political heroes. In the absence of printing, when most human knowledge was passed by word of mouth from one generation to another, it was very easy for myths to become traditions and for traditions eventually to become accepted as facts.

Moses had taught the Jews that every first-born son belonged to the Lord, and that, in lieu of his sacrifice as was the custom among the heathen nations, such a son might live provided his parents would redeem him by the payment of five shekels to any authorized priest. There was also a Mosaic ordinance which directed that a mother, after the passing of a certain period of time, should present herself (or have someone make the proper sacrifice for her) at the temple for purification. It was customary to perform both of these ceremonies at the same time. Accordingly, Joseph and Mary went up to the temple at Jerusalem in person to present Jesus to the priests and effect his redemption and also to make the proper sacrifice to insure Mary's ceremonial purification from the alleged uncleanness of childbirth.

There lingered constantly about the courts of the temple two remarkable characters, Simeon a singer and Anna a poetess. Simeon was a Judean, but Anna was a Galilean. This couple were frequently in each other's company, and both were intimates of the priest Zacharias, who had confided the secret of John and Jesus to them. Both Simeon and Anna longed for the coming of the Messiah, and their confidence in Zacharias led them to believe that Jesus was the expected deliverer of the Jewish people.

Zacharias knew the day Joseph and Mary were expected to appear at the temple with Jesus, and he had prearranged with Simeon and Anna to indicate, by the salute of his upraised hand, which one in the procession of first-born children was Jesus.

For this occasion Anna had written a poem which Simeon proceeded to sing, much to the astonishment of Joseph, Mary, and all who were assembled in the temple courts. And this was their hymn of the redemption of the first-born son:

> Blessed be the Lord, the God of Israel,
> For he has visited us and wrought redemption for his people;
> He has raised up a horn of salvation for all of us
> In the house of his servant David.
> Even as he spoke by the mouth of his holy prophets
> Salvation from our enemies and from the hand of all who hate us;
> To show mercy to our fathers, and remember his holy covenant
> The oath which he swore to Abraham our father,
> To grant us that we, being delivered out of the hand of our enemies,
> Should serve him without fear,
> In holiness and righteousness before him all our days.

Yes, and you, child of promise, shall be called the prophet of the Most
High;
For you shall go before the face of the Lord to establish his kingdom;
To give knowledge of salvation to his people
In the remission of their sins.
Rejoice in the tender mercy of our God because the dayspring from on
high has now visited us
To shine upon those who sit in darkness and the shadow of death;
To guide our feet into ways of peace.
And now let your servant depart in peace, O Lord, according to your
word,
For my eyes have seen your salvation,
Which you have prepared before the face of all peoples;
A light for even the unveiling of the gentiles
And the glory of your people Israel.

On the way back to Bethlehem, Joseph and Mary were silent — confused and
overawed. Mary was much disturbed by the farewell salutation of Anna, the aged
poetess, and Joseph was not in harmony with this premature effort to make Jesus
out to be the expected Messiah of the Jewish people.

But the watchers for Herod were not inactive. When they reported to him the
visit of the priests of Ur to Bethlehem, Herod summoned these Chaldeans to
appear before him. He inquired diligently of these wise men about the new "king
of the Jews," but they gave him little satisfaction, explaining that the babe had been
born of a woman who had come down to Bethlehem with her husband for the census enrollment. Herod, not being satisfied with this answer, sent them forth with a
purse and directed that they should find the child so that he too might come and
worship him, since they had declared that his kingdom was to be spiritual, not
temporal. But when the wise men did not return, Herod grew suspicious. As he
turned these things over in his mind, his informers returned and made full report
of recent occurrences in the temple, bringing him a copy of parts of a worshipful
song which had been sung at the redemption ceremonies of Jesus. But they had
failed to follow Joseph and Mary, and Herod was very angry with them when they
could not tell him whither the pair had taken the babe. He then dispatched search-
ers to locate Joseph and Mary. Knowing Herod pursued the Nazareth family,
Zacharias and Elizabeth remained away from Bethlehem. The boy baby was se-
creted with Joseph's relatives.

Joseph was afraid to seek work, and their small savings were rapidly disap-
pearing. Even at the time of the purification ceremonies at the temple, Joseph
deemed himself sufficiently poor to warrant his offering for Mary two young pi-

geons as Moses had directed for the purification of recent mothers among the poor.

When, after more than a year of searching, Herod's spies had not located Jesus, and because of the suspicion that the babe was still concealed in Bethlehem, he prepared an order directing that a systematic search be made of every house in Bethlehem, and that all boy babies under two years of age should be killed. In this manner Herod hoped to make sure that this child who was to become "king of the Jews" would be destroyed. And thus perished in one day sixteen boy babies in Bethlehem of Judea.

The massacre of these infants took place about the middle of October, 6 B.C., when Jesus was a little over one year of age. But there were believers in the coming Messiah even among Herod's court attachés, and one of these, learning of the order to slaughter the Bethlehem boy babies, communicated with Zacharias, who in turn dispatched a messenger to Joseph; and the night before the massacre Joseph and Mary departed from Bethlehem with the babe for Alexandria in Egypt. In order to avoid attracting attention, they journeyed alone to Egypt with Jesus. They went to Alexandria on funds provided by Zacharias, and there Joseph worked at his trade while Mary and Jesus lodged with well-to-do relatives of Joseph's family. They sojourned in Alexandria two full years, not returning to Bethlehem until after the death of Herod.

LATER CHILDHOOD OF JESUS

A S A BABE and young child Jesus experienced the normal ups and downs of physical life as a human child of that time. Nothing of extraordinary occurrence happened during these times, save the gradual unfolding of his awreness of the dual nature of his origin. It is beyond the scope of this narrative to explore these years.

The family grew in due course and at the time of Jesus' twelfth year the family consisted of Mary, Joseph, Jesus and his four brothers and two sisters. The last sister, Ruth, and baby boy, Amos had yet to arrive.

Although Jesus might have enjoyed a better opportunity for schooling at Alexandria than in Galilee, he could not have had such a splendid environment for working out his own life problems with a minimum of educational guidance, at the same time enjoying the great advantage of constantly contacting with such a large number of all classes of men and women hailing from every part of the civilized world. Had he remained at Alexandria, his education would have been directed by Jews and along exclusively Jewish lines. At Nazareth he secured an education and received a training which more acceptably prepared him to understand the gentiles, and which gave him a better and more balanced idea of the relative merits of the Eastern, or Babylonian, and the Western, or Hellenic, views of Hebrew theology.

A .D. 6, his twelfth year on Earth, was an eventful year for Jesus. He continued to make progress at school and was indefatigable in his study of nature, while increasingly he prosecuted his study of the methods whereby men make a living. He began doing regular work in the home carpenter shop and was permitted to manage his own earnings, a very unusual arrangement to obtain in a Jewish family.

Throughout this year he experienced many seasons of uncertainty, if not actual doubt, regarding the nature of his mission. His naturally developing human mind did not yet fully grasp the reality of his dual nature. The fact that he had a single personality rendered it difficult for his consciousness to recognize the double origin of those factors which composed the nature associated with that selfsame personality.

From this time on he became more successful in getting along with his brothers and sisters. He was increasingly tactful, always compassionate and considerate of their welfare and happiness, and enjoyed good relations with them up to the beginning of his public ministry. To be more explicit: He got along with James, Miriam, and the two younger (as yet unborn) children, Amos and Ruth, most excellently. He always got along with Martha fairly well. What trouble he had at home largely arose out of friction with Joseph and Jude, particularly the latter.

It was a trying experience for Joseph and Mary to undertake the rearing of this unprecedented combination of divinity and humanity, and they deserve great credit for so faithfully and successfully discharging their parental responsibilities. Increasingly Jesus' parents realized that there was something superhuman resident within this eldest son, but they never even faintly dreamed that this son of promise was indeed and in truth the actual creator of this local universe of things and beings. Joseph and Mary lived and died without ever learning that their son Jesus really was the Universe Creator incarnate in mortal flesh.

This year Jesus paid more attention than ever to music, and he continued to teach the home school for his brothers and sisters. It was at about this time that the lad became keenly conscious of the difference between the viewpoints of Joseph and Mary regarding the nature of his mission. He pondered much over his parents' differing opinions, often hearing their discussions when they thought he was sound asleep. More and more he inclined to the view of his father that he was to be a spiritual leader, so that his mother was destined to be hurt by the realization that her son was gradually rejecting her guidance in matters having to do with his life career. And, as the years passed, this breach of understanding widened. Less and less did Mary comprehend the significance of Jesus' mission, and increasingly was this good mother hurt by the failure of her favorite son to fulfill her fond expectations.

As time passed, Jesus did much to modify their practice of religious forms, such as the family prayers and other customs. And it was possible to do many such things at Nazareth, for its synagogue was under the influence of a liberal school of rabbis, exemplified by the renowned Nazareth teacher, Jose.

Throughout this and the two following years Jesus suffered great mental distress as the result of his constant effort to adjust his personal views of religious practices and social amenities to the established beliefs of his parents. He was distraught by the conflict between the urge to be loyal to his own convictions and the conscientious admonition of dutiful submission to his parents; his supreme conflict was between two great commands that were uppermost in his youthful mind.

The one was: "Be loyal to the dictates of your highest convictions of truth and righteousness." The other was: "Honor your father and mother, for they have given you life and the nurture thereof." However, he never shirked the responsibility of making the necessary daily adjustments between these realms of loyalty to one's personal convictions and duty toward one's family, and he achieved the satisfaction of effecting an increasingly harmonious blending of personal convictions and family obligations into a masterful concept of group solidarity based upon loyalty, fairness, tolerance, and love.

In his thirteenth year the lad of Nazareth passed from boyhood to the beginning of young manhood; his voice began to change, and other features of mind and body gave evidence of the oncoming status of manhood.

On Sunday night, January 9, A.D. 7, his baby brother, Amos, was born. Jude was not yet two years of age, and the baby sister, Ruth, was yet to come; so it may be seen that Jesus had a sizable family of small children left to his watchcare when his father met his accidental death the following year.

It was about the middle of February that Jesus became humanly assured that he was destined to perform a mission on earth for the enlightenment of man and the revelation of God. Momentous decisions, coupled with far-reaching plans, were formulating in the mind of this youth, who was, to outward appearances, an average Jewish lad of Nazareth. The intelligent life of all the local creation looked on with fascination and amazement as all this began to unfold in the thinking and acting of the now adolescent carpenter's son.

On the first day of the week, March 20, A.D. 7, Jesus graduated from the course of training in the local school connected with the Nazareth synagogue. This was a great day in the life of any ambitious Jewish family, the day when the firstborn son was pronounced a "son of the commandment" and the ransomed firstborn of the Lord God of Israel, a "child of the Most High" and servant of the Lord of all the earth.

Friday of the week before, Joseph had come over from Sepphoris, where he was in charge of the work on a new public building, to be present on this glad occasion. Jesus' teacher confidently believed that his alert and diligent pupil was destined to some outstanding career, some distinguished mission. The elders of the temple, notwithstanding all their trouble with Jesus' nonconformist tendencies, were very proud of the lad and had already begun laying plans which would enable him to go to Jerusalem to continue his education in the renowned Hebrew academies.

As Jesus heard these plans discussed from time to time, he became increasingly sure that he would never go to Jerusalem to study with the rabbis. But he little dreamed of the tragedy, so soon to occur, which would insure the abandonment of all such plans by causing him to assume the responsibility for the support and direction of a large family, presently to consist of five brothers and three sisters as well as his mother and himself. Jesus had a larger and longer experience rearing this family than was accorded to Joseph, his father; and he did measure up to the standard which he subsequently set for himself: to become a wise, patient, understanding, and effective teacher and eldest brother to this family — his family — so suddenly sorrow-stricken and so unexpectedly bereaved.

Jesus having now reached the threshold of young manhood and having been formally graduated from the synagogue schools, was qualified to proceed to Jerusalem with his parents to participate with them in the celebration of his first Passover. The Passover feast of this year fell on Saturday, April 9, A.D. 7. A considerable company (103) made ready to depart from Nazareth early Monday morning, April 4, for Jerusalem. They journeyed south toward Samaria, but on reaching Jezreel, they turned east, going around Mount Gilboa into the Jordan valley in order to avoid passing through Samaria. Joseph and his family would have enjoyed going down through Samaria by way of Jacob's well and Bethel, but since the Jews disliked dealing with the Samaritans, they decided to go with their neighbors by way of the Jordan valley.

The much-dreaded Archelaus, son of Herod had been deposed, and they had little to fear in taking Jesus to Jerusalem. Twelve years had passed since the first Herod had sought to destroy the babe of Bethlehem, and no one would now think of associating that affair with this obscure lad of Nazareth.

Before reaching the Jezreel junction, and as they journeyed on, very soon, on the left, they passed the ancient village of Shunem, and Jesus heard about the most beautiful maiden of all Israel who once lived there and also about the wonderful works Elisha performed there. In passing by Jezreel, Jesus' parents recounted the doings of Ahab and Jezebel and the exploits of Jehu. In passing around Mount Gilboa they talked much about Saul, who took his life on the slopes of this mountain, King David, and the associations of this historic spot.

As they rounded the base of Gilboa, the pilgrims could see the Greek city of Scythopolis on the right. They gazed upon the marble structures from a distance but went not near the gentile city lest they so defile themselves that they could not participate in the forthcoming solemn and sacred ceremonies of the Passover at Jerusalem.

On their second day's journey they passed by where the Jabbok, from the east, flows into the Jordan, and looking east up this river valley, they recounted the days of Gideon, when the Midianites poured into this region to overrun the land. Toward the end of the second day's journey they camped near the base of the highest mountain overlooking the Jordan valley, Mount Sartaba, whose summit was occupied by the Alexandrian fortress where Herod had imprisoned one of his wives and buried his two strangled sons

The third day they passed by two villages which had been recently built by Herod and noted their superior architecture and their beautiful palm gardens. By nightfall they reached Jericho. That evening Joseph, Mary, and Jesus walked a mile and a half to the site of the ancient Jericho, where Joshua, for whom Jesus was named, had performed his renowned exploits, according to Jewish tradition.

By the fourth and last day's journey the road was a continuous procession of pilgrims. They now began to climb the hills leading up to Jerusalem. As they neared the top, they could look across the Jordan to the mountains beyond and south over the sluggish waters of the Dead Sea. About halfway up to Jerusalem, Jesus gained his first view of the Mount of Olives and Joseph pointed out to him that the Holy City lay just beyond this ridge, and the lad's heart beat fast with joyous anticipation of soon beholding the city and house of his heavenly Father.

On the eastern slopes of Olivet they paused for rest in the borders of a little village called Bethany. The hospitable villagers poured forth to minister to the pilgrims, and it happened that Joseph and his family had stopped near the house of one Simon, who had three children about the same age as Jesus — Mary, Martha, and Lazarus. They invited the Nazareth family in for refreshment, and a lifelong friendship sprang up between the two families. Many times afterward, in his eventful life, Jesus stopped in this home.

They pressed on, soon standing on the brink of Olivet, and Jesus saw for the first time (in his memory) the Holy City, the ambitious palaces, and the inspiring temple of his Father. At no time in his life did Jesus ever experience such a purely human thrill as that which at this time so completely enthralled him as he stood there on this April afternoon on the Mount of Olives, drinking in his first view of Jerusalem. And in after years, on this same spot he stood and wept over the city, which was about to reject another prophet, the last and the greatest of her heavenly teachers.

But they hurried on to Jerusalem. It was now Thursday afternoon. On reaching the city, they journeyed past the temple, and never had Jesus beheld such throngs of human beings. He meditated deeply on how these Jews had assembled here from the uttermost parts of the known world.

Soon they reached the place prearranged for their accommodation during the Passover week, the large home of a well-to-do relative of Mary's, one who knew something of the early history of both John and Jesus, through Zacharias. The following day, the day of preparation, they made ready for the appropriate celebration of the Passover Sabbath.

While all Jerusalem was astir in preparation for the Passover, Joseph found time to take his son around to visit the academy where it had been arranged for him to resume his education two years later, as soon as he reached the required age of fifteen. Joseph was truly puzzled when he observed how little interest Jesus evinced in all these carefully laid plans.

The temple and all the associated services and other activities profoundly impressed Jesus. For the first time since he was four years old, he was too much preoccupied with his own meditations to ask many questions. He did, however, ask his father several embarrassing questions (as he had on previous occasions) as to why the heavenly Father required the slaughter of so many innocent and helpless animals. And his father well knew from the expression on the lad's face that his answers and attempts at explanation were unsatisfactory to his deep-thinking and keen-reasoning son.

On the day before the Passover Sabbath, flood tides of spiritual illumination swept through the mortal mind of Jesus and filled his human heart to overflowing with affectionate pity for the spiritually blind and morally ignorant multitudes assembled for the celebration of the ancient Passover commemoration. This was one of the most extraordinary days that the Son of God spent in the flesh; and during the night, for the first time in his earth career, there appeared to him an assigned messenger from Salvington, commissioned by Immanuel, who said: "The hour has come. It is time that you began to be about your Father's business."

And so, even ere the heavy responsibilities of the Nazareth family descended upon his youthful shoulders, there now arrived the celestial messenger to remind this lad, not quite thirteen years of age, that the hour had come to begin the resumption of the responsibilities of a universe. This was the first act of a long succession of events which finally culminated in the completion of the Son's bestowal on Earth and the replacing of "the government of a universe on his human-divine shoulders."

As time passed, the mystery of the incarnation became, to all of us, more and more unfathomable. We could hardly comprehend that this lad of Nazareth was the creator of all the local universe. Neither do we nowadays understand how the spirit of this same Creator Son and his Paradise Father are associated with the souls of mankind. With the passing of time, we could see that his human mind was increasingly discerning that, while he lived his life in the flesh, in spirit on his shoulders rested the responsibility of a universe.

Thus ends the career of the Nazareth lad, and begins the narrative of that adolescent youth — the increasingly self-conscious divine human — who now begins the contemplation of his world career as he strives to integrate his expanding life purpose with the desires of his parents and his obligations to his family and the society of his day and age.

JESUS AT JERUSALEM

N O INCIDENT in all Jesus' eventful earth career was more engaging, more humanly thrilling, than this, his first remembered visit to Jerusalem. He was especially stimulated by the experience of attending the temple discussions by himself, and it long stood out in his memory as the great event of his later childhood and early youth. This was his first opportunity to enjoy a few days of independent living, the exhilaration of going and coming without restraint and restrictions. This brief period of undirected living, during the week following the Passover, was the first complete freedom from responsibility he had ever enjoyed. And it was many years subsequent to this before he again had a like period of freedom from all sense of responsibility, even for a short time.

Women seldom went to the Passover feast at Jerusalem; they were not required to be present. Jesus, however, had virtually refused to go unless his mother would accompany them. And when Mary decided to go, many other village women were led to make the journey, so that the company of pilgrims contained the largest number of women, in proportion to men, ever to go up to the Passover from Nazareth.

From the time they left Nazareth until they reached the summit of the Mount of Olives, Jesus experienced one long stress of expectant anticipation. All through a joyful childhood he had reverently heard of Jerusalem and its temple; now he was soon to behold them in reality. From the Mount of Olives and from the outside, on closer inspection, the temple had been all and more than Jesus had expected; but when he once entered its sacred portals, the great disillusionment began.

In company with his parents Jesus passed through the temple precincts on his way to join that group of new sons of the law who were about to be consecrated as citizens of Israel. He was a little disappointed by the general demeanor of the temple throngs, but the first great shock of the day came when his mother took leave of them on her way to the women's gallery. It had never occurred to Jesus that his mother was not to accompany him to the consecration ceremonies, and he was thoroughly indignant that she was made to suffer from such unjust discrimination. While he strongly resented this, aside from a few remarks of protest to his father, he said nothing. But he thought, and thought deeply, as his questions to the scribes and teachers a week later disclosed.

He passed through the consecration rituals but was disappointed by their perfunctory and routine natures. He missed that personal interest which characterized the ceremonies of the synagogue at Nazareth. He then returned to greet his mother and prepared to accompany his father on his first trip about the temple and its various courts, galleries, and corridors. The temple precincts could accommodate over two hundred thousand worshipers at one time, and while the vastness of these buildings — in comparison with any he had ever seen — greatly impressed his mind, he was more intrigued by the contemplation of the spiritual significance of the temple ceremonies and their associated worship.

Though many of the temple rituals very touchingly impressed his sense of the beautiful and the symbolic, he was always disappointed by the explanation of the real meanings of these ceremonies that his parents would offer in answer to his many searching inquiries. Jesus simply would not accept explanations of worship and religious devotion which involved belief in the wrath of God or the anger of the Almighty. In further discussion of these questions, after the conclusion of the temple visit, when his father became mildly insistent that he acknowledge acceptance of the orthodox Jewish beliefs, Jesus turned suddenly upon his parents and, looking appealingly into the eyes of Joseph, said: "My father, it cannot be true — the Father in heaven cannot so regard His erring children on earth. The heavenly Father cannot love His children less than you love me. And I well know, no matter what unwise thing I might do, you would never pour out wrath upon me nor vent anger against me. If you, my earthly father, possess such human reflections of the Divine, how much more must the heavenly Father be filled with goodness and overflowing with mercy. I refuse to believe that my Father in heaven loves me less than my father on earth."

When Joseph and Mary heard these words of their first-born son, they held their peace. And never again did they seek to change his mind about the love of God and the mercifulness of the Father in heaven.

Everywhere Jesus went throughout the temple courts, he was shocked and sickened by the spirit of irreverence that he observed. He deemed the conduct of the temple throngs to be inconsistent with their presence in "his Father's house." But he received the shock of his young life when his father escorted him into the court of the gentiles with its noisy jargon, loud talking and cursing, mingled indiscriminately with the bleating of sheep and the babble of noises which betrayed the presence of the money-changers and the vendors of sacrificial animals and sundry other commercial commodities.

But most of all was his sense of propriety outraged by the sight of the frivolous courtesans parading about within this precinct of the temple, just such painted women as he had so recently seen when on a visit to Sepphoris. This profanation of the temple fully aroused all his youthful indignation, and he did not hesitate to express himself freely to Joseph.

Jesus admired the sentiment and service of the temple, but he was shocked by the spiritual ugliness that he beheld on the faces of so many of the unthinking worshipers.

They now passed down to the priests' court beneath the rock ledge in front of the temple, where the altar stood, to observe the killing of the droves of animals and the washing away of the blood from the hands of the officiating slaughter priests at the bronze fountain. The bloodstained pavement, the gory hands of the priests, and the sounds of the dying animals were more than this nature-loving lad could stand. The terrible sight sickened this boy of Nazareth; he clutched his father's arm and begged to be taken away. They walked back through the court of the gentiles, and even the coarse laughter and profane jesting which he there heard were a relief from the sights he had just beheld.

Joseph saw how his son had sickened at the sight of the temple rites and wisely led him around to view the "gate beautiful," the artistic gate made of Corinthian bronze. But Jesus had had enough for his first visit at the temple. They returned to the upper court for Mary and walked about in the open air and away from the crowds for an hour, viewing the Asmonean palace, the stately home of Herod, and the tower of the Roman guards. During this stroll Joseph explained to Jesus that only the inhabitants of Jerusalem were permitted to witness the daily sacrifices in the temple, and that the dwellers in Galilee came up only three times a year to participate in the temple worship: at the Passover, at the feast of Pentecost, and at the feast of tabernacles in October. These feasts were established by Moses. They then discussed the two later established feasts of the dedication and of Purim. Afterward they went to their lodgings and made ready for the celebration of the Passover.

Five Nazareth families were guests of, or associates with, the family of Simon of Bethany in the celebration of the Passover, Simon having purchased the paschal lamb for the company. It was the slaughter of these lambs in such enormous numbers that had so affected Jesus on his temple visit. It had been the plan to eat the Passover with Mary's relatives, but Jesus persuaded his parents to accept the invitation to go to Bethany.

That night they assembled for the Passover rites, eating the roasted flesh with unleavened bread and bitter herbs. Jesus, being a new son of the covenant, was asked to recount the origin of the Passover, and this he well did, but he somewhat disconcerted his parents by the inclusion of numerous remarks mildly reflecting the impressions made on his youthful but thoughtful mind by the things which he had so recently seen and heard. This was the beginning of the seven-day ceremonies of the feast of the Passover.

Even at this early date, though he said nothing about such matters to his parents, Jesus had begun to turn over in his mind the propriety of celebrating the Passover without the slaughtered lamb. He felt assured in his own mind that the Father in heaven was not pleased with this spectacle of sacrificial offerings, and as the years passed, he became increasingly determined someday to establish the celebration of a bloodless Passover.

Jesus slept very little that night. His rest was greatly disturbed by revolting dreams of slaughter and suffering. His mind was distraught and his heart torn by the inconsistencies and absurdities of the theology of the whole Jewish ceremonial system. His parents likewise slept little. They were greatly disconcerted by the events of the day just ended. They were completely upset in their own hearts by the lad's, to them, strange and determined attitude. Mary became nervously agitated during the fore part of the night, but Joseph remained calm, though he was equally puzzled. Both of them feared to talk frankly with the lad about these problems, though Jesus would gladly have talked with his parents if they had dared to encourage him.

The next day's services at the temple were more acceptable to Jesus and did much to relieve the unpleasant memories of the previous day. The following morning young Lazarus took Jesus in hand, and they began a systematic exploration of Jerusalem and its environs. Before the day was over, Jesus discovered the various places about the temple where teaching and question conferences were in progress; and aside from a few visits to the holy of holies to gaze in wonder as to what really was behind the veil of separation, he spent most of his time about the temple at these teaching conferences.

Throughout the Passover week, Jesus kept his place among the new sons of the commandment, and this meant that he must seat himself outside the rail which segregated all persons who were not full citizens of Israel. Being thus made conscious of his youth, he refrained from asking the many questions that surged back and forth in his mind; at least he refrained until the Passover celebration had ended and these restrictions on the newly consecrated youths were lifted.

On Wednesday of the Passover week, Jesus was permitted to go home with Lazarus to spend the night at Bethany. This evening, Lazarus, Martha, and Mary heard Jesus discuss things temporal and eternal, human and divine, and from that night on they all three loved him as if he had been their own brother.

By the end of the week, Jesus saw less of Lazarus since he was not eligible for admission to even the outer circle of the temple discussions, though he attended some of the public talks delivered in the outer courts. Lazarus was the same age as

Jesus, but in Jerusalem youths were seldom admitted to the consecration of sons of the law until they were a full thirteen years of age.

Again and again, during the Passover week, his parents would find Jesus sitting off by himself with his youthful head in his hands, profoundly thinking. They had never seen him behave like this, and not knowing how much he was confused in mind and troubled in spirit by the experience through which he was passing, they were sorely perplexed; they did not know what to do. They welcomed the passing of the days of the Passover week and longed to have their strangely acting son safely back in Nazareth.

Day by day Jesus was thinking through his problems. By the end of the week he had made many adjustments; but when the time came to return to Nazareth, his youthful mind was still swarming with perplexities and beset by a host of unanswered questions and unsolved problems.

Before Joseph and Mary left Jerusalem, in company with Jesus' Nazareth teacher they made definite arrangements for Jesus to return when he reached the age of fifteen to begin his long course of study in one of the best-known academies of the rabbis. Jesus accompanied his parents and teacher on their visits to the school, but they were distressed to observe how indifferent he seemed to all they said and did. Mary was deeply pained at his reactions to the Jerusalem visit, and Joseph was profoundly perplexed at the lad's strange remarks and unusual conduct.

After all, Passover week had been a great event in Jesus' life. He had enjoyed the opportunity of meeting scores of boys about his own age, fellow candidates for the consecration, and he utilized such contacts as a means of learning how people lived in Mesopotamia, Turkestan, and Parthia, as well as in the Far-Western provinces of Rome. He was already fairly conversant with the way in which the youth of Egypt and other regions near Palestine grew up. There were thousands of young people in Jerusalem at this time, and the Nazareth lad personally met, and more or less extensively interviewed, more than one hundred and fifty. He was particularly interested in those who hailed from the Far-Eastern and the remote Western countries. As a result of these contacts the lad began to entertain a desire to travel about the world for the purpose of learning how the various groups of his fellow men toiled for their livelihood.

It had been arranged that the Nazareth party should gather in the region of the temple at midmorning on the first day of the week after the Passover festival had ended. This they did and started out on the return journey to Nazareth. Jesus had gone into the temple to listen to the discussions while his parents awaited the assembly of their fellow travelers. Presently the company prepared to depart, the men going in one group and the women in another, as was their custom in journeying to and from the Jerusalem festivals. Jesus had gone up to Jerusalem in company with his mother and the women. Being now a young man of the consecration, he was supposed to journey back to Nazareth in company with his father and the men. But as the Nazareth party moved on toward Bethany, Jesus was completely absorbed in the discussion of angels taking place in the temple. He was wholly unmindful of the passing of the time for the departure of his parents. And he did not realize that he had been left behind until the noontime adjournment of the temple conferences.

The Nazareth travelers did not miss Jesus because Mary surmised he journeyed with the men, while Joseph thought he traveled with the women since he had gone up to Jerusalem with them, leading Mary's donkey. They did not discover his absence until they reached Jericho and prepared to tarry for the night. After making inquiry of the last of the party to reach Jericho and learning that none of them had seen their son, they spent a sleepless night, turning over in their minds what might have happened to him, recounting many of his unusual reactions to the events of Passover week, and mildly chiding each other for not seeing to it that he was in the group before they left Jerusalem.

In the meantime, Jesus had remained in the temple throughout the afternoon, listening to the discussions and enjoying the more quiet and decorous atmosphere, the great crowds of Passover week having about disappeared. At the conclusion of the afternoon discussions, in none of which Jesus participated, he betook himself to Bethany, arriving just as Simon's family made ready to partake of their evening meal. The three youngsters were overjoyed to greet Jesus, and he remained in Simon's house for the night. He visited very little during the evening, spending much of the time alone in the garden meditating.

Early next day Jesus was up and on his way to the temple. On the brow of Olivet he paused and wept over the sight his eyes beheld — a spiritually impoverished people, tradition bound and living under the surveillance of the Roman legions. Early forenoon found him in the temple with his mind made up to take part in the discussions. Meanwhile, Joseph and Mary also had arisen with the early dawn with the intention of retracing their steps to Jerusalem. First, they hastened to the house of their relatives, where they had lodged as a family during the Passover week, but inquiry elicited the fact that no one had seen Jesus. After searching all day and finding no trace of him, they returned to their relatives for the night.

At the second conference Jesus had made bold to ask questions, and in a very amazing way he participated in the temple discussions but always in a manner consistent with his youth. Sometimes his pointed questions were somewhat embarrassing to the learned teachers of the Jewish law, but he evinced such a spirit of candid fairness, coupled with an evident hunger for knowledge, that the majority of the temple teachers were disposed to treat him with every consideration. But when he presumed to question the justice of putting to death a drunken gentile who had wandered outside the court of the gentiles and unwittingly entered the forbidden and reputedly sacred precincts of the temple, one of the more intolerant teachers grew impatient with the lad's implied criticisms and, glowering down upon him, asked how old he was.

Jesus replied, "Thirteen years lacking a trifle more than four months."

"Then," rejoined the now irate teacher, "why are you here, since you are not of age as a son of the law?"

Jesus explained that he had received consecration during the Passover, and that he was a finished student of the Nazareth schools.

The teachers with one accord derisively replied, "We might have known; he is from Nazareth."

But the leader insisted that Jesus was not to be blamed if the rulers of the synagogue at Nazareth had graduated him, technically, when he was twelve instead of thirteen; and notwithstanding that several of his detractors got up and left, it was ruled that the lad might continue undisturbed as a pupil of the temple discussions. When this, his second day in the temple, was finished, again he went to Bethany for the night. And again he went out in the garden to meditate and pray. His mind was concerned with the contemplation of weighty problems.

Jesus' third day with the scribes and teachers in the temple witnessed the gathering of many spectators who, having heard of this youth from Galilee, came to enjoy the experience of seeing a lad confuse the wise men of the law. Simon also came down from Bethany to see what the boy was up to. Throughout this day Joseph and Mary continued their anxious search for Jesus, even going several times into the temple but never thinking to scrutinize the several discussion groups, although they once came almost within hearing distance of his fascinating voice.

Before the day had ended, the entire attention of the chief discussion group of the temple had become focused upon the questions being asked by Jesus. Among his many questions were:

1. What really exists in the holy of holies, behind the veil?

2. Why should mothers in Israel be segregated from the male temple worshipers?

3. If God is a father who loves his children, why all this slaughter of animals to gain divine favor — has the teaching of Moses been misunderstood?

4. Since the temple is dedicated to the worship of the Father in heaven, is it consistent to permit the presence of those who engage in secular barter and trade?

5. Is the expected Messiah to become a temporal prince to sit on the throne of David, or is he to function as the light of life in the establishment of a spiritual kingdom?

And all the day through, those who listened marveled at these questions, and none was more astonished than Simon. For more than four hours this Nazareth youth plied these Jewish teachers with thought-provoking and heart-searching questions. He made few comments on the remarks of his elders. He conveyed his teaching by the questions he would ask. By the deft and subtle phrasing of a question he would at one and the same time challenge their teaching and suggest his own. In the manner of his asking a question there was an appealing combination of sagacity and humor which endeared him even to those who more or less resented his youthfulness. He was always eminently fair and considerate in the asking of these penetrating questions. On this eventful afternoon in the temple he exhibited that same reluctance to take unfair advantage of an opponent which characterized his entire subsequent public ministry. As a youth, and later on as a man, he seemed to be utterly free from all egoistic desire to win an argument merely to experience logical triumph over his fellows, being interested supremely in just one thing: to proclaim everlasting truth and thus effect a fuller revelation of the eternal God.

When the day was over, Simon and Jesus wended their way back to Bethany. For most of the distance both the man and the boy were silent. Again Jesus paused on the brow of Olivet, but as he viewed the city and its temple, he did not weep; he only bowed his head in silent devotion.

After the evening meal at Bethany he again declined to join the merry circle but instead went to the garden, where he lingered long into the night, vainly endeavoring to think out some definite plan of approach to the problem of his lifework and to decide how best he might labor to reveal to his spiritually blinded countrymen a more beautiful concept of the heavenly Father and so set them free from their terrible bondage to law, ritual, ceremonial, and musty tradition. But the clear light did not come to the truth-seeking lad.

Jesus was strangely unmindful of his earthly parents; even at breakfast, when Lazarus's mother remarked that his parents must be about home by that time, Jesus did not seem to comprehend that they would be somewhat worried about his having lingered behind.

Again he journeyed to the temple, but he did not pause to meditate at the brow of Olivet. In the course of the morning's discussions much time was devoted to the law and the prophets, and the teachers were astonished that Jesus was so familiar with the Scriptures, in Hebrew as well as Greek. But they were amazed not so much by his knowledge of truth as by his youth.

At the afternoon conference they had hardly begun to answer his question relating to the purpose of prayer when the leader invited the lad to come forward and, sitting beside him, bade him state his own views regarding prayer and worship.

The evening before, Jesus' parents had heard about this strange youth who so deftly sparred with the expounders of the law, but it had not occurred to them that this lad was their son. They had about decided to journey out to the home of Zacharias as they thought Jesus might have gone thither to see Elizabeth and John. Thinking Zacharias might perhaps be at the temple, they stopped there on their way to the City of Judah. As they strolled through the courts of the temple, imagine their surprise and amazement when they recognized the voice of the missing lad and beheld him seated among the temple teachers.

Joseph was speechless, but Mary gave vent to her long-pent-up fear and anxiety when, rushing up to the lad, now standing to greet his astonished parents, she said, "My child, why have you treated us like this? It is now more than three days that your father and I have searched for you sorrowing. Whatever possessed you to desert us?" It was a tense moment. All eyes were turned on Jesus to hear what he would say. His father looked reprovingly at him but said nothing.

It should be remembered that Jesus was supposed to be a young man. He had finished the regular schooling of a child, had been recognized as a son of the law, and had received consecration as a citizen of Israel. And yet his mother more than mildly upbraided him before all the people assembled, right in the midst of the most serious and sublime effort of his young life, thus bringing to an inglorious termination one of the greatest opportunities ever to be granted him to function as a teacher of truth, a preacher of righteousness, a revealer of the loving character of his Father in heaven.

But the lad was equal to the occasion. When you take into fair consideration all the factors which combined to make up this situation, you will be better prepared to fathom the wisdom of the boy's reply to his mother's unintended rebuke. After a moment's thought, Jesus answered his mother, saying: "Why is it that you have so long sought me? Would you not expect to find me in my Father's house since the time has come when I should be about my Father's business?"

Everyone was astonished at the lad's manner of speaking. Silently they all withdrew and left him standing alone with his parents. Presently the young man relieved the embarrassment of all three when he quietly said, "Come, my parents, none has done aught but that which he thought best. Our Father in heaven has ordained these things; let us depart for home."

In silence they started out, arriving at Jericho for the night. Only once did they pause, and that on the brow of Olivet, when the lad raised his staff aloft and, quivering from head to foot under the surging of intense emotion, said, "O Jerusalem, Jerusalem, and the people thereof, what slaves you are — subservient to the Roman yoke and victims of your own traditions — but I will return to cleanse yonder temple and deliver my people from this bondage!"

On the three days' journey to Nazareth Jesus said little; neither did his parents say much in his presence. They were truly at a loss to understand the conduct of their first-born son, but they did treasure in their hearts his sayings, even though they could not fully comprehend their meanings.

Upon reaching home, Jesus made a brief statement to his parents, assuring them of his affection and implying that they need not fear he would again give any occasion for their suffering anxiety because of his conduct. He concluded this momentous statement by saying: "While I must do the will of my Father in heaven, I will also be obedient to my father on earth. I will await my hour."

Though Jesus, in his mind, would many times refuse to *consent* to the well-intentioned but misguided efforts of his parents to dictate the course of his thinking or to establish the plan of his work on earth, still, in every manner consistent with his dedication to the doing of his Paradise Father's will, he did most gracefully *conform* to the desires of his earthly father and of his family in the flesh. Even when he could not consent, he would do everything possible to conform. He was an artist in the matter of adjusting his dedication to duty to his obligations of family loyalty and social service.

Joseph was puzzled, but Mary, as she reflected on these experiences, gained comfort, eventually viewing his utterance on Olivet as prophetic of the Messianic mission of her son as Israel's deliverer. She set to work with renewed energy to mold his thoughts into patriotic and nationalistic channels and enlisted the efforts of her brother, Jesus' favorite uncle; and in every other way did the mother of Jesus address herself to the task of preparing her first-born son to assume the leadership of those who would restore the throne of David and forever cast off the gentile yoke of political bondage.

THE TWO CRUCIAL YEARS

OF ALL Jesus' earth-life experiences, the fourteenth and fifteenth years were the most crucial. These two years, after he began to be self-conscious of divinity and destiny, and before he achieved a large measure of communication with his indwelling Father Fragment –the divine spark of the Source and Center that every normal minded human receives- were the most trying of his eventful life on Earth. It is this period of two years that should be called the great test, the real temptation. No human youth, in passing through the early confusions and adjustment problems of adolescence, ever experienced a more crucial testing than that which Jesus passed through during his transition from childhood to young manhood.

This important period in Jesus' youthful development began with the conclusion of the Jerusalem visit and with his return to Nazareth. At first Mary was happy in the thought that she had her boy back once more, that Jesus had returned home to be a dutiful son — not that he was ever anything else — and that he would henceforth be more responsive to her plans for his future life. But she was not for long to bask in this sunshine of maternal delusion and unrecognized family pride; very soon she was to be more completely disillusioned. More and more the boy was in the company of his father; less and less did he come to her with his problems, while increasingly both his parents failed to comprehend his frequent alternation between the affairs of this world and the contemplation of his relation to his Father's business. Frankly, they did not understand him, but they did truly love him.

As he grew older, Jesus' pity and love for the Jewish people deepened, but with the passing years, there developed in his mind a growing righteous resentment of the presence in the Father's temple of the politically appointed priests. Jesus had great respect for the sincere Pharisees and the honest scribes, but he held the hypocritical Pharisees and the dishonest theologians in great contempt;

he looked with disdain upon all those religious leaders who were not sincere. When he scrutinized the leadership of Israel, he was sometimes tempted to look with favor on the possibility of his becoming the Messiah of Jewish expectation, but he never yielded to such a temptation.

The story of his exploits among the wise men of the temple in Jerusalem was gratifying to all Nazareth, especially to his former teachers in the synagogue school. For a time his praise was on everybody's lips. The entire village recounted his childhood wisdom and praiseworthy conduct and predicted that he was destined to become a great leader in Israel; at last a really great teacher was to come out of Nazareth in Galilee. And they all looked forward to the time when he would be fifteen years of age so that he might be permitted regularly to read the Scriptures in the synagogue on the Sabbath day.

The year 8 A.D. was the calendar year of his fourteenth birthday. He had become a good yoke maker and worked well with both canvas and leather. He was also rapidly developing into an expert carpenter and cabinetmaker. This summer he made frequent trips to the top of the hill to the northwest of Nazareth for prayer and meditation. He was gradually becoming more self-conscious of the nature of his bestowal on earth.

This hill, a little more than one hundred years previously, had been the "high place of Baal," and now it was the site of the tomb of Simeon, a reputed holy man of Israel. From the summit of this hill of Simeon, Jesus looked out over Nazareth and the surrounding country. He would gaze upon Megiddo and recall the story of the Egyptian army winning its first great victory in Asia; and how, later on, another such army defeated the Judean king Josiah. Not far away he could look upon Taanach, where Deborah and Barak defeated Sisera. In the distance he could view the hills of Dothan, where he had been taught Joseph's brethren sold him into Egyptian slavery. He then would shift his gaze over to Ebal and Gerizim and recount to himself the traditions of Abraham, Jacob, and Abimelech. And thus he recalled and turned over in his mind the historic and traditional events of his father Joseph's people.

He continued to carry on his advanced courses of reading under the synagogue teachers, and he also continued with the home education of his brothers and sisters as they grew up to suitable ages.

Early this year Joseph arranged to set aside the income from his Nazareth and Capernaum property to pay for Jesus' long course of study at Jerusalem, it having been planned that he should go to Jerusalem in August of the following year when he would be fifteen years of age.

By the beginning of this year both Joseph and Mary entertained frequent doubts about the destiny of their first-born son. He was indeed a brilliant and lovable child, but he was so difficult to understand, so hard to fathom, and again, nothing extraordinary or miraculous ever happened. Scores of times had his proud mother stood in breathless anticipation, expecting to see her son engage in some superhuman or miraculous performance, but always were her hopes dashed down in cruel disappointment. And all this was discouraging, even dis- heartening. The devout people of those days truly believed that prophets and men of promise always demonstrated their calling and established their divine authority by performing miracles and working wonders. But Jesus did none of these things; wherefore was the confusion of his parents steadily increased as they contemplated his future.

The improved economic condition of the Nazareth family was reflected in many ways about the home and especially in the increased number of smooth white boards which were used as writing slates, the writing being done with charcoal. Jesus was also permitted to resume his music lessons; he was very fond of playing the harp.

Throughout this year it can truly be said that Jesus "grew in favor with man and with God." The prospects of the family seemed good; the future was bright.

All did go well until that fateful day of Tuesday, September 25, when a runner from Sepphoris brought to this Nazareth home the tragic news that Joseph had been severely injured by the falling of a derrick while at work on the governor's residence. The messenger from Sepphoris had stopped at the shop on the way to Joseph's home, informing Jesus of his father's accident, and they went together to the house to break the sad news to Mary. Jesus desired to go immediately to his father, but Mary would hear to nothing but that she must hasten to her husband's side. She directed that James, then ten years of age, should accompany her to Sepphoris while Jesus remained home with the younger children until she should return, as she did not know how seriously Joseph had been injured. But Joseph died of his injuries before Mary arrived. They brought him to Nazareth, and on the following day he was laid to rest with his fathers.

Just at the time when prospects were good and the future looked bright, an apparently cruel hand struck down the head of this Nazareth household, the affairs of this home were disrupted, and every plan for Jesus and his future education was demolished. This carpenter lad, now just past fourteen years of age, awakened to the realization that he had not only to fulfill the commission of his heavenly Father to reveal the divine nature on earth and in the flesh, but that his young human nature must also shoulder the responsibility of caring for his widowed mother and seven brothers and sisters — and another yet to be born. This lad of Nazareth now became the sole support and comfort of this so suddenly bereaved family. Thus were permitted those occurrences of the natural order of events on Earth which would force this young man of destiny so early to assume these heavy but highly educational and disciplinary responsibilities attendant upon becoming the head of a human family, of becoming father to his own brothers and sisters, of supporting and protecting his mother, of functioning as guardian of his father's home, the only home he was to know while on this world.

Jesus cheerfully accepted the responsibilities so suddenly thrust upon him, and he carried them faithfully to the end. At least one great problem and antici-pated difficulty in his life had been tragically solved — he would not now be ex-pected to go to Jerusalem to study under the rabbis. It remained always true that Jesus "sat at no man's feet." He was ever willing to learn from even the humblest of little children, but he never derived authority to teach truth from human sources.

As the years passed, this young carpenter of Nazareth increasingly measured every institution of society and every usage of religion by the unvarying test: What does it do for the human soul? Does it bring God to man? Does it bring man to God? While this youth did not wholly neglect the recreational and social aspects of life, more and more he devoted his time and energies to just two purposes: the care of his family and the preparation to do his Father's heavenly will on earth.

This year it became the custom for the neighbors to drop in during the winter evenings to hear Jesus play upon the harp, to listen to his stories (for the lad was a master storyteller), and to hear him read from the Greek scriptures.

The economic affairs of the family continued to run fairly smoothly, as there was quite a sum of money on hand at the time of Joseph's death. Jesus early dem-onstrated the possession of keen business judgment and financial sagacity. He was liberal but frugal; he was saving but generous. He proved to be a wise and efficient administrator of his father's estate.

But in spite of all that Jesus and the Nazareth neighbors could do to bring cheer into the home, Mary, and even the children, were overcast with sadness. Jo-seph was gone. Joseph was an unusual husband and father, and they all missed him. And it seemed all the more tragic to think that he died before they could speak to him or hear his farewell blessing.

By the middle of his fifteenth year, A.D. 9 Jesus had taken a firm grasp upon the management of his family. Before this year had passed, their savings had about disappeared, and they were face to face with the necessity of disposing of one of the Nazareth houses which Joseph and his neighbor Jacob owned in partnership.

On Wednesday evening, April 17, A.D. 9, Ruth, the baby of the family, was born, and to the best of his ability Jesus endeavored to take the place of his father in comforting and ministering to his mother during this trying and peculiarly sad ordeal. For almost a score of years (until he began his public ministry) no father could have loved and nurtured his daughter any more affectionately and faithfully than Jesus cared for little Ruth. And he was an equally good father to all the other members of his family.

During this year Jesus first formulated the prayer which he subsequently taught to his apostles, and which to many has become known as "The Lord's Prayer." In a way it was an evolution of the family altar; they had many forms of praise and several formal prayers. After his father's death Jesus tried to teach the older children to express themselves individually in prayer — much as he so enjoyed doing — but they could not grasp his thought and would invariably fall back upon their memorized prayer forms. It was in this effort to stimulate his older brothers and sisters to say individual prayers that Jesus would endeavor to lead them along by suggestive phrases, and presently, without intention on his part, it developed that they were all using a form of prayer which was largely built up from these suggestive lines which Jesus had taught them.

At last Jesus gave up the idea of having each member of the family formulate spontaneous prayers, and one evening in October he sat down by the little squat lamp on the low stone table, and, on a piece of smooth cedar board about eighteen inches square, with a piece of charcoal he wrote out the prayer which became from that time on the standard family petition.

This year Jesus was much troubled with confused thinking. Family responsibility had quite effectively removed all thought of immediately carrying out any plan for responding to the Jerusalem visitation directing him to "be about his Father's business." Jesus rightly reasoned that the watchcare of his earthly father's family must take precedence of all duties; that the support of his family must become his first obligation.

In the course of this year Jesus found a passage in the so-called Book of Enoch which influenced him in the later adoption of the term "Son of Man" as a designation for his bestowal mission on Earth. He had thoroughly considered the idea of the Jewish Messiah and was firmly convinced that he was not to be that Messiah. He longed to help his father's people, but he never expected to lead Jewish armies in overthrowing the foreign domination of Palestine. He knew he would never sit on the throne of David at Jerusalem. Neither did he believe that his mission was that of a spiritual deliverer or moral teacher solely to the Jewish people. In no sense, therefore, could his life mission be the fulfillment of the intense longings and supposed Messianic prophecies of the Hebrew scriptures; at least, not as the Jews understood these predictions of the prophets. Likewise he was certain he was never to appear as the Son of Man depicted by the Prophet Daniel.

But when the time came for him to go forth as a world teacher, what would he call himself? What claim should he make concerning his mission? By what name would the people who would become believers in his teachings call him?

While turning all these problems over in his mind, he found in the synagogue library at Nazareth, among the apocalyptic books which he had been studying, this manuscript called "The Book of Enoch"; and though he was certain that it had not been written by Enoch of old, it proved very intriguing to him, and he read and re-read it many times. There was one passage that particularly impressed him, a passage in which this term "Son of Man" appeared. The writer of this so-called Book of Enoch went on to tell about this Son of Man, describing the work he would do on earth and explaining that this Son of Man, before coming down on this earth to bring salvation to mankind, had walked through the courts of heavenly glory with his Father, the Father of all; and that he had turned his back upon all this grandeur and glory to come down on earth to proclaim salvation to needy mortals. As Jesus would read these passages (well understanding that much of the Eastern mysticism which had become admixed with these teachings was erroneous), he responded in his heart and recognized in his mind that of all the Messianic predictions of the Hebrew scriptures and of all the theories about the Jewish deliverer, none was so near the truth as this story tucked away in this only partially accredited Book of Enoch; and he then and there decided to adopt as his inaugural title "the Son of Man." And this he did when he subsequently began his public work. Jesus had an unerring ability for the recognition of truth, and truth he never hesitated to embrace, no matter from what source it appeared to emanate.

By this time he had quite thoroughly settled many things about his forthcoming work for the world, but he said nothing of these matters to his mother, who still held stoutly to the idea of his being the Jewish Messiah.

The great confusion of Jesus' younger days now arose. Having settled something about the nature of his mission on earth, "to be about his Father's business" — to show forth his Father's loving nature to all mankind — he began to ponder anew the many statements in the Scriptures referring to the coming of a national deliverer, a Jewish teacher or king. To what event did these prophecies refer? Was not he a Jew? Or was he? Was he or was he not of the house of David? His mother averred he was; his father had ruled that he was not. He decided he was not. But had the prophets confused the nature and mission of the Messiah?

After all, could it be possible that his mother was right? In most matters, when differences of opinion had arisen in the past, she had been right. If he were a new teacher and *not* the Messiah, then how should he recognize the Jewish Messiah if such a one should appear in Jerusalem during the time of his earth mission; and, further, what should be his relation to this Jewish Messiah? And what should be his relation, after embarking on his life mission, to his family? To the Jewish commonwealth and religion? To the Roman Empire? To the gentiles and their religions? Each of these momentous problems this young Galilean turned over in his mind and seriously pondered while he continued to work at the carpenter's bench, laboriously making a living for himself, his mother, and eight other hungry mouths.

Before the end of this year Mary saw the family funds diminishing. She turned the sale of doves over to James. Presently they bought a second cow, and with the aid of Miriam they began the sale of milk to their Nazareth neighbors.

His profound periods of meditation, his frequent journeys to the hilltop for prayer, and the many strange ideas which Jesus advanced from time to time, thoroughly alarmed his mother. Sometimes she thought the lad was beside himself, and then she would steady her fears, remembering that he was, after all, a child of promise and in some manner different from other youths.

But Jesus was learning not to speak of all his thoughts, not to present all his ideas to the world, not even to his own mother. From this year on, Jesus' disclosures about what was going on in his mind steadily diminished; that is, he talked less about those things which an average person could not grasp, and which would lead to his being regarded as peculiar or different from ordinary folks. To all appearances he became commonplace and conventional, though he did long for someone who could understand his problems. He craved a trustworthy and confidential friend, but his problems were too complex for his human associates to comprehend. The uniqueness of the unusual situation compelled him to bear his burdens alone.

With the coming of his fifteenth birthday, Jesus could officially occupy the synagogue pulpit on the Sabbath day. Many times before, in the absence of speakers, Jesus had been asked to read the Scriptures, but now the day had come when, according to law, he could conduct the service. Therefore on the first Sabbath after his fifteenth birthday the chazan arranged for Jesus to conduct the morning service of the synagogue. And when all the faithful in Nazareth had assembled, the young man, having made his selection of Scriptures, stood up and began to read:

"The spirit of the Lord God is upon me, for the Lord has anointed me; he has sent me to bring good news to the meek, to bind up the brokenhearted, to proclaim liberty to the captives, and to set the spiritual prisoners free; to proclaim the year of God's favor and the day of our God's reckoning; to comfort all mourners, to give them beauty for ashes, the oil of joy in the place of mourning, a song of praise instead of the spirit of sorrow, that they may be called trees of righteousness, the planting of the Lord, wherewith he may be glorified.

"Seek good and not evil that you may live, and so the Lord, the God of hosts, shall be with you. Hate the evil and love the good; establish judgment in the gate. Perhaps the Lord God will be gracious to the remnant of Joseph.

"Wash yourselves, make yourselves clean; put away the evil of your doings from before my eyes; cease to do evil and learn to do good; seek justice, relieve the oppressed. Defend the fatherless and plead for the widow.

"Wherewith shall I come before the Lord, to bow myself before the Lord of all the earth? Shall I come before him with burnt offerings, with calves a year old? Will the Lord be pleased with thousands of rams, ten thousands of sheep, or with rivers of oil? Shall I give my first-born for my transgression, the fruit of my body for the sin of my soul? For the Lord has showed us, O men, what is good. And what does the Lord require of you but to deal justly, love mercy, and walk humbly with your God?

"To whom, then, will you liken God who sits upon the circle of the earth? Lift up your eyes and behold who has created all these worlds, who brings forth their host by number and calls them all by their names. He does all these things by the greatness of His might, and because He is strong in power, not one fails. He gives power to the weak, and to those who are weary He increases strength. Fear not, for I am with you; be not dismayed, for I am your God. I will strengthen you and I will help you; yes, I will uphold you with the right hand of my righteousness, for I am the Lord your God. And I will hold your right hand, saying to you, fear not, for I will help you.

"And you are my witness, says the Lord, and my servant whom I have chosen that all may know and believe me and understand that I am the Eternal. I, even I, am the Lord, and beside me there is no savior."

And when he had thus read, he sat down, and the people went to their homes, pondering over the words that he had so graciously read to them. Never had his townspeople seen him so magnificently solemn; never had they heard his voice so earnest and so sincere; never had they observed him so manly and decisive, so authoritative.

This Sabbath afternoon Jesus climbed the Nazareth hill with James and, when they returned home, wrote out the Ten Commandments in Greek on two smooth boards in charcoal. Subsequently Martha colored and decorated these boards, and for long they hung on the wall over James's small workbench.

Gradually Jesus and his family returned to the simple life of their earlier years. Their clothes and even their food became simpler. They had plenty of milk, butter, and cheese. In season they enjoyed the produce of their garden, but each passing month necessitated the practice of greater frugality. Their breakfasts were very plain; they saved their best food for the evening meal. However, among these Jews lack of wealth did not imply social inferiority.

Already had this youth well-nigh encompassed the comprehension of how men live in his day. And how well he understood life in the home, field, and workshop is shown by his subsequent teachings, which so abundantly reveal his intimate contact with all phases of human experience.

The Nazareth chazan continued to cling to the belief that Jesus was to become a great teacher, probably the successor of the renowned Gamaliel at Jerusalem.

Apparently all Jesus' plans for a career were thwarted. The future did not look bright as matters now developed. But he did not falter; he was not discouraged. He lived on, day by day, doing well the present duty and faithfully discharging the *immediate* responsibilities of his station in life. Jesus' life is the everlasting comfort of all disappointed idealists.

The pay of a common day-laboring carpenter was slowly diminishing. By the end of this year Jesus could earn, by working early and late, only the equivalent of about two dollars a day. By the next year they found it difficult to pay the civil taxes, not to mention the synagogue assessments and the temple tax of one-half shekel. During this year the tax collector tried to squeeze extra revenue out of Jesus, even threatening to take his harp.

Fearing that his copy of the Greek scriptures might be discovered and confiscated by the tax collectors, Jesus, on his fifteenth birthday, presented it to the Nazareth synagogue library as his maturity offering to the Lord.

The great shock of his fifteenth year came when Jesus went over to Sepphoris to receive the decision of Herod regarding the appeal taken to him in the dispute about the amount of money due Joseph at the time of his accidental death. Jesus and Mary had hoped for the receipt of a considerable sum of money when the treasurer at Sepphoris had offered them a paltry amount. Joseph's brothers had taken an appeal to Herod himself, and now Jesus stood in the palace and heard Herod decree that his father had nothing due him at the time of his death. And for such an unjust decision Jesus never again trusted Herod Antipas. It is not surprising that he once alluded to Herod as "that fox."

The close work at the carpenter's bench during this and subsequent years deprived Jesus of the opportunity of mingling with the caravan passengers. The family supply shop had already been taken over by his uncle, and Jesus worked altogether in the home shop, where he was near to help Mary with the family. About this time he began sending James up to the camel lot to gather information about world events, in this way he sought to keep in touch with the news of the day.

As he grew up to manhood, he passed through all those conflicts and confusions which the average young persons of previous and subsequent ages have undergone. And the rigorous experience of supporting his family was a sure safeguard against his having overmuch time for idle meditation or the indulgence of mystic tendencies.

This was the year that Jesus rented a considerable piece of land just to the north of their home, which was divided up as a family garden plot. Each of the older children had an individual garden, and they entered into keen competition in their agricultural efforts. Their eldest brother spent some time with them in the garden each day during the season of vegetable cultivation. As Jesus worked with his younger brothers and sisters in the garden, he many times entertained the wish that they were all located on a farm out in the country where they could enjoy the liberty and freedom of an unhampered life. But they did not find themselves growing up in the country; and Jesus, being a thoroughly practical youth as well as an idealist, intelligently and vigorously attacked his problem just as he found it, and did everything within his power to adjust himself and his family to the realities of their situation and to adapt their condition to the highest possible satisfaction of their individual and collective longings.

At one time Jesus faintly hoped that he might be able to gather up sufficient means, provided they could collect the considerable sum of money due his father for work on Herod's palace, to warrant undertaking the purchase of a small farm. He had really given serious thought to this plan of moving his family out into the country. But when Herod refused to pay them any of the funds due Joseph, they gave up the ambition of owning a home in the country. As it was, they contrived to enjoy much of the experience of farm life as they now had three cows, four sheep,a flock of chickens, a donkey, and a dog, in addition to the doves. Even the little tots had their regular duties to perform in the well-regulated scheme of management that characterized the home life of this Nazareth family.

With the close of this fifteenth year Jesus completed the traversal of that dangerous and difficult period in human existence, that time of transition between the more complacent years of childhood and the consciousness of approaching manhood with its increased responsibilities and opportunities for the acquirement of advanced experience in the development of a noble character. The growth period for mind and body had ended, and now began the real career of this young man of Nazareth.

THE ADOLESCENT YEARS

AS JESUS entered upon his adolescent years, he found himself the head and sole support of a large family. Within a few years after his father's death all their property was gone. As time passed, he became increasingly conscious of his pre-existence; at the same time he began more fully to realize that he was present on earth and in the flesh for the express purpose of revealing his Paradise Father to the children of men.

No adolescent youth who has lived or ever will live on this world or any other world has had or ever will have more weighty problems to resolve or more intricate difficulties to untangle. No youth of Earth will ever be called upon to pass through more testing conflicts or more trying situations than Jesus himself endured during those strenuous years from fifteen to twenty.

Having thus tasted the actual experience of living these adolescent years on a world beset by evil and distraught by sin, the Son of Man became possessed of full knowledge about the life experience of the youth of all the realms of his local creation, and thus forever he became the understanding refuge for the distressed and perplexed adolescents of all ages and on all worlds throughout this local universe.

Slowly, but certainly and by actual experience, this divine Son is *earning* the right to become sovereign of his universe, the unquestioned and supreme ruler of all created intelligences on all local universe worlds, the understanding refuge of the beings of all ages and of all degrees of personal endowment and experience.

The incarnated Son passed through infancy and experienced an uneventful childhood. Then he emerged from that testing and trying transition stage between childhood and young manhood — he became the adolescet Jesus.

This year, 10 A.D. he attained his full physical growth. He was a virile and comely youth. He became increasingly sober and serious, but he was kind and sympathetic. His eye was kind but searching; his smile was always engaging and reassuring. His voice was musical but authoritative; his greeting cordial but unaffected. Always, even in the most commonplace of contacts, there seemed to be in evidence the touch of a twofold nature, the human and the divine. Ever he displayed this combination of the sympathizing friend and the authoritative teacher. And these personality traits began early to become manifest, even in these adolescent years.

This physically strong and robust youth also acquired the full growth of his human intellect, not the full experience of human thinking but the fullness of capacity for such intellectual development. He possessed a healthy and well-proportioned body, a keen and analytical mind, a kind and sympathetic disposition, a somewhat fluctuating but aggressive temperament, all of which were becoming organized into a strong, striking, and attractive personality.

As time went on, it became more difficult for his mother and his brothers and sisters to understand him; they stumbled over his sayings and misinterpreted his doings. They were all unfitted to comprehend their eldest brother's life because their mother had given them to understand that he was destined to become the deliverer of the Jewish people. After they had received from Mary such intimations as family secrets, imagine their confusion when Jesus would make frank denials of all such ideas and intentions.

This year Simon started to school, and they were compelled to sell another house. James now took charge of the teaching of his three sisters, two of whom were old enough to begin serious study. As soon as Ruth grew up, she was taken in hand by Miriam and Martha. Ordinarily the girls of Jewish families received little education, but Jesus maintained (and his mother agreed) that girls should go to school the same as boys, and since the synagogue school would not receive them, there was nothing to do but conduct a home school especially for them.

Throughout this year Jesus was closely confined to the workbench. Fortunately he had plenty of work; his was of such a superior grade that he was never idle no matter how slack work might be in that region. At times he had so much to do that James would help him.

By the end of this year he had just about made up his mind that he would, after rearing his family and seeing them married, enter publicly upon his work as a teacher of truth and as a revealer of the heavenly Father to the world. He knew he was not to become the expected Jewish Messiah, and he concluded that it was next to useless to discuss these matters with his mother; he decided to allow her to entertain whatever ideas she might choose since all he had said in the past had made little or no impression upon her and he recalled that his father had never been able to say anything that would change her mind. From this year on he talked less and less with his mother, or anyone else, about these problems. His was such a peculiar mission that no one living on earth could give him advice concerning its prosecution.

He was a real though youthful father to the family; he spent every possible hour with the youngsters, and they truly loved him. His mother grieved to see him work so hard; she sorrowed that he was day by day toiling at the carpenter's bench earning a living for the family instead of being, as they had so fondly planned, at Jerusalem studying with the rabbis. While there was much about her son that Mary could not understand, she did love him, and she most thoroughly appreciated the willing manner in which he shouldered the responsibility of the home.

At about the time of his seventeenth year, A.D. 11, there was considerable agitation, especially at Jerusalem and in Judea, in favor of rebellion against the payment of taxes to Rome. There was coming into existence a strong nationalist party, presently to be called the Zealots who, unlike the Pharisees, were not willing to await the coming of the Messiah. They proposed to bring things to a head through political revolt.

A group of organizers from Jerusalem arrived in Galilee and were making good headway until they reached Nazareth. When they came to see Jesus, he listened carefully to them and asked many questions but refused to join the party. He declined fully to disclose his reasons for not enlisting, and his refusal had the effect of keeping out many of his youthful fellows in Nazareth.

Mary did her best to induce him to enlist, but she could not budge him. She went so far as to intimate that his refusal to espouse the nationalist cause at her behest was insubordination, a violation of his pledge made upon their return from Jerusalem that he would be subject to his parents; but in answer to this insinuation he only laid a kindly hand on her shoulder and, looking into her face, said, "My mother, how could you?" And Mary withdrew her statement.

One of Jesus' uncles (Mary's brother Simon) had already joined this group, subsequently becoming an officer in the Galilean division. And for several years there was something of an estrangement between Jesus and his uncle.

But trouble began to brew in Nazareth. Jesus' attitude in these matters had resulted in creating a division among the Jewish youths of the city. About half had joined the nationalist organization, and the other half began the formation of an opposing group of more moderate patriots, expecting Jesus to assume the leadership. They were amazed when he refused the honor offered him, pleading as an excuse his heavy family responsibilities, which they all allowed. But the situation was still further complicated when, presently, a wealthy Jew, Isaac, a moneylender to the gentiles, came forward agreeing to support Jesus' family if he would lay down his tools and assume leadership of these Nazareth patriots.

Jesus, then scarcely seventeen years of age, was confronted with one of the most delicate and difficult situations of his early life. Patriotic issues, especially when complicated by tax-gathering foreign oppressors, are always difficult for spiritual leaders to relate themselves to, and it was doubly so in this case since the Jewish religion was involved in all this agitation against Rome.

Jesus' position was made more difficult because his mother and uncle, and even his younger brother James, all urged him to join the nationalist cause. All the better Jews of Nazareth had enlisted, and those young men who had not joined the movement would all enlist the moment Jesus changed his mind. He had but one wise counselor in all Nazareth, his old teacher, the chazan, who counseled him about his reply to the citizens' committee of Nazareth when they came to ask for his answer to the public appeal which had been made. In all Jesus' young life this was the very first time he had consciously resorted to public strategy. Always before had he depended upon a frank statement of truth to clarify the situation, but now he could not declare the full truth. He could not intimate that he was more than a man; he could not disclose his idea of the mission which awaited his attainment of a riper manhood. Despite these limitations his religious fealty and national loyalty were directly challenged. His family was in turmoil, his youthful friends in division, and the entire Jewish contingent of the town in a hubbub. And to think that he was to blame for it all! And how innocent he had been of all intention to make trouble of any kind, much less a disturbance of this sort.

Something had to be done. He must state his position, and this he did bravely and diplomatically to the satisfaction of many, but not all. He adhered to the terms of his original plea, maintaining that his first duty was to his family, that a widowed mother and eight brothers and sisters needed something more than mere money could buy — the physical necessities of life — that they were entitled to a father's watchcare and guidance, and that he could not in clear conscience release himself from the obligation which a cruel accident had thrust upon him. He paid compliment to his mother and eldest brother for being willing to release him but reiterated that loyalty to a dead father forbade his leaving the family no matter how much money was forthcoming for their material support, making his never-to-be-forgotten statement that "money cannot love." In the course of this address Jesus made several veiled references to his "life mission" but explained that, regardless of whether or not it might be inconsistent with the military idea, it, along with everything else in his life, had been given up in order that he might be able to discharge faithfully his obligation to his family. Everyone in Nazareth well knew he was a good father to his family, and this was a matter so near the heart of every noble Jew that Jesus' plea found an appreciative response in the hearts of many of his hearers; and some of those who were not thus minded were disarmed by a speech made by James, which, while not on the program, was delivered at this time. That very day the chazan had rehearsed James in his speech, but that was their secret.

James stated that he was sure Jesus would help to liberate his people if he (James) were only old enough to assume responsibility for the family, and that, if they would only consent to allow Jesus to remain "with us, to be our father and teacher, then you will have not just one leader from Joseph's family, but presently you will have five loyal nationalists, for are there not five of us boys to grow up and come forth from our brother-father's guidance to serve our nation?" And thus did the lad bring to a fairly happy ending a very tense and threatening situation.

The crisis for the time being was over, but never was this incident forgotten in Nazareth. The agitation persisted; not again was Jesus in universal favor; the division of sentiment was never fully overcome. And this, augmented by other and subsequent occurrences, was one of the chief reasons why he moved to Capernaum in later years. Henceforth Nazareth maintained a division of sentiment regarding the Son of Man.

James graduated at school this year and began full-time work at home in the carpenter shop. He had become a clever worker with tools and now took over the making of yokes and plows while Jesus began to do more house finishing and expert cabinetwork.

This year Jesus made great progress in the organization of his mind. Gradually he had brought his divine and human natures together, and he accomplished all this organization of intellect by the force of his own *decisions* and with only the aid of his indwelling Father Fragment, just such a Mystery Monitor as indwells the minds of all normal mortals on all worlds of time and space. Truly is man 'created in our image.' And still, nothing supernatural had happened in this young man's career except the visit of a messenger dispatched by his elder brother Immanuel, who once appeared to him during the night at Jerusalem.

In the course of his eighteenth year, all the family property, except the home and garden, was disposed of. The last piece of Capernaum property (except an equity in one other), already mortgaged, was sold. The proceeds were used for taxes, to buy some new tools for James, and to make a payment on the old family supply and repair shop near the caravan lot, which Jesus now proposed to buy back since James was old enough to work at the house shop and help Mary about the home. With the financial pressure thus eased for the time being, Jesus decided to take James to the Passover. They went up to Jerusalem a day early, to be alone, going by way of Samaria. They walked, and Jesus told James about the historic places en route as his father had taught him on a similar journey five years before.

In passing through Samaria, they saw many strange sights. On this journey they talked over many of their problems, personal, family, and national. James was a very religious type of lad, and while he did not fully agree with his mother regarding the little he knew of the plans concerning Jesus' lifework, he did look forward to the time when he would be able to assume responsibility for the family so that Jesus could begin his mission. He was very appreciative of Jesus' taking him up to the Passover, and they talked over the future more fully than ever before.

Jesus did much thinking as they journeyed through Samaria, particularly at Bethel and when drinking from Jacob's well. He and his brother discussed the traditions of Abraham, Isaac, and Jacob. He did much to prepare James for what he was about to witness at Jerusalem, thus seeking to lessen the shock such as he himself had experienced on his first visit to the temple. But James was not so sensitive to some of these sights. He commented on the perfunctory and heartless manner in which some of the priests performed their duties but on the whole greatly enjoyed his sojourn at Jerusalem.

Jesus took James to Bethany for the Passover supper. Simon had been laid to rest with his fathers, and Jesus presided over this household as the head of the Passover family, having brought the paschal lamb from the temple.

After the Passover supper Mary sat down to talk with James while Martha, Lazarus, and Jesus talked together far into the night. The next day they attended the temple services, and James was received into the commonwealth of Israel. That morning, as they paused on the brow of Olivet to view the temple, while James exclaimed in wonder, Jesus gazed on Jerusalem in silence. James could not comprehend his brother's demeanor. That night they again returned to Bethany and would have departed for home the next day, but James was insistent on their going back to visit the temple, explaining that he wanted to hear the teachers. And while this was true, secretly in his heart he wanted to hear Jesus participate in the discussions, as he had heard his mother tell about. Accordingly, they went to the temple and heard the discussions, but Jesus asked no questions. It all seemed so puerile and insignificant to this awakening mind of man and God — he could only pity them. James was disappointed that Jesus said nothing. To his inquiries Jesus only made reply, "My hour has not yet come."

The next day they journeyed home by Jericho and the Jordan valley, and Jesus recounted many things by the way, including his former trip over this road when he was thirteen years old.

Upon returning to Nazareth, Jesus began work in the old family repair shop and was greatly cheered by being able to meet so many people each day from all parts of the country and surrounding districts. Jesus truly loved people — just common folks. Each month he made his payments on the shop and, with James's help, continued to provide for the family.

Several times a year, when visitors were not present thus to function, Jesus continued to read the Sabbath scriptures at the synagogue and many times offered comments on the lesson, but usually he so selected the passages that comment was unnecessary. He was skillful, so arranging the order of the reading of the various passages that the one would illuminate the other. He never failed, weather permitting, to take his brothers and sisters out on Sabbath afternoons for their nature strolls.

About this time the chazan inaugurated a young men's club for philosophic discussion which met at the homes of different members and often at his own home, and Jesus became a prominent member of this group. By this means he was enabled to regain some of the local prestige which he had lost at the time of the recent nationalistic controversies.

His social life, while restricted, was not wholly neglected. He had many warm friends and stanch admirers among both the young men and the young women of Nazareth.

In September, Elizabeth and John came to visit the Nazareth family. John, having lost his father, intended to return to the Judean hills to engage in agriculture and sheep raising unless Jesus advised him to remain in Nazareth to take up carpentry or some other line of work. They did not know that the Nazareth family was practically penniless. The more Mary and Elizabeth talked about their sons, the more they became convinced that it would be good for the two young men to work together and see more of each other.

Jesus and John had many talks together; and they talked over some very intimate and personal matters. When they had finished this visit, they decided not again to see each other until they should meet in their public service after "the heavenly Father should call" them to their work. John was tremendously impressed by what he saw at Nazareth that he should return home and labor for the support of his mother. He became convinced that he was to be a part of Jesus' life mission, but he saw that Jesus was to occupy many years with the rearing of his family; so he was much more content to return to his home and settle down to the care of their little farm and to minister to the needs of his mother. And never again did John and Jesus see each other until that day by the Jordan when the Son of Man presented himself for baptism.

On Saturday afternoon, December 3, of this year, death for the second time struck at this Nazareth family. Little Amos, their baby brother, died after a week's illness with a high fever. After passing through this time of sorrow with her first-born son as her only support, Mary at last and in the fullest sense recognized Jesus as the real head of the family; and he was truly a worthy holder of the designation.

For four years their standard of living had steadily declined; year by year they felt the pinch of increasing poverty. By the close of this year they faced one of the most difficult experiences of all their uphill struggles. James had not yet begun to earn much, and the expenses of a funeral on top of everything else staggered them. But Jesus would only say to his anxious and grieving mother: "Mother-Mary, sorrow will not help us; we are all doing our best, and mother's smile, perchance, might even inspire us to do better. Day by day we are strengthened for these tasks by our hope of better days ahead." His sturdy and practical optimism was truly contagious; all the children lived in an atmosphere of anticipation of better times and better things. And this hopeful courage contributed mightily to the development of strong and noble characters, in spite of the depressing nature of their poverty.

Jesus possessed the ability effectively to mobilize all his powers of mind, soul, and body on the task immediately in hand. He could concentrate his deep-thinking mind on the one problem which he wished to solve, and this, in connection with his untiring *patience,* enabled him serenely to endure the trials of a difficult mortal existence — to live as if he were "seeing Him who is invisible."

By his nineteenth year Jesus and Mary were getting along much better. She regarded him less as a son; he had become to her more a father to her children. Each day's life swarmed with practical and immediate difficulties. Less frequently they spoke of his lifework, for, as time passed, all their thought was mutually devoted to the support and upbringing of their family of four boys and three girls.

By the beginning of this year Jesus had fully won his mother to the acceptance of his methods of child training — the positive injunction to do good in the place of the older Jewish method of forbidding to do evil. In his home and throughout his public-teaching career Jesus invariably employed the *positive* form of exhortation. Always and everywhere did he say, "You shall do this — you ought to do that." Never did he employ the negative mode of teaching derived from the ancient taboos. He refrained from placing emphasis on evil by forbidding it, while he exalted the good by commanding its performance. Prayer time in this household was the occasion for discussing anything and everything relating to the welfare of the family.

Jesus began wise discipline upon his brothers and sisters at such an early age that little or no punishment was ever required to secure their prompt and wholehearted obedience. The only exception was Jude, upon whom on sundry occasions Jesus found it necessary to impose penalties for his infractions of the rules of the home. On three occasions when it was deemed wise to punish Jude for self-confessed and deliberate violations of the family rules of conduct, his punishment was fixed by the unanimous decree of the older children and was assented to by Jude himself before it was inflicted.

While Jesus was most methodical and systematic in everything he did, there was also in all his administrative rulings a refreshing elasticity of interpretation and an individuality of adaptation that greatly impressed all the children with the spirit of justice which actuated their father-brother. He never arbitrarily disciplined his brothers and sisters, and such uniform fairness and personal consideration greatly endeared Jesus to all his family.

James and Simon grew up trying to follow Jesus' plan of placating their belli-
cose and sometimes irate playmates by persuasion and nonresistance, and they
were fairly successful; but Joseph and Jude, while assenting to such teachings at
home, made haste to defend themselves when assailed by their comrades; in particular was Jude guilty of violating the spirit of these teachings. But nonresistance
was not a *rule* of the family. No penalty was attached to the violation of personal
teachings.

In general, all of the children, particularly the girls, would consult Jesus
about their childhood troubles and confide in him just as they would have in an affectionate father.

James was growing up to be a well-balanced and even-tempered youth, but
he was not so spiritually inclined as Jesus. He was a much better student than Joseph, who, while a faithful worker, was even less spiritually minded. Joseph was a
plodder and not up to the intellectual level of the other children. Simon was a well-
meaning boy but too much of a dreamer. He was slow in getting settled down in
life and was the cause of considerable anxiety to Jesus and Mary. But he was always a good and well-intentioned lad. Jude was a firebrand. He had the highest of
ideals, but he was unstable in temperament. He had all and more of his mother's
determination and aggressiveness, but he lacked much of her sense of proportion
and discretion.

Miriam was a well-balanced and level-headed daughter with a keen appreciation of things noble and spiritual. Martha was slow in thought and action but a very
dependable and efficient child. Baby Ruth was the sunshine of the home; though
thoughtless of speech, she was most sincere of heart. She just about worshiped her
big brother and father. But they did not spoil her. She was a beautiful child but not
quite so comely as Miriam, who was the belle of the family, if not of the city.

As time passed, Jesus did much to liberalize and modify the family teachings
and practices related to Sabbath observance and many other phases of religion,
and to all these changes Mary gave hearty assent. By this time Jesus had become
the unquestioned head of the house.

This year Jude started to school, and it was necessary for Jesus to sell his harp
in order to defray these expenses. Thus disappeared the last of his recreational
pleasures. He much loved to play the harp when tired in mind and weary in body,
but he comforted himself with the thought that at least the instrument was safe
from seizure by the tax collector.

Although Jesus was poor, his social standing in Nazareth was in no way impaired.
He was one of the foremost young men of the city and very highly regarded by
most of the young women. Since Jesus was such a splendid specimen of robust and
intellectual manhood, and considering his reputation as a spiritual leader, it was
not strange that Rebecca, the eldest daughter of Ezra, a wealthy merchant and trader

of Nazareth, should discover that she was slowly falling in love with this son of Joseph. She first confided her affection to Miriam, Jesus' sister, and Miriam in turn talked all this over with her mother. Mary was intensely aroused. Was she about to lose her son, now become the indispensable head of the family? Would troubles never cease? What next could happen? And then she paused to contemplate what effect marriage would have upon Jesus' future career; not often, but at least sometimes, did she recall the fact that Jesus was a "child of promise." After she and Miriam had talked this matter over, they decided to make an effort to stop it before Jesus learned about it, by going direct to Rebecca, laying the whole story before her, and honestly telling her about their belief that Jesus was a son of destiny; that he was to become a great religious leader, perhaps the Messiah.

Rebecca listened intently; she was thrilled with the recital and more than ever determined to cast her lot with this man of her choice and to share his career of leadership. She argued (to herself) that such a man would all the more need a faithful and efficient wife. She interpreted Mary's efforts to dissuade her as a natural reaction to the dread of losing the head and sole support of her family; but knowing that her father approved of her attraction for the carpenter's son, she rightly reckoned that he would gladly supply the family with sufficient income fully to compensate for the loss of Jesus' earnings. When her father agreed to such a plan, Rebecca had further conferences with Mary and Miriam, and when she failed to win their support, she made bold to go directly to Jesus. This she did with the co-operation of her father, who invited Jesus to their home for the celebration of Rebecca's seventeenth birthday.

Jesus listened attentively and sympathetically to the recital of these things, first by the father, then by Rebecca herself. He made kindly reply to the effect that no amount of money could take the place of his obligation personally to rear his father's family, to "fulfill the most sacred of all human trusts — loyalty to one's own flesh and blood." Rebecca's father was deeply touched by Jesus' words of family devotion and retired from the conference. His only remark to Mary, his wife, was: "We can't have him for a son; he is too noble for us."

Then began that eventful talk with Rebecca. Thus far in his life, Jesus had made little distinction in his association with boys and girls, with young men and young women. His mind had been altogether too much occupied with the pressing problems of practical earthly affairs and the intriguing contemplation of his eventual career "about his Father's business" ever to have given serious consideration to the consummation of personal love in human marriage. But now he was face to face with another of those problems that every average human being must confront and decide. Indeed was he "tested in all points like as you are."

After listening attentively, he sincerely thanked Rebecca for her expressed admiration, adding, "It shall cheer and comfort me all the days of my life." He explained that he was not free to enter into relations with any woman other than those of simple brotherly regard and pure friendship. He made it clear that his first and paramount duty was the rearing of his father's family, that he could not consider marriage until that was accomplished; and then he added: "If I am a son of destiny, I must not assume obligations of lifelong duration until such a time as my destiny shall be made manifest."

Rebecca was heartbroken. She refused to be comforted and importuned her father to leave Nazareth until he finally consented to move to Sepphoris. In after years, to the many men who sought her hand in marriage, Rebecca had but one answer. She lived for only one purpose — to await the hour when this, to her, the greatest man who ever lived would begin his career as a teacher of living truth. And she followed him devotedly through his eventful years of public labor, being present (unobserved by Jesus) that day when he rode triumphantly into Jerusalem; and she stood "among the other women" by the side of Mary on that fateful and tragic afternoon when the Son of Man hung upon the cross, to her, as well as to countless worlds on high, "the one altogether lovely and the greatest among ten thousand."

The story of Rebecca's love for Jesus was whispered about Nazareth and later on at Capernaum, so that, while in the years to follow many women loved Jesus even as men loved him, not again did he have to reject the personal proffer of another good woman's devotion. From this time on human affection for Jesus partook more of the nature of worshipful and adoring regard. Both men and women loved him devotedly and for what he was, not with any tinge of self-satisfaction or desire for affectionate possession. But for many years, whenever the story of Jesus' human personality was recited, the devotion of Rebecca was recounted.

Although they could hardly afford it, Jesus had a strange longing to go up to Jerusalem for the Passover in A.D. 14, his twentieth year on Earth. His mother, knowing of his recent experience with Rebecca, wisely urged him to make the journey. He was not markedly conscious of it, but what he most wanted was an opportunity to talk with Lazarus and to visit with Martha and Mary. Next to his own family he loved these three most of all.

In making this trip to Jerusalem, he went by way of Megiddo, Antipatris, and Lydda, in part covering the same route traversed when he was brought back as a babe to Nazareth on the return from Egypt. He spent four days going up to the Passover and thought much about the past events that had transpired in and around Megiddo, the international battlefield of Palestine.

Jesus passed on through Jerusalem, only pausing to look upon the temple and the gathering throngs of visitors. He had a strange and increasing aversion to this Herod-built temple with its politically appointed priesthood. He wanted most of all to see Lazarus, Martha, and Mary. Lazarus was the same age as Jesus and now head of the house; by the time of this visit Lazarus's mother had also been laid to rest. Martha was a little over one year older than Jesus, while Mary was two years younger. And Jesus was the idolized ideal of all three of them.

On this visit occurred one of those periodic outbreaks of rebellion against tradition — the expression of resentment for those ceremonial practices which Jesus deemed misrepresentative of his Father in heaven. Not knowing Jesus was coming, Lazarus had arranged to celebrate the Passover with friends in an adjoining village down the Jericho road. Jesus now proposed that they celebrate the feast where they were, at Lazarus's house. "But," said Lazarus, "we have no paschal lamb."

And then Jesus entered upon a prolonged and convincing dissertation to the effect that the Father in heaven was not truly concerned with such childlike and meaningless rituals. After solemn and fervent prayer they rose, and Jesus said, "Let the childlike and darkened minds of my people serve their God as Moses directed; it is better that they do, but let us who have seen the light of life no longer approach our Father by the darkness of death. Let us be free in the knowledge of the truth of our Father's eternal love."

That evening about twilight these four sat down and partook of the first Passover feast ever to be celebrated by devout Jews without the paschal lamb. The unleavened bread and the wine had been made ready for this Passover, and these emblems, which Jesus termed "the bread of life" and "the water of life," he served to his companions, and they ate in solemn conformity with the teachings just imparted. It was his custom to engage in this sacramental ritual whenever he paid subsequent visits to Bethany. When he returned home, he told all this to his mother. She was shocked at first but came gradually to see his viewpoint; nevertheless, she was greatly relieved when Jesus assured her that he did not intend to introduce this new idea of the Passover in their family. At home with the children he continued, year by year, to eat the Passover "according to the law of Moses."

It was during this year that Mary had a long talk with Jesus about marriage. She frankly asked him if he would get married if he were free from his family responsibilities. Jesus explained to her that, since immediate duty forbade his marriage, he had given the subject little thought. He expressed himself as doubting that he would ever enter the marriage state; he said that all such things must await "...my hour," the time when "...my Father's work must begin." Having settled already in his mind that he was not to become the father of children in the flesh, he gave very little thought to the subject of human marriage.

This year he began anew the task of further weaving his mortal and divine natures into a simple and effective *human individuality.* And he continued to grow in moral status and spiritual understanding.

Although all their Nazareth property (except their home) was gone, this year they received a little financial help from the sale of an equity in a piece of property in Capernaum. This was the last of Joseph's entire estate. This real estate deal in Capernaum was with a boat builder named Zebedee.

Joseph graduated at the synagogue school this year and prepared to begin work at the small bench in the home carpenter shop. Although the estate of their father was exhausted, there were prospects that they would successfully fight off poverty since three of them were now regularly at work.

Jesus is rapidly becoming a man, not just a young man but an adult. He has learned well to bear responsibility. He knows how to carry on in the face of disappointment. He bears up bravely when his plans are thwarted and his purposes temporarily defeated. He has learned how to be fair and just even in the face of injustice. He is learning how to adjust his ideals of spiritual living to the practical demands of earthly existence. He is learning how to plan for the achievement of a higher and distant goal of idealism while he toils earnestly for the attainment of a nearer and immediate goal of necessity. He is steadily acquiring the art of adjusting his aspirations to the commonplace demands of the human occasion. He has very nearly mastered the technique of utilizing the energy of the spiritual drive to turn the mechanism of material achievement. He is slowly learning how to live the heavenly life while he continues on with the earthly existence. More and more he depends upon the ultimate guidance of his heavenly Father while he assumes the fatherly role of guiding and directing the children of his earth family. He is becoming experienced in the skillful wresting of victory from the very jaws of defeat; he is learning how to transform the difficulties of time into the triumphs of eternity.

And so, as the years pass, this young man of Nazareth continues to experience life as it is lived in mortal flesh on the worlds of time and space. He lives a full, representative, and replete life on Earth. He left this world ripe in the experience that his creatures pass through during the short and strenuous years of their first life, the life in the flesh. And all this human experience is an eternal possession of the Universe Sovereign. He is our understanding brother, sympathetic friend, experienced sovereign, and merciful father.

As a child he accumulated a vast body of knowledge; as a youth he sorted, classified, and correlated this information; and now as a man of the realm he begins to organize these mental possessions preparatory to utilization in his subsequent teaching, ministry, and service in behalf of his fellow mortals on this world and on all other spheres of habitation throughout his entire local universe of beings and things.

Born into the world a babe of the realm, he has lived his childhood life and passed through the successive stages of youth and young manhood; he now stands on the threshold of full manhood, rich in the experience of human living, replete in the understanding of human nature, and full of sympathy for the frailties of human beings. He is becoming expert in the divine art of revealing his Paradise Father to all ages and stages of mortal creatures.

And now as a full-grown man — an adult of the realm — he prepares to continue his supreme mission of revealing God to men and leading men to God.

JESUS' EARLY MANHOOD

A S JESUS of Nazareth entered upon the early years of his adult life, he had lived, and continued to live, a normal and average human life on earth. Jesus came into this world just as other children come; he had nothing to do with selecting his parents. He did choose this particular world as the planet whereon to carry out his seventh and final bestowal, his incarnation in the likeness of mortal flesh, but otherwise he entered the world in a natural manner, growing up as a child of the realm and wrestling with the vicissitudes of his environment just as do other mortals on this and on similar worlds.

Always be mindful of the twofold purpose of Michael's bestowal on Earth:

1. The mastering of the experience of living the full life of a human creature in mortal flesh, the completion of his sovereignty in the local creation.
2. The revelation of the Universal Father to the mortal dwellers on the worlds of time and space and the more effective leading of these same mortals to a better understanding of the Universal Father.

All other creature benefits and universe advantages were incidental and secondary to these major purposes of the mortal bestowal.

A .D. 15 was his twenty-first year on Earth. With the attainment of adult years Jesus began in earnest and with full self-consciousness the task of completing the experience of mastering the knowledge of the life of his lowest form of intelligent creatures, thereby finally and fully earning the right of unqualified rulership of his self-created universe. He entered upon this stupendous task fully realizing his dual nature. But he had already effectively combined these two natures into one — Jesus of Nazareth.

Joshua ben Joseph knew full well that he was a man, a mortal man, born of woman. This is shown in the selection of his first title, the *Son of Man*. He was truly a partaker of flesh and blood, and even now, as he presides in sovereign authority over the destinies of a universe, he still bears among his numerous well-earned titles that of Son of Man. It is literally true that the creative Word — the Creator Son — of the Universal Father was "made flesh and dwelt as a man of the realm on Earth." He labored, grew weary, rested, and slept. He hungered and satisfied such cravings with food; he thirsted and quenched his thirst with water. He experienced the full gamut of human feelings and emotions; he was "in all things tested, even as you are," and he suffered and died.

He obtained knowledge, gained experience, and combined these into wisdom, just as do other mortals of the realm. Until after his baptism he availed himself of no supernatural power. He employed no agency not a part of his human endowment as a son of Joseph and Mary.

As to the attributes of his pre-human existence, he emptied himself. Prior to the beginning of his public work his knowledge of men and events was wholly self-limited. He was a true man among men.

It is forever and gloriously true: "We have a high ruler who can be touched with the feeling of our infirmities. We have a Sovereign who was in all points tested and tempted like as we are, yet without sin." And since he himself has suffered, being tested and tried, he is abundantly able to understand and minister to those who are confused and distressed.

The Nazareth carpenter now fully understood the work before him, but he chose to live his human life in the channel of its natural flowing. And in some of these matters he is indeed an example to his mortal creatures, even as it is recorded: "Let this mind be in you which was also in Christ Jesus, who, being of the nature of God, thought it not strange to be equal with God. But he made himself to be of little import and, taking upon himself the form of a creature, was born in the likeness of mankind. And being thus fashioned as a man, he humbled himself and became obedient to death, even the death of the cross."

He lived his mortal life just as all others of the human family may live theirs, "who in the days of the flesh so frequently offered up prayers and supplications, even with strong feelings and tears, to Him who is able to save from all evil, and his prayers were effective because he believed." Wherefore it behooved him *in every respect* to be made like his brethren that he might become a merciful and understanding sovereign ruler over them.

Of his human nature he was never in doubt; it was self-evident and always present in his consciousness. But of his divine nature there was always room for doubt and conjecture, at least this was true right up to the event of his baptism. The self-realization of divinity was a slow and, from the human standpoint, a natural evolutionary revelation. This revelation and self-realization of divinity began in Jerusalem when he was not quite thirteen years old with the first supernatural occurrence of his human existence. This experience of effecting the self-realization of his divine nature was completed at the time of his second supernatural experience while in the flesh, the episode attendant upon his baptism by John in the Jordan, which event marked the beginning of his public career of ministry and teaching.

Between these two celestial visitations, one in his thirteenth year and the other at his baptism, there occurred nothing supernatural or superhuman in the life of this incarnated Creator Son. Notwithstanding this, the babe of Bethlehem, the lad, youth, and man of Nazareth, was in reality the incarnated Creator of a universe; but he never once used aught of this power, nor did he utilize the guidance of celestial personalities, aside from that of his guardian seraphim, in the living of his human life up to the day of his baptism by John. And we who thus testify know whereof we speak.

And yet, throughout all these years of his life in the flesh he was truly divine. He was actually a Creator Son of the Paradise Father. When once he had espoused his public career, subsequent to the technical completion of his purely mortal experience of sovereignty acquirement, he did not hesitate publicly to admit that he was the Son of God. He did not hesitate to declare, "I am Alpha and Omega, the beginning and the end, the first and the last." He made no protest in later years when he was called Lord of Glory, Ruler of a Universe, the Lord God of all creation, the Holy One of Israel, the Lord of all, our Lord and our God, God with us, having a name above every name and on all worlds, the Omnipotence of a universe, the Universe Mind of this creation, the One in whom are hid all treasures of wisdom and knowledge, the fullness of Him who fills all things, the eternal Word of the eternal God, the One who was before all things and in whom all things consist, the Creator of the heavens and the earth, the Upholder of our local universe, the Judge of all the earth, the Giver of life eternal, the True Shepherd, the Deliverer of the worlds, and the Captain of our salvation.

He never objected to any of these titles as they were applied to him subsequent to the emergence from his purely human life into the later years of his self-consciousness of the ministry of divinity in humanity, for humanity, and to humanity on this world and for all other worlds in his local creation. Jesus objected to but one title as applied to him: When he was once called Immanuel, he merely replied, "Not I, that is my elder brother."

Always, even after his emergence into the larger life on earth, Jesus was submissively subject to the will of the Father in heaven.

After his baptism he thought nothing of permitting his sincere believers and grateful followers to worship him. Even while he wrestled with poverty and toiled with his hands to provide the necessities of life for his family, his awareness that he was a Son of God was growing; he knew that he was the maker of the heavens and this very earth whereon he was now living out his human existence. And the hosts of celestial beings throughout the great and onlooking universe likewise knew that this man of Nazareth was their beloved Sovereign and Creator-father. A profound suspense pervaded the universe of the local creation throughout these years; all celestial eyes were continuously focused on Earth — on Palestine.

This year Jesus went up to Jerusalem with Joseph to celebrate the Passover. Having taken James to the temple for consecration, he deemed it his duty to take Joseph. Jesus never exhibited any degree of partiality in dealing with his family. He went with Joseph to Jerusalem by the usual Jordan valley route, but he returned to Nazareth by the east Jordan way, which led through Amathus. Going down the Jordan, Jesus narrated Jewish history to Joseph and on the return trip told him about the experiences of the reputed tribes of Ruben, Gad, and Gilead that traditionally had dwelt in these regions east of the river.

Joseph asked Jesus many leading questions concerning his life mission, but to most of these inquiries Jesus would only reply, "My hour has not yet come." However, in these intimate discussions many words were dropped which Joseph remembered during the stirring events of subsequent years. Jesus, with Joseph, spent this Passover with his three friends at Bethany, as was his custom when in Jerusalem attending these festival commemorations.

His twenty-second year was one of several during which Jesus' brothers and sisters were facing the trials and tribulations peculiar to the problems and readjustments of adolescence. Jesus now had brothers and sisters ranging in ages from seven to eighteen, and he was kept busy helping them to adjust themselves to the new awakenings of their intellectual and emotional lives. He had thus to grapple with the problems of adolescence as they became manifest in the lives of his younger brothers and sisters.

This year Simon graduated from school and began work with Jesus' old boyhood playmate and ever-ready defender, Jacob the stone mason. As a result of several family conferences it was decided that it was unwise for all the boys to take up carpentry. It was thought that by diversifying their trades they would be prepared to take contracts for putting up entire buildings. Again, they had not all kept busy since three of them had been working as full-time carpenters.

Jesus continued this year at house finishing and cabinetwork but spent most of his time at the caravan repair shop. James was beginning to alternate with him in attendance at the shop. The latter part of this year, when carpenter work was slack about Nazareth, Jesus left James in charge of the repair shop and Joseph at the home bench while he went over to Sepphoris to work with a smith. He worked six months with metals and acquired considerable skill at the anvil.

Before taking up his new employment at Sepphoris, Jesus held one of his periodic family conferences and solemnly installed James, then just past eighteen years old, as acting head of the family. He promised his brother hearty support and full co-operation and exacted formal promises of obedience to James from each member of the family. From this day James assumed full financial responsibility for the family, Jesus making his weekly payments to his brother. Never again did Jesus take the reins out of James's hands. While working at Sepphoris he could have walked home every night if necessary, but he purposely remained away, assigning weather and other reasons, but his true motive was to train James and Joseph in the bearing of the family responsibility. He had begun the slow process of weaning his family. Each Sabbath Jesus returned to Nazareth, and sometimes during the week when occasion required, to observe the working of the new plan, to give advice and offer helpful suggestions.

Living much of the time in Sepphoris for six months afforded Jesus a new opportunity to become better acquainted with the gentile viewpoint of life. He worked with gentiles, lived with gentiles, and in every possible manner did he make a close and painstaking study of their habits of living and of the gentile mind.

The moral standards of this home city of Herod Antipas were so far below those of even the caravan city of Nazareth that after six months' sojourn at Sepphoris Jesus was not averse to finding an excuse for returning to Nazareth. The group he worked for were to become engaged on public work in both Sepphoris and the new city of Tiberias, and Jesus was disinclined to have anything to do with any sort of employment under the supervision of Herod Antipas. And there were still other reasons that made it wise, in the opinion of Jesus, for him to go back to Nazareth. When he returned to the repair shop, he did not again assume the personal direction of family affairs. He worked in association with James at the shop and as far as possible permitted him to continue oversight of the home. James's management of family expenditures and his administration of the home budget were undisturbed.

It was by just such wise and thoughtful planning that Jesus prepared the way for his eventual withdrawal from active participation in the affairs of his family. When James had had two years' experience as acting head of the family — and two full years before he (James) was to be married — Joseph was placed in charge of the household funds and entrusted with the general management of the home.

★ ★ ★

During his twenty-third year the financial pressure was slightly relaxed as four were at work. Miriam earned considerable by the sale of milk and butter; Martha had become an expert weaver. The purchase price of the repair shop was over one third paid. The situation was such that Jesus stopped work for three weeks to take Simon to Jerusalem for the Passover, and this was the longest period away from daily toil he had enjoyed since the death of his father.

They journeyed to Jerusalem by way of the Decapolis and through Pella, Gerasa, Philadelphia, Heshbon, and Jericho. They returned to Nazareth by the coast route, touching Lydda, Joppa, Caesarea, thence around Mount Carmel to Ptolemais and Nazareth. This trip fairly well acquainted Jesus with the whole of Palestine north of the Jerusalem district.

At Philadelphia Jesus and Simon became acquainted with a merchant from Damascus who developed such a great liking for the Nazareth couple that he insisted they stop with him at his Jerusalem headquarters. While Simon gave attendance at the temple, Jesus spent much of his time talking with this well-educated and much-traveled man of world affairs. This merchant owned over four thousand caravan camels; he had interests all over the Roman world and was now on his way to Rome. He proposed that Jesus come to Damascus to enter his Oriental import business, but Jesus explained that he did not feel justified in going so far away from his family just then. But on the way back home he thought much about these distant cities and the even more remote countries of the Far West and the Far East, countries he had so frequently heard spoken of by the caravan passengers and conductors.

Simon greatly enjoyed his visit to Jerusalem. He was duly received into the commonwealth of Israel at the Passover consecration of the new sons of the commandment. While Simon attended the Passover ceremonies, Jesus mingled with the throngs of visitors and engaged in many interesting personal conferences with numerous gentile proselytes.

Perhaps the most notable of all these contacts was the one with a young Hellenist named Stephen. This young man was on his first visit to Jerusalem and chanced to meet Jesus on Thursday afternoon of Passover week. While they both strolled about viewing the Asmonean palace, Jesus began the casual conversation that resulted in their becoming interested in each other, and which led to a four-hour discussion of the way of life and the true God and his worship. Stephen was tremendously impressed with what Jesus said; he never forgot his words.

And this was the same Stephen who subsequently became a believer in the teachings of Jesus, and whose boldness in preaching this early gospel resulted in his being stoned to death by irate Jews. Some of Stephen's extraordinary boldness in proclaiming his view of the new gospel was the direct result of this earlier interview with Jesus. But Stephen never even faintly surmised that the Galilean he had talked with some fifteen years previously was the very same person whom he later proclaimed the world's Savior, and for whom he was so soon to die, thus becoming the first martyr of the newly evolving Christian faith. When Stephen yielded up his life as the price of his attack upon the Jewish temple and its traditional practices, there stood by one named Saul, a citizen of Tarsus. And when Saul saw how this Greek could die for his faith, there were aroused in his heart those emotions which eventually led him to espouse the cause for which Stephen died; later on he became the aggressive and indomitable Paul, the philosopher, if not the sole founder, of the Christian religion.

On the Sunday after Passover week Simon and Jesus started on their way back to Nazareth. Simon never forgot what Jesus taught him on this trip. He had always loved Jesus, but now he felt that he had begun to know his father-brother. They had many heart-to-heart talks as they journeyed through the country and prepared their meals by the wayside. They arrived home Thursday noon, and Simon kept the family up late that night relating his experiences.

Mary was much upset by Simon's report that Jesus spent most of the time when in Jerusalem "visiting with the strangers, especially those from the far countries." Jesus' family never could comprehend his great interest in people, his urge to visit with them, to learn about their way of living, and to find out what they were thinking about.

More and more the Nazareth family became engrossed with their immediate and human problems; not often was mention made of the future mission of Jesus, and very seldom did he himself speak of his future career. His mother rarely thought about his being a child of promise. She was slowly giving up the idea that Jesus was to fulfill any divine mission on earth, yet at times her faith was revived when she paused to recall the Gabriel visitation before the child was born.

The last four months of this year Jesus spent in Damascus as the guest of the merchant whom he first met at Philadelphia when on his way to Jerusalem. A representative of this merchant had sought out Jesus when passing through Nazareth and escorted him to Damascus. This part-Jewish merchant proposed to devote an extraordinary sum of money to establish a school of religious philosophy at Damascus. He planned to create a center of learning that would out-rival Alexandria. And he proposed that Jesus should immediately begin a long tour of the world's educational centers preparatory to becoming the head of this new project. This was one of the greatest temptations that Jesus ever faced in the course of his purely human career.

Presently this merchant brought before Jesus a group of twelve merchants and bankers who agreed to support this newly projected school. Jesus manifested deep interest in the project, helped them plan for its organization, but always expressed the fear that his other and unstated but prior obligations would prevent his accepting the direction of such an ambitious enterprise. His would-be benefactor was persistent, and he profitably employed Jesus at his home doing some translating while he, his wife, and their sons and daughters sought to prevail upon Jesus to accept the proffered honor. But he would not consent. He well knew that his mission on earth was not to be supported by institutions of learning; he knew that he must not obligate himself in the least to be directed by the "councils of men," no matter how well-intentioned.

He who was rejected by the Jerusalem religious leaders, even after he had demonstrated his leadership, was recognized and hailed as a master teacher by the businessmen and bankers of Damascus, and all this when he was an obscure and unknown carpenter of Nazareth.

He never spoke about this offer to his family, and the end of the year A.D. 17 found him back in Nazareth going about his daily duties just as if he had never been tempted by the flattering propositions of his Damascus friends. Neither did these men of Damascus ever associate the later citizen of Capernaum who turned all Jewry upside down with the former carpenter of Nazareth who had dared to refuse the honor which their combined wealth might have procured.

Jesus most cleverly and intentionally contrived to detach various episodes of his life so that they never became, in the eyes of the world, associated together as the doings of a single individual. Many times in subsequent years he listened to the recital of this very story of the strange Galilean who declined the opportunity of founding a school in Damascus to compete with Alexandria.

One purpose which Jesus had in mind, when he sought to segregate certain features of his earthly experience, was to prevent the building up of such a versatile and spectacular career as would cause subsequent generations to venerate the teacher in place of obeying the truth which he had lived and taught. Jesus did not want to build up such a human record of achievement as would attract attention *from his teaching*. Very early he recognized that his followers would be tempted to formulate a religion *about* him that might become a competitor of the gospel of the kingdom that he intended to proclaim to the world. Accordingly, he consistently sought to suppress everything during his eventful career that he thought might be made to serve this natural human tendency to exalt the teacher in place of proclaiming his teachings.

This same motive also explains why he permitted himself to be known by different titles during various epochs of his diversified life on earth. Again, he did not want to bring any undue influence to bear upon his family or others that would lead them to believe in him against their honest convictions. He always refused to take undue or unfair advantage of the human mind. He did not want men to believe in him unless their hearts were responsive to the spiritual realities revealed in his teachings.

By the end of this year the Nazareth home was running fairly smoothly. The children were growing up, and Mary was becoming accustomed to Jesus' being away from home. He continued to turn over his earnings to James for the support of the family, retaining only a small portion for his immediate personal expenses.

As the years passed, it became more difficult to realize that this man was a Son of God on earth. He seemed to become quite like an individual of the realm, just another man among men. And it was ordained by the Father in heaven that the bestowal should unfold in this very way.

His twenty-fourth on earth was Jesus' first year of comparative freedom from family responsibility. James was very successful in managing the home with Jesus' help in counsel and finances.

The week following the Passover of this year a young man from Alexandria came down to Nazareth to arrange for a meeting, later in the year, between Jesus and a group of Alexandrian Jews at some point on the Palestinian coast. This conference was set for the middle of June, and Jesus went over to Caesarea to meet with five prominent Jews of Alexandria, who besought him to establish himself in their city as a religious teacher, offering as an inducement to begin with, the position of assistant to the chazan in their chief synagogue.

The spokesmen for this committee explained to Jesus that Alexandria was destined to become the headquarters of Jewish culture for the entire world; that the Hellenistic trend of Jewish affairs had virtually outdistanced the Babylonian school of thought. They reminded Jesus of the ominous rumblings of rebellion in Jerusalem and throughout Palestine and assured him that any uprising of the Palestinian Jews would be equivalent to national suicide, that the iron hand of Rome would crush the rebellion in three months, and that Jerusalem would be destroyed and the temple demolished, that not one stone would be left upon another.

Jesus listened to all they had to say, thanked them for their confidence, and, in declining to go to Alexandria, in substance said, "My hour has not yet come." They were nonplused by his apparent indifference to the honor they had sought to confer upon him. Before taking leave of Jesus, they presented him with a purse in token of the esteem of his Alexandrian friends and in compensation for the time and expense of coming over to Caesarea to confer with them. But he likewise refused the money, saying: "The house of Joseph has never received alms, and we cannot eat another's bread as long as I have strong arms and my brothers can labor."

His friends from Egypt set sail for home, and in subsequent years, when they heard rumors of the Capernaum boatbuilder who was creating such a commotion in Palestine, few of them surmised that he was the babe of Bethlehem grown up and the same strange-acting Galilean who had so unceremoniously declined the invitation to become a great teacher in Alexandria.

Jesus returned to Nazareth. The remainder of this year was the most uneventful six months of his whole career. He enjoyed this temporary respite from the usual program of problems to solve and difficulties to surmount. He communed much with his Father in heaven and made tremendous progress in the mastery of his human mind.

But human affairs on the worlds of time and space do not run smoothly for long. In December James had a private talk with Jesus, explaining that he was much in love with Esta, a young woman of Nazareth, and that they would sometime like to be married if it could be arranged. He called attention to the fact that Joseph would soon be eighteen years old, and that it would be a good experience for him to have a chance to serve as the acting head of the family. Jesus gave consent for James's marriage two years later, provided he had, during the intervening time, properly trained Joseph to assume direction of the home.

And now things began to happen; marriage was in the air. James's success in gaining Jesus' assent to his marriage emboldened Miriam to approach her brother-father with her plans. Jacob, the younger stone mason, the same self-appointed champion of Jesus during their childhood days, now business associate of James and Joseph, had long sought to gain Miriam's hand in marriage. After Miriam had laid her plans before Jesus, he directed that Jacob should come to him making formal request for her and promised his blessing for the marriage just as soon as she felt that Martha was competent to assume her duties as eldest daughter.

When at home, he continued to teach the evening school three times a week, read the Scriptures often in the synagogue on the Sabbath, visited with his mother, taught the children, and in general conducted himself as a worthy and respected citizen of Nazareth in the commonwealth of Israel.

His twenty-fifth year began with the Nazareth family all in good health and witnessed the finishing of the regular schooling of all the children with the exception of certain work that Martha must do for Ruth.

Jesus was one of the most robust and refined specimens of manhood to appear on earth since the days of Adam. His physical development was superb. His mind was active, keen, and penetrating — compared with the average mentality of his contemporaries, it had developed gigantic proportions — and his spirit was indeed humanly divine.

The family finances were in the best condition since the disappearance of Joseph's estate. The final payments had been made on the caravan repair shop; they owed no man and for the first time in years had some funds ahead. This being true, and since he had taken his other brothers to Jerusalem for their first Passover ceremonies, Jesus decided to accompany Jude (who had just graduated from the synagogue school) on his first visit to the temple.

They went up to Jerusalem and returned by the same route, the Jordan valley, as Jesus feared trouble if he took his young brother through Samaria. Already at Nazareth Jude had got into slight trouble several times because of his hasty disposition, coupled with his strong patriotic sentiments.

They arrived at Jerusalem in due time and were on their way for a first visit to the temple, the very sight of which had stirred and thrilled Jude to the very depths of his soul, when they chanced to meet Lazarus of Bethany. While Jesus talked with Lazarus and sought to arrange for their joint celebration of the Passover, Jude started up real trouble for them all. Close at hand stood a Roman guard who made some improper remarks regarding a Jewish girl who was passing. Jude flushed with fiery indignation and was not slow in expressing his resentment of such an impropriety directly to and within hearing of the soldier. Now the Roman legionnaires were very sensitive to anything bordering on Jewish disrespect; so the guard promptly placed Jude under arrest. This was too much for the young patriot, and before Jesus could caution him by a warning glance, he had delivered himself of a voluble denunciation of pent-up anti-Roman feelings, all of which only made a bad matter worse. Jude, with Jesus by his side, was taken at once to the military prison.

Jesus endeavored to obtain either an immediate hearing for Jude or else his release in time for the Passover celebration that evening, but he failed in these attempts. Since the next day was a "holy convocation" in Jerusalem, even the Romans would not presume to hear charges against a Jew. Accordingly, Jude remained in confinement until the morning of the second day after his arrest, and Jesus stayed at the prison with him. They were not present in the temple at the ceremony of receiving the sons of the law into the full citizenship of Israel. Jude did not pass through this formal ceremony for several years, until he was next in Jerusalem at a Passover and in connection with his propaganda work in behalf of the Zealots, the patriotic organization to which he belonged and in which he was very active.

The morning following their second day in prison Jesus appeared before the military magistrate in behalf of Jude. By making apologies for his brother's youth and by a further explanatory but judicious statement with reference to the provocative nature of the episode which had led up to the arrest of his brother, Jesus so handled the case that the magistrate expressed the opinion that the young Jew might have had some possible excuse for his violent outburst. After warning Jude not to allow himself again to be guilty of such rashness, he said to Jesus in dismissing them, "You had better keep your eye on the lad; he's liable to make a lot of trouble for all of you." And the Roman judge spoke the truth. Jude did make considerable trouble for Jesus, and always was the trouble of this same nature — clashes with the civil authorities because of his thoughtless and unwise patriotic outbursts.

Jesus and Jude walked over to Bethany for the night, explaining why they had failed to keep their appointment for the Passover supper, and set out for Nazareth the following day. Jesus did not tell the family about his young brother's arrest at Jerusalem, but he had a long talk with Jude about this episode some three weeks after their return. After this talk with Jesus Jude himself told the family. He never forgot the patience and forbearance his brother-father manifested throughout the whole of this trying experience.

This was the last Passover Jesus attended with any member of his own family. Increasingly the Son of Man was to become separated from close association with his own flesh and blood.

This year his seasons of deep meditation were often broken into by Ruth and her playmates. And always was Jesus ready to postpone the contemplation of his future work for the world and the universe that he might share in the childish joy and youthful gladness of these youngsters, who never tired of listening to Jesus relate the experiences of his various trips to Jerusalem. They also greatly enjoyed his stories about animals and nature.

The children were always welcome at the repair shop. Jesus provided sand, blocks, and stones by the side of the shop, and bevies of youngsters flocked there to amuse themselves. When they tired of their play, the more intrepid ones would peek into the shop, and if its keeper was not busy, they would make bold to go in and say, "Uncle Joshua, come out and tell us a big story." Then they would lead him out by tugging at his hands until he was seated on the favorite rock by the corner of the shop, with the children on the ground in a semicircle before him. And how the little folks did enjoy their Uncle Joshua. They were learning to laugh, and to laugh heartily. It was customary for one or two of the smallest of the children to climb upon his knees and sit there, looking up in wonderment at his expressive features as he told his stories. The children loved Jesus, and Jesus loved the children, and the celestial observers wondered at the sight of it all.

It was difficult for his friends to comprehend the range of his intellectual activities, how he could so suddenly and so completely swing from the profound discussion of politics, philosophy, or religion to the lighthearted and joyous playfulness of these tots of from five to ten years of age. As his own brothers and sisters grew up, as he gained more leisure, and before the grandchildren arrived, he paid a great deal of attention to these little ones. But he did not live on earth long enough to enjoy the grandchildren very much.

★ ★ ★

A.D. 20 was his twenty-sixth year on earth. As this year began, Jesus of Nazareth became strongly conscious that he possessed a wide range of potential power. But he was likewise fully persuaded that this power was not to be employed by his personality as the Son of Man, at least not until his hour should come.

At this time he thought much but said little about the relation of himself to his Father in heaven. And the conclusion of all this thinking was expressed once in his prayer on the hilltop, when he said: "Regardless of who I am and what power I may or may not wield, I always have been, and always will be, subject to the will of my Paradise Father." And yet, as this man walked about Nazareth to and from his work, it was literally true — as concerned his vast local universe — that "in him were hidden all the treasures of wisdom and knowledge."

All this year the family affairs ran smoothly except for Jude. For years James had trouble with his youngest brother, who was not inclined to settle down to work, nor was he to be depended upon for his share of the home expenses. While he would live at home, he was not conscientious about earning his share of the family upkeep.

Jesus was a man of peace, and all too often was he embarrassed by Jude's belligerent exploits and numerous patriotic outbursts. James and Joseph were in favor of casting him out, but Jesus would not consent. When their patience would be severely tried, Jesus would only advise: "Be patient. Be wise in your counsel and eloquent in your lives, that your young brother may first know the better way and then be constrained to follow you in it." The wise and loving counsel of Jesus prevented a break in the family; they remained together. But Jude never was brought to his sober senses until after his marriage.

Mary seldom spoke of Jesus' future mission. Whenever this subject was referred to, Jesus only replied, "My hour has not yet come." Jesus had about completed the difficult task of weaning his family from dependence on the immediate presence of his personality. He was rapidly preparing for the day when he could consistently leave this Nazareth home to begin the more active prelude to his real mimistry for men.

Never lose sight of the fact that the prime mission of Jesus in his seventh bestowal was the acquirement of creature experience, the achievement of the sovereignty of his local creation. And in the gathering of this very experience he made the supreme revelation of the Paradise Father to Earth and to his entire local universe. Incidental to these purposes he also undertook to untangle the complicated affairs of this planet as they were related to the Lucifer rebellion.

This year Jesus enjoyed more than usual leisure, and he devoted much time to training James in the management of the repair shop and Joseph in the direction of home affairs. Mary sensed that he was making ready to leave them. Leave them to go where? To do what? She had about given up the thought that Jesus was the

Messiah. She could not understand him; she simply could not fathom her first-born son.

Jesus spent a great deal of time this year with the individual members of his family. He would take them for long and frequent strolls up the hill and through the countryside. Before harvest he took Jude to the farmer uncle south of Nazareth, but Jude did not remain long after the harvest. He ran away, and Simon later found him with the fishermen at the lake. When Simon brought him back home, Jesus talked things over with the runaway lad and, since he wanted to be a fisherman, went over to Magdala with him and put him in the care of a fisherman relative; and Jude worked fairly well and regularly from that time on until his marriage, and he continued as a fisherman after his marriage.

At last the day had come when all Jesus' brothers had chosen, and were established in, their lifework. The stage was being set for Jesus' departure from home.

In November a double wedding occurred. James and Esta, and Miriam and Jacob were married. It was truly a joyous occasion. Even Mary was once more happy except every now and then when she realized that Jesus was preparing to go away. She suffered under the burden of a great uncertainty: If Jesus would only sit down and talk it all over freely with her as he had done when he was a boy, but he was consistently uncommunicative; he was profoundly silent about the future.

James and his bride, Esta, moved into a neat little home on the west side of town, the gift of her father. While James continued his support of his mother's home, his quota was cut in half because of his marriage, and Joseph was formally installed by Jesus as head of the family. Jude was now very faithfully sending his share of funds home each month. The weddings of James and Miriam had a very beneficial influence on Jude, and when he left for the fishing grounds, the day after the double wedding, he assured Joseph that he could depend on him "to do my full duty, and more if it is needed." And he kept his promise.

Miriam lived next door to Mary in the home of Jacob, Jacob the elder having been laid to rest with his fathers. Martha took Miriam's place in the home, and the new organization was working smoothly before the year ended.

The day after this double wedding Jesus held an important conference with James. He told James, confidentially, that he was preparing to leave home. He presented full title to the repair shop to James, formally and solemnly abdicated as head of Joseph's house, and most touchingly established his brother James as "head and protector of my father's house." He drew up, and they both signed, a secret compact in which it was stipulated that, in return for the gift of the repair shop, James would henceforth assume full financial responsibility for the family, thus releasing Jesus from all further obligations in these matters. After the contract was signed, after the budget was so arranged that the actual expenses of the family would be met without any contribution from Jesus, Jesus said to James, "But, my son, I will continue to send you something each month until my hour shall have come, but what I send shall be used by you as the occasion demands. Apply my funds to the family necessities or pleasures as you see fit. Use them in case of sickness or apply them to meet the unexpected emergencies which may befall any individual member of the family."

And thus did Jesus make ready to enter upon the second and home-detached phase of his adult life before the public entrance upon his Father's business.

THE LATER ADULT LIFE OF JESUS

JESUS HAD fully and finally separated himself from the management of the domestic affairs of the Nazareth family and from the immediate direction of its individuals. He continued, right up to the event of his baptism, to contribute to the family finances and to take a keen personal interest in the spiritual welfare of every one of his brothers and sisters. And always was he ready to do everything humanly possible for the comfort and happiness of his widowed mother.

The Son of Man had now made every preparation for detaching himself permanently from the Nazareth home; and this was not easy for him to do. Jesus naturally loved his people; he loved his family, and this natural affection had been tremendously augmented by his extraordinary devotion to them. The more fully we bestow ourselves upon our fellows, the more we come to love them; and since Jesus had given himself so fully to his family, he loved them with a great and fervent affection.

All the family had slowly awakened to the realization that Jesus was making ready to leave them. The sadness of the anticipated separation was only tempered by this graduated method of preparing them for the announcement of his intended departure. For more than four years they discerned that he was planning for this eventual separation.

In January of the year, A.D. 21, on a rainy Sunday morning, Jesus took unceremonious leave of his family, only explaining that he was going over to Tiberias and then on a visit to other cities about the Sea of Galilee. And thus he left them, never again to be a regular member of that household.

He spent one week at Tiberias, the new city which was soon to succeed Sepphoris as the capital of Galilee; and finding little to interest him, he passed on successively through Magdala and Bethsaida to Capernaum, where he stopped to pay a visit to his father's friend Zebedee. Zebedee's sons were fishermen; he himself was a boatbuilder. Jesus of Nazareth was an expert in both designing and building; he was a master at working with wood; and Zebedee had long known of the skill of the Nazareth craftsman. For a long time Zebedee had contemplated making improved boats; he now laid his plans before Jesus and invited the visiting carpenter to join him in the enterprise, and Jesus readily consented.

Jesus worked with Zebedee only a little more than one year, but during that time he created a new style of boat and established entirely new methods of boatmaking. By superior technique and greatly improved methods of steaming the boards, Jesus and Zebedee began to build boats of a very superior type, craft that were far safer for sailing the lake than were the older types. For several years Zebedee had more work, turning out these new-style boats, than his small establishment could handle; in less than five years practically all the craft on the lake had been built in the shop of Zebedee at Capernaum. Jesus became well known to the Galilean fisherfolk as the designer of the new boats.

Zebedee was a moderately well-to-do man; his boatbuilding shops were on the lake to the south of Capernaum, and his home was situated down the lake shore near the fishing headquarters of Bethsaida. Jesus lived in the home of Zebedee during the year and more he remained at Capernaum. He had long worked alone in the world, that is, without a father, and greatly enjoyed this period of working with a father-partner.

Zebedee's wife, Salome, was a relative of Annas, onetime high priest at Jerusalem and still the most influential of the Sadducean group, having been deposed only eight years previously. Salome became a great admirer of Jesus. She loved him as she loved her own sons, James, John, and David, while her four daughters looked upon Jesus as their elder brother. Jesus often went out fishing with James, John, and David, and they learned that he was an experienced fisherman as well as an expert boatbuilder.

All this year Jesus sent money each month to James. He returned to Nazareth in October to attend Martha's wedding, and he was not again in Nazareth for over two years, when he returned shortly before the double wedding of Simon and Jude.

Throughout this year Jesus built boats and continued to observe how men lived on earth. Frequently he would go down to visit at the caravan station, Capernaum being on the direct travel route from Damascus to the south. Capernaum was a strong Roman military post, and the garrison's commanding officer was a gentile believer in Yahweh, "a devout man," as the Jews were wont to designate such proselytes. This officer belonged to a wealthy Roman family, and he took it upon himself to build a beautiful synagogue in Capernaum, which had been presented to the Jews a short time before Jesus came to live with Zebedee. Jesus conducted the services in this new synagogue more than half the time this year, and some of the caravan people who chanced to attend remembered him as the carpenter from Nazareth.

When it came to the payment of taxes, Jesus registered himself as a "skilled craftsman of Capernaum." From this day on to the end of his earth life he was known as a resident of Capernaum. He never claimed any other legal residence, although he did, for various reasons, permit others to assign his residence to Damascus, Bethany, Nazareth, and even Alexandria.

At the Capernaum synagogue he found many new books in the library chests, and he spent at least five evenings a week at intense study. One evening he devoted to social life with the older folks, and one evening he spent with the young people. There was something gracious and inspiring about the personality of Jesus which invariably attracted young people. He always made them feel at ease in his presence. Perhaps his great secret in getting along with them consisted in the twofold fact that he was always interested in what they were doing, while he seldom offered them advice unless they asked for it.

The Zebedee family almost worshiped Jesus, and they never failed to attend the conferences of questions and answers which he conducted each evening after supper before he departed for the synagogue to study. The youthful neighbors also came in frequently to attend these after-supper meetings. To these little gatherings Jesus gave varied and advanced instruction, just as advanced as they could comprehend. He talked quite freely with them, expressing his ideas and ideals about politics, sociology, science, and philosophy, but never presumed to speak with authoritative finality except when discussing religion — the relation of man to God.

Once a week Jesus held a meeting with the entire household, shop, and shore helpers, for Zebedee had many employees. And it was among these workers that Jesus was first called "the Master." They all loved him. He enjoyed his labors with Zebedee in Capernaum, but he missed the children playing out by the side of the Nazareth carpenter shop.

Of the sons of Zebedee, James was the most interested in Jesus as a teacher, as a philosopher. John cared most for his religious teaching and opinions. David respected him as a mechanic but took little stock in his religious views and philosophic teachings.

Frequently Jude came over on the Sabbath to hear Jesus talk in the synagogue and would tarry to visit with him. And the more Jude saw of his eldest brother, the more he became convinced that Jesus was a truly great man.

This year Jesus made great advances in the ascendant mastery of his human mind and attained new and high levels of conscious contact with his indwelling Father Fragment.

This was the last year of his settled life. Never again did Jesus spend a whole year in one place or at one undertaking. The days of his earth pilgrimages were rapidly approaching. Periods of intense activity were not far in the future, but there were now about to intervene between his simple but intensely active life of the past and his still more intense and strenuous public ministry, a few years of extensive travel and highly diversified personal activity. His training as a man of the realm had to be completed before he could enter upon his career of teaching and preaching as the perfected God-man of the divine and post-human phases of his earthly bestowal.

In March, A.D. 22, Jesus took leave of Zebedee and of Capernaum. He asked for a small sum of money to defray his expenses to Jerusalem. While working with Zebedee he had drawn only small sums of money, which each month he would send to the family at Nazareth. One month Joseph would come down to Capernaum for the money; the next month Jude would come over to Capernaum, get the money from Jesus, and take it up to Nazareth. Jude's fishing headquarters was only a few miles south of Capernaum.

When Jesus took leave of Zebedee's family, he agreed to remain in Jerusalem until Passover time, and they all promised to be present for that event. They even arranged to celebrate the Passover supper together. They all sorrowed when Jesus left them, especially the daughters of Zebedee.

Before leaving Capernaum, Jesus had a long talk with his new-found friend and close companion, John Zebedee. He told John that he contemplated traveling extensively until "my hour shall come" and asked John to act in his stead in the matter of sending some money to the family at Nazareth each month until the funds due him should be exhausted. And John made him this promise: "My Teacher, go about your business, do your work in the world; I will act for you in this or any other matter, and I will watch over your family even as I would foster my own mother and care for my own brothers and sisters. I will disburse your funds which my father holds as you have directed and as they may be needed, and when your money has been expended, if I do not receive more from you, and if your mother is in need, then will I share my own earnings with her. Go your way in peace. I will act in your stead in all these matters."

Therefore, after Jesus had departed for Jerusalem, John consulted with his father, Zebedee, regarding the money due Jesus, and he was surprised that it was such a large sum. As Jesus had left the matter so entirely in their hands, they agreed that it would be the better plan to invest these funds in property and use the income for assisting the family at Nazareth; and since Zebedee knew of a little house in Capernaum which carried a mortgage and was for sale, he directed John to buy this house with Jesus' money and hold the title in trust for his friend. And John did as his father advised him. For two years the rent of this house was applied

on the mortgage, and this, augmented by a certain large fund which Jesus presently sent up to John to be used as needed by the family, almost equaled the amount of
this obligation; and Zebedee supplied the difference, so that John paid up the remainder of the mortgage when it fell due, thereby securing clear title to this two
room house. In this way Jesus became the owner of a house in Capernaum, but he
had not been told about it.

When the family at Nazareth heard that Jesus had departed from Capernaum,
they, not knowing of this financial arrangement with John, believed the time had
come for them to get along without any further help from Jesus. James remembered his contract with Jesus and, with the help of his brothers, forthwith assumed
full responsibility for the care of the family.

But let us go back to observe Jesus in Jerusalem. For almost two months he
spent the greater part of his time listening to the temple discussions with occa-
sional visits to the various schools of the rabbis. Most of the Sabbath days he spent
at Bethany.

Jesus had carried with him to Jerusalem a letter from Salome, Zebedee's wife,
introducing him to the former high priest, Annas, as "one, the same as my own
son." Annas spent much time with him, personally taking him to visit the many
academies of the Jerusalem religious teachers. While Jesus thoroughly inspected
these schools and carefully observed their methods of teaching, he never so much
as asked a single question in public. Although Annas looked upon Jesus as a great
man, he was puzzled as to how to advise him. He recognized the foolishness of
suggesting that he enter any of the schools of Jerusalem as a student, and yet he
well knew Jesus would never be accorded the status of a regular teacher inasmuch
as he had never been trained in these schools.

Presently the time of the Passover drew near, and along with the throngs from
every quarter there arrived at Jerusalem from Capernaum, Zebedee and his entire
family. They all stopped at the spacious home of Annas, where they celebrated the
Passover as one happy family.

Before the end of this Passover week, by apparent chance, Jesus met a
wealthy traveler and his son, a young man about seventeen years of age. These
travelers hailed from India, and being on their way to visit Rome and various other
points on the Mediterranean, they had arranged to arrive in Jerusalem during the
Passover, hoping to find someone whom they could engage as interpreter for both
and tutor for the son. The father was insistent that Jesus consent to travel with
them. Jesus told him about his family and that it was hardly fair to go away for almost two years, during which time they might find themselves in need. Where-
upon, this traveler from the Orient proposed to advance to Jesus the wages of one
year so that he could entrust such funds to his friends for the safeguarding of his
family against want. And Jesus agreed to make the trip.

Jesus turned this large sum over to John the son of Zebedee. And you have been told how John applied this money toward the liquidation of the mortgage on the Capernaum property. Jesus took Zebedee fully into his confidence regarding this Mediterranean journey, but he enjoined him to tell no man, not even his own flesh and blood, and Zebedee never did disclose his knowledge of Jesus' whereabouts during this long period of almost two years. Before Jesus' return from this trip the family at Nazareth had just about given him up as dead. Only the assurances of Zebedee, who went up to Nazareth with his son John on several occasions, kept hope alive in Mary's heart.

During this time the Nazareth family got along very well; Jude had considerably increased his quota and kept up this extra contribution until he was married. Notwithstanding that they required little assistance, it was the practice of John Zebedee to take presents each month to Mary and Ruth, as Jesus had instructed him.

The whole of Jesus' twenty-ninth year was spent finishing up the tour of the Mediterranean world. The main events, as far as we have permission to reveal these experiences, constitute the subjects of the narratives that immediately follow this chapter.

Throughout this tour of the Roman world, for many reasons, Jesus was known as the *Damascus scribe*. At Corinth and other stops on the return trip he was, however, known as the *Jewish tutor*.

This was an eventful period in Jesus' life. While on this journey he made many contacts with his fellow men, but this experience is a phase of his life that he never revealed to any member of his family nor to any of the apostles. Jesus lived out his life in the flesh and departed from this world without anyone (save Zebedee of Bethsaida) knowing that he had made this extensive trip. Some of his friends thought he had returned to Damascus; others thought he had gone to India. His own family inclined to the belief that he was in Alexandria, as they knew that he had once been invited to go there for the purpose of becoming an assistant chazan.

When Jesus returned to Palestine, he did nothing to change the opinion of his family that he had gone from Jerusalem to Alexandria; he permitted them to continue in the belief that all the time he had been absent from Palestine had been spent in that city of learning and culture. Only Zebedee the boatbuilder of Bethsaida knew the facts about these matters, and Zebedee told no one.

In all your efforts to decipher the meaning of Jesus' life on Earth, you must be mindful of the motivation of the Michael bestowal. If you would comprehend the meaning of many of his apparently strange doings, you must discern the purpose of his sojourn on the world. He was consistently careful not to build up an over-attractive and attention-consuming personal career. He wanted to make no unusual or overpowering appeals to his fellow men. He was dedicated to the work of revealing the heavenly Father to his fellow mortals and at the same time was consecrated to the sublime task of living his mortal earth life all the while subject to the will of the same Paradise Father.

It will also always be helpful in understanding Jesus' life on earth if all mortal students of this divine bestowal will remember that, while he lived this life of incarnation *on* Earth, he lived it *for* his entire universe. There was something special and inspiring associated with the life he lived in the flesh of mortal nature for every single inhabited sphere throughout all the universe of his local creation. The same is also true of all those worlds that have become habitable since the eventful times of his sojourn on Earth. And it will likewise be equally true of all worlds that may become inhabited by will creatures in all the future history of this local universe.

The Son of Man, during the time and through the experiences of this tour of the Roman world, practically completed his educational contact-training with the diversified peoples of the world of his day and generation. By the time of his return to Nazareth, through the medium of this travel-training he had just about learned how man lived and wrought out his existence on Earth.

The real purpose of his trip around the Mediterranean basin was to *know men.* He came very close to hundreds of humankind on this journey. He met and loved all manner of mortals, rich and poor, high and low, black and white, educated and uneducated, cultured and uncultured, animalistic and spiritual, religious and irreligious, moral and immoral.

On this Mediterranean journey Jesus made great advances in his human task of mastering the material and mortal mind, and his indwelling Father Fragment made great progress in the ascension and spiritual conquest of this same human intellect. By the end of this tour Jesus virtually knew — with all human certainty — that he was a Son of God, a Creator Son of the Universal Father. The Father Fragment more and more was able to bring up in the mind of the Son of Man shadowy memories of his Paradise experience in association with his divine Father ere he ever came to organize and administer this local universe. Thus did the Mystery Monitor (a Father Fragment in all respects except prior experience like unto that which indwells the minds of all normal humans), little by little, bring to Jesus' human consciousness those necessary memories of his former and divine existence in the various epochs of the well-nigh eternal past. The last episode of his pre-human experience to be brought forth by the Mystery Monitor was his farewell conference with Immanuel of Salvington just before his surrender of conscious personality to embark upon the Earth incarnation. And this final memory picture of pre-human existence was made clear in Jesus' consciousness on the very day of his baptism by John in the Jordan.

★ ★ ★

To the onlooking celestial intelligences of the local universe, this Mediterranean trip was the most enthralling of all Jesus' earth experiences, at least of all his career right up to the event of his crucifixion and mortal death. This was the fascinating period of his *personal ministry* in contrast with the soon-following epoch of public ministry. This unique episode was all the more engrossing because he was at this time still the carpenter of Nazareth, the boatbuilder of Capernaum, the scribe of Damascus; he was still the Son of Man. He had not yet achieved the complete mastery of his human mind; the Mystery Monitor had not fully mastered and counterparted the mortal identity. He was still a man among men.

The purely human religious experience - the personal spiritual growth - of the Son of Man came near to reaching the apex of attainment during this, his twenty-ninth year on earth. This experience of spiritual development was a consistently gradual growth from the moment of the arrival of his Father Fragment until the day of the completion and confirmation of that natural and normal human relationship between the material mind of man and the mind-endowment of the spirit — the phenomenon of the making of these two minds one, the experience which the Son of Man attained in completion and finality, as an incarnated mortal of the realm, on the day of his baptism in the Jordan.

Throughout these years, while he did not appear to engage in so many seasons of formal communion with his Father in heaven, he perfected increasingly effective methods of personal communication with the indwelling spirit presence of the Paradise Father, the Mystery Monitor. He lived a real life, a full life, and a truly normal, natural, and average life in the flesh. He knows from personal experience the equivalent of the actuality of the entire sum and substance of the living of the life of human beings on the material worlds of time and space.

The Son of Man experienced those wide ranges of human emotion, which reach from superb joy to profound sorrow. He was a child of joy and a being of rare good humor; likewise was he a "man of sorrows and acquainted with grief." In a spiritual sense, he did live through the mortal life from the bottom to the top, from the beginning to the end. From a material point of view, he might appear to have escaped living through both social extremes of human existence, but intellectually he became wholly familiar with the entire and complete experience of humankind.

Jesus knows about the thoughts and feelings, the urges and impulses, of the evolutionary and ascendant mortals of the realms, from birth to death. He has lived the human life from the beginnings of physical, intellectual, and spiritual selfhood up through infancy, childhood, youth, and adulthood — even to the human experience of death. He not only passed through these usual and familiar human periods of intellectual and spiritual advancement, but he *also* fully experienced those higher and more advanced phases of human and Father Fragment reconciliation which so few Earth mortals ever attain. And thus he experienced the full life of mortal man, not only as it is lived on your world, but also as it is lived on all other evolutionary worlds of time and space, even on the highest and most advanced of all the worlds settled in light and life.

Although this perfect life which he lived in the likeness of mortal flesh may not have received the unqualified and universal approval of his fellow mortals, those who chanced to be his contemporaries on earth, still, the life which Jesus of Nazareth lived in the flesh and on earth did receive full and unqualified acceptance by the Universal Father as constituting at one and the same time, and in one and the same personality-life, the fullness of the revelation of the eternal God to mortal man and the presentation of perfected human personality to the satisfaction of the Infinite Creator.

And this was his true and supreme purpose. He did not come down to live on Earth as the perfect and detailed example for any child or adult, any man or woman, in that age or any other. True it is, indeed, that in his full, rich, beautiful, and noble life we may all find much that is exquisitely exemplary, divinely inspiring, but this is because he lived a true and genuinely human life. Jesus did not live his life on earth in order to set an example for all other human beings to copy. He lived this life in the flesh by the same mercy ministry that we all may live our lives on earth; and as he lived his mortal life in his day and *as he was,* so did he thereby set the example for all of us thus to live our lives in our day and *as we are.* You may not aspire to live his life, but you can resolve to *live your lives* even as, and by the same means that, he lived his. Jesus may not be the technical and detailed example for all the mortals of all ages on all the realms of this local universe, but he is everlastingly the inspiration and guide of all Paradise pilgrims from the worlds of initial ascension up through a universe of universes and on through Havona to Paradise. Jesus is the *new and living way* from man to God, from the partial to the perfect, from the earthly to the heavenly, from time to eternity.

By the end of the twenty-ninth year Jesus of Nazareth had virtually finished the living of the life required of mortals as sojourners in the flesh. He came on earth the fullness of God to be manifest to man; he had now become well nigh the perfection of man awaiting the occasion to become manifest to God. And he did all of this before he was thirty years of age.

ON THE WAY TO ROME

THE TOUR of the Roman world consumed most of the twenty-eighth and the entire twenty-ninth year of Jesus' life on earth. Jesus and the two natives from India — Gonod and his son Ganid — left Jerusalem on a Sunday morning, April 26, A.D. 22. They made their journey according to schedule, and Jesus said good-bye to the father and son in the city of Charax on the Persian Gulf on the tenth day of December the following year, A.D. 23.

From Jerusalem they went to Caesarea by way of Joppa. At Caesarea they took a boat for Alexandria. From Alexandria they sailed for Lasea in Crete. From Crete they sailed for Carthage, touching at Cyrene. At Carthage they took a boat for Naples, stopping at Malta, Syracuse, and Messina. From Naples they went to Capua, whence they traveled by the Appian Way to Rome.

After their stay in Rome they went overland to Tarentum, where they set sail for Athens in Greece, stopping at Nicopolis and Corinth. From Athens they went to Ephesus by way of Troas. From Ephesus they sailed for Cyprus, putting in at Rhodes on the way. They spent considerable time visiting and resting on Cyprus and then sailed for Antioch in Syria. From Antioch they journeyed south to Sidon and then went over to Damascus. From there they traveled by caravan to Mesopotamia, passing through Thapsacus and Larissa. They spent some time in Babylon, visited Ur and other places, and then went to Susa. From Susa they journeyed to Charax, from which place Gonod and Ganid embarked for India.

It was while working four months at Damascus that Jesus had picked up the rudiments of the language spoken by Gonod and Ganid. While there he had labored much of the time on translations from Greek into one of the languages of India, being assisted by a native of Gonod's home district.

On this Mediterranean tour Jesus spent about half of each day teaching Ganid and acting as interpreter during Gonod's business conferences and social contacts. The remainder of each day, which was at his disposal, he devoted to making those close personal contacts with his fellow men, those intimate associations with the mortals of the realm, which so characterized his activities during these years that just preceded his public ministry.

From firsthand observation and actual contact Jesus acquainted himself with the higher material and intellectual civilization of the Occident and the Levant; from Gonod and his brilliant son he learned a great deal about the civilization and culture of India and China, for Gonod, himself a citizen of India, had made three extensive trips to the empire of the yellow race.

Ganid, the young man, learned much from Jesus during this long and intimate association. They developed a great affection for each other, and the lad's father many times tried to persuade Jesus to return with them to India, but Jesus always declined, pleading the necessity for returning to his family in Palestine.

During their stay in Joppa, Jesus met Gadiah, a Philistine interpreter who worked for one Simon a tanner. Gonod's agents in Mesopotamia had transacted much business with this Simon; so Gonod and his son desired to pay him a visit on their way to Caesarea. While they tarried at Joppa, Jesus and Gadiah became warm friends. This young Philistine was a truth seeker. Jesus was a truth giver; he *was* the truth for that generation on Earth. When a great truth seeker and a great truth giver meet, the result is a great and liberating enlightenment born of the experience of new truth.

One day after the evening meal Jesus and the young Philistine strolled down by the sea, and Gadiah, not knowing that this "scribe of Damascus" was so well versed in the Hebrew traditions, pointed out to Jesus the ship landing from which it was reputed that Jonah had embarked on his ill-fated voyage to Tarshish. And when he had concluded his remarks, he asked Jesus this question: "But do you suppose the big fish really did swallow Jonah?"

Jesus perceived that this young man's life had been tremendously influenced by this tradition, and that its contemplation had impressed upon him the folly of trying to run away from duty; Jesus therefore said nothing that would suddenly destroy the foundations of Gadiah's present motivation for practical living. In answering this question, Jesus said, "My friend, we are all Jonahs with lives to live in accordance with the will of God, and at all times when we seek to escape the present duty of living by running away to far-off enticements, we thereby put ourselves in the immediate control of those influences which are not directed by the powers of truth and the forces of righteousness. The flight from duty is the sacrifice of truth.

The escape from the service of light and life can only result in those distressing conflicts with the difficult whales of selfishness which lead eventually to darkness and death unless such God-forsaking Jonahs shall turn their hearts, even when in the very depths of despair, to seek after God and his goodness. And when such disheartened souls sincerely seek for God — hunger for truth and thirst for righteousness — there is nothing that can hold them in further captivity. No matter into what great depths they may have fallen, when they seek the light with a whole heart, the spirit of the Lord God of heaven will deliver them from their captivity; the evil circumstances of life will spew them out upon the dry land of fresh opportunities for renewed service and wiser living."

Gadiah was mightily moved by Jesus' teaching, and they talked long into the night by the seaside, and before they went to their lodgings, they prayed together and for each other. This was the same Gadiah who listened to the later preaching of Peter, became a profound believer in Jesus of Nazareth, and held a memorable argument with Peter one evening at the home of Dorcas. And Gadiah had very much to do with the final decision of Simon, the wealthy leather merchant, to embrace Christianity.

(In this narrative of the personal work of Jesus with his fellow mortals on this tour of the Mediterranean, we shall, in accordance with our mandate, freely translate his words into modern phraseology current on Earth at the time of this presentation.)

Jesus' last visit with Gadiah had to do with a discussion of good and evil. This young Philistine was much troubled by a feeling of injustice because of the presence of evil in the world alongside the good. He said, "How can God, if he is infinitely good, permit us to suffer the sorrows of evil; after all, who creates evil?" It was still believed by many in those days that God creates both good and evil, but Jesus never taught such error.

In answering this question, Jesus said, "My brother, God is love; therefore He must be good, and His goodness is so great and real that it cannot contain the small and unreal things of evil. God is so positively good that there is absolutely no place in Him for negative evil. Evil is the immature choosing and the unthinking misstep of those who are resistant to goodness, rejectful of beauty, and disloyal to truth. Evil is only the misadaptation of immaturity or the disruptive and distorting influence of ignorance. Evil is the inevitable darkness that follows upon the heels of the unwise rejection of light. Evil is that which is dark and untrue, and which, when consciously embraced and willfully endorsed, becomes sin.

"Your Father in heaven, by endowing you with the power to choose between truth and error, created the potential negative of the positive way of light and life; but such errors of evil are really nonexistent until such a time as an intelligent creature wills their existence by mischoosing the way of life. And then are such evils later exalted into sin by the knowing and deliberate choice of such a willful and rebellious creature. This is why our Father in heaven permits the good and the evil to go along together until the end of life, just as nature allows the wheat and the tares to grow side by side until the harvest." Gadiah was fully satisfied with Jesus' answer to his question after their subsequent discussion had made clear to his mind the real meaning of these momentous statements.

Jesus and his friends tarried in Caesarea beyond the time expected because one of the huge steering paddles of the vessel on which they intended to embark was discovered to be in danger of cleaving. The captain decided to remain in port while a new one was being made. There was a shortage of skilled woodworkers for this task, so Jesus volunteered to assist. During the evenings Jesus and his friends strolled about on the beautiful wall which served as a promenade around the port. Ganid greatly enjoyed Jesus' explanation of the water system of the city and the technique whereby the tides were utilized to flush the city's streets and sewers. This youth of India was much impressed with the temple of Augustus, situated upon an elevation and surmounted by a colossal statue of the Roman emperor. The second afternoon of their stay the three of them attended a performance in the enormous amphitheater, which could seat twenty thousand persons, and that night they went to a Greek play at the theater. These were the first exhibitions of this sort Ganid had ever witnessed, and he asked Jesus many questions about them. On the morning of the third day they paid a formal visit to the governor's palace, for Caesarea was the capital of Palestine and the residence of the Roman procurator.

At their inn there also lodged a merchant from Mongolia, and since this Far-Easterner spoke Greek fairly well, Jesus had several long visits with him. This man was much impressed with Jesus' philosophy of life and never forgot his words of wisdom regarding "the living of the heavenly life while on earth by means of daily submission to the will of the heavenly Father." This merchant was a Taoist, and he had thereby become a strong believer in the doctrine of a universal Deity. When he returned to Mongolia, he began to teach these advanced truths to his neighbors and to his business associates, and as a direct result of such activities, his eldest son decided to become a Taoist priest. This young man exerted a great influence in behalf of advanced truth throughout his lifetime and was followed by a son and a grandson who likewise were devotedly loyal to the doctrine of the One God — the Supreme Ruler of Heaven.

While the eastern branch of the early Christian church, having its headquarters at Philadelphia, held more faithfully to the teachings of Jesus than did the Jerusalem brethren, it was regrettable that there was no one like Peter to go into China, or like Paul to enter India, where the spiritual soil was then so favorable for planting the seed of the new gospel of the kingdom. These very teachings of Jesus, as they were held by the Philadelphians, would have made just such an immediate and effective appeal to the minds of the spiritually hungry Asiatic peoples as did the preaching of Peter and Paul in the West.

One of the young men who worked with Jesus one day on the steering paddle became much interested in the words that he dropped from hour to hour as they toiled in the shipyard. When Jesus intimated that the Father in heaven was interested in the welfare of his children on earth, this young Greek, Anaxand, said: "If the Gods are interested in me, then why do they not remove the cruel and unjust foreman of this workshop?" He was startled when Jesus replied, "Since you know the ways of kindness and value justice, perhaps the Gods have brought this erring man near that you may lead him into this better way. Maybe you are the salt which is to make this brother more agreeable to all other men; that is, if you have not lost your savor. As it is, this man is your master in that his evil ways unfavorably influence you. Why not assert your mastery of evil by virtue of the power of goodness and thus become the master of all relations between the two of you? I predict that the good in you could overcome the evil in him if you gave it a fair and living chance. There is no adventure in the course of mortal existence more enthralling than to enjoy the exhilaration of becoming the material life partner with spiritual energy and divine truth in one of their triumphant struggles with error and evil. It is a marvelous and transforming experience to become the living channel of spiritual light to the mortal who sits in spiritual darkness. If you are more blessed with truth than is this man, his need should challenge you. Surely you are not the coward who could stand by on the seashore and watch a fellow man who could not swim perish! How much more of value is this man's soul floundering in darkness compared to his body drowning in water!"

Anaxand was mightily moved by Jesus' words. Presently he told his superior what Jesus had said, and that night they both sought Jesus' advice as to the welfare of their souls. And later on, after the Christian message had been proclaimed in Caesarea, both of these men, one a Greek and the other a Roman, believed Philip's preaching and became prominent members of the church which he founded. Later this young Greek was appointed the steward of a Roman centurion, Cornelius, who became a believer through Peter's ministry. Anaxand continued to minister light to those who sat in darkness until the days of Paul's imprisonment at Caesarea, when he perished, by accident, in the great slaughter of twenty thousand Jews while he ministered to the suffering and dying.

Ganid was, by this time, beginning to learn how his tutor spent his leisure in this unusual personal ministry to his fellow men, and the young Indian set about to find out the motive for these incessant activities.

He asked, "Why do you occupy yourself so continuously with these visits with strangers?"

And Jesus answered, "Ganid, no man is a stranger to one who knows God. In the experience of finding the Father in heaven you discover that all men are your brothers, and does it seem strange that one should enjoy the exhilaration of meeting a newly discovered brother? To become acquainted with one's brothers and sisters, to know their problems and to learn to love them, is the supreme experience of living."

This was a conference that lasted well into the night, in the course of which the young man requested Jesus to tell him the difference between the will of God and that human mind act of choosing which is also called will.

In substance Jesus said: The will of God is the way of God, partnership with the choice of God in the face of any potential alternative. To do the will of God, therefore, is the progressive experience of becoming more and more like God, and God is the source and destiny of all that is good and beautiful and true. The will of man is the way of man, the sum and substance of that which the mortal chooses to be and do. Will is the deliberate choice of a self-conscious being which leads to decision-conduct based on intelligent reflection.

That afternoon Jesus and Ganid had both enjoyed playing with a very intelligent shepherd dog, and Ganid wanted to know whether the dog had a soul, whether it had a will. In response to his questions Jesus said, "The dog has a mind which can know material man, his master, but cannot know God, who is spirit; therefore the dog does not possess a spiritual nature and cannot enjoy a spiritual experience. The dog may have a will derived from nature and augmented by training, but such a power of mind is not a spiritual force, neither is it comparable to the human will, inasmuch as it is not *reflective* — it is not the result of discriminating higher and moral meanings or choosing spiritual and eternal values. It is the possession of such powers of spiritual discrimination and truth choosing that makes mortal man a moral being, a creature endowed with the attributes of spiritual responsibility and the potential of eternal survival." Jesus went on to explain that it is the absence of such mental powers in the animal which makes it forever impossible for the animal world to develop language in time or to experience anything equivalent to personality survival in eternity. As a result of this day's instruction Ganid never again entertained belief in the transmigration of the souls of men into the bodies of animals.

The next day Ganid talked all this over with his father, and it was in answer to Gonod's question that Jesus explained that "human wills which are fully occupied with passing only upon temporal decisions having to do with the material problems of animal existence are doomed to perish in time. Those who make wholehearted moral decisions and unqualified spiritual choices are thus progressively identified with the indwelling and divine spirit, and thereby are they increasingly transformed into the values of eternal survival - unending progression of divine service."

It was on this same day that the celestial observers first heard that momentous truth which, stated in modern terms, would signify: "Will is that manifestation of the human mind which enables the subjective consciousness to express itself objectively and to experience the phenomenon of aspiring to be Godlike." And it is in this same sense that every reflective and spiritually minded human being can become *creative*.

It had been an eventful visit at Caesarea, and when the boat was ready, Jesus and his two friends departed at noon one day for Alexandria in Egypt.

The three enjoyed a most pleasant passage to Alexandria. Ganid was delighted with the voyage and kept Jesus busy answering questions. As they approached the city's harbor, the young man was thrilled by the great lighthouse of Pharos, located on the island which Alexander had joined by a breakwater to the mainland, thus creating two magnificent harbors and thereby making Alexandria the maritime commercial crossroads of Africa, Asia, and Europe. This great lighthouse was one of the Seven Wonders of the World and was the forerunner of all subsequent lighthouses. They arose early in the morning to view this splendid lifesaving device of man, and amidst the exclamations of Ganid Jesus said, "And you, my son, will be like this lighthouse when you return to India, even after your father is laid to rest; you will become like the light of life to those who sit about you in darkness, showing all who so desire the way to reach the harbor of salvation in safety."

And as Ganid squeezed Jesus' hand, he said, "I will."

And again we remark that the early teachers of the Christian religion made a great mistake when they so exclusively turned their attention to the western civilization of the Roman world. The teachings of Jesus, as they were held by the Mesopotamian believers of the first century, would have been readily received by the various groups of Asiatic religionists.

By the fourth hour after landing they were settled near the eastern end of the long and broad avenue, one hundred feet wide and five miles long, which stretched on out to the western limits of this city of one million people. After the first survey of the city's chief attractions — university (museum), library, the royal mausoleum of Alexander, the palace, temple of Neptune, theater, and gymnasium — Gonod addressed himself to business while Jesus and Ganid went to the library, the greatest in the world. Here were assembled nearly a million manuscripts from the entire civilized world: Greece, Rome, Palestine, Parthia, India, China, and even Japan. In this library Ganid saw the largest collection of Indian literature in the entire world; and they spent some time here each day throughout their stay in Alexandria. Jesus told Ganid about the translation of the Hebrew scriptures into Greek at this place. And they discussed again and again all the religions of the world, Jesus endeavoring to point out to this young mind the truth in each, always adding: "But Yahweh is the God developed from the revelations of Melchizedek and the covenant of Abraham. The Jews were the offspring of Abraham and subsequently occupied the very land wherein Melchizedek had lived and taught, and from which he sent teachers to all the world; and their religion eventually portrayed a clearer recognition of the Lord God of Israel as the Universal Father in heaven than any other world religion."

Under Jesus' direction Ganid made a collection of the teachings of all those religions of the world which recognized a Universal Deity, even though they might also give more or less recognition to subordinate deities. After much discussion Jesus and Ganid decided that the Romans had no real God in their religion, that their religion was hardly more than emperor worship. The Greeks, they concluded, had a philosophy but hardly a religion with a personal God. The mystery cults they discarded because of the confusion of their multiplicity, and because their varied concepts of Deity seemed to be derived from other and older religions.

Although these translations were made at Alexandria, Ganid did not finally arrange these selections and add his own personal conclusions until near the end of their sojourn in Rome. He was much surprised to discover that the best of the authors of the world's sacred literature all more or less clearly recognized the existence of an eternal God and were much in agreement with regard to His character and His relationship with mortal man.

Jesus and Ganid spent much time in the museum during their stay in Alexandria. This museum was not a collection of rare objects but rather a university of fine art, science, and literature. Learned professors here gave daily lectures, and in those times this was the intellectual center of the Occidental world. Day by day Jesus interpreted the lectures to Ganid; one day during the second week the young man exclaimed, "Teacher Joshua, you know more than these professors; you should stand up and tell them the great things you have told me; they are befogged by much thinking. I shall speak to my father and have him arrange it."

Jesus smiled, saying, "You are an admiring pupil, but these teachers are not minded that you and I should instruct them. The pride of unspiritualized learning is a treacherous thing in human experience. The true teacher maintains his intellectual integrity by ever remaining a learner."

Alexandria was the city of the blended culture of the Occident and next to Rome the largest and most magnificent in the world. Here was located the largest Jewish synagogue in the world, the seat of government of the Alexandria Sanhedrin, the seventy ruling elders.

Among the many men with whom Gonod transacted business was a certain Jewish banker, Alexander, whose brother, Philo, was a famous religious philospher of that time. Philo was engaged in the laudable but exceedingly difficult task of harmonizing Greek philosophy and Hebrew theology. Ganid and Jesus talked much about Philo's teachings and expected to attend some of his lectures, but throughout their stay at Alexandria this famous Hellenistic Jew lay sick abed.

Jesus commended to Ganid much in the Greek philosophy and the Stoic doctrines, but he impressed upon the lad the truth that these systems of belief, like the indefinite teachings of some of his own people, were religions only in the sense that they led men to find God and enjoy a living experience in knowing the Eternal.

The night before they left Alexandria Ganid and Jesus had a long visit with one of the government professors at the university who lectured on the teachings of Plato. Jesus interpreted for the learned Greek teacher but injected no teaching of his own in refutation of the Greek philosophy. Gonod was away on business that evening; so, after the professor had departed, the teacher and his pupil had a long and heart-to-heart talk about Plato's doctrines. While Jesus gave qualified approval of some of the Greek teachings which had to do with the theory that the material things of the world are shadowy reflections of invisible but more substantial spiritual realities, he sought to lay a more trustworthy foundation for the lad's thinking; so he began a long dissertation concerning the nature of reality in the universe. In substance and in modern phraseology Jesus said to Ganid:

The source of universe reality is the Infinite. The material things of finite creation are the time-space repercussions of the Paradise Pattern and the Universal Mind of the eternal God. Causation in the physical world, self-consciousness in the intellectual world, and progressing selfhood in the spirit world — these realities, projected on a universal scale, combined in eternal relatedness, and experienced with perfection of quality and divinity of value — constitute the *reality of the Supreme.* But in an ever-changing universe the Original Personality of causation, intelligence, and spirit experience is changeless, absolute. All things, even in an eternal universe of limitless values and divine qualities, may, and oftentimes do, change except the Absolutes and that which has attained the physical status, intellectual embrace, or spiritual identity which is absolute.

The highest level to which a finite creature can progress is the recognition of the Universal Father and the knowing of the Supreme. And even then such beings of finality destiny go on experiencing change in the motions of the physical world and in its material phenomena. Likewise do they remain aware of selfhood progression in their continuing ascension of the spiritual universe and of growing consciousness in their deepening appreciation of, and response to, the intellectual cosmos. Only in the perfection, harmony, and unanimity of will can the creature become as one with the Creator; and such a state of divinity is attained and maintained only by the creature's continuing to live in time and eternity by consistently conforming his finite personal will to the divine will of the Creator. Always must the desire to do the Father's will be supreme in the soul and dominant over the mind of an ascending son of God.

A one-eyed person can never hope to visualize depth of perspective. Neither can single-eyed material scientists nor single-eyed spiritual mystics and allegorists correctly visualize and adequately comprehend the true depths of universe reality. All true values of creature experience are concealed in depth of recognition.

Mindless causation cannot evolve the refined and complex from the crude and the simple, neither can spiritless experience evolve the divine characters of eternal survival from the material minds of the mortals of time. The one attribute of the universe which so exclusively characterizes the infinite Deity is this unending creative bestowal of personality which can survive in progressive Deity attainment.

Personality is that cosmic endowment, that phase of universal reality, which can coexist with unlimited change and at the same time retain its identity in the very presence of all such changes, and forever afterward.

Life is an adaptation of the original cosmic causation to the demands and possibilities of universe situations, and it comes into being by the action of the Universal Mind and the activation of the spirit spark of the God who is spirit. The meaning of life is its adaptability; the value of life is its progressability - even to the heights of God-consciousness.

Misadaptation of self-conscious life to the universe results in cosmic disharmony. Final divergence of personality will from the trend of the universes terminates in intellectual isolation, personality segregation. Loss of the indwelling spirit pilot (the Father Fragment) supervenes in spiritual cessation of existence. Intelligent and progressing life becomes then, in and of itself, an incontrovertible proof of the existence of a purposeful universe expressing the will of a divine Creator. And this life, in the aggregate, struggles toward higher values, having for its final goal the Universal Father.

Only in degree does man possess mind above the animal level aside from the higher and quasi-spiritual ministrations of intellect. Therefore animals (not having worship and wisdom) cannot experience superconsciousness, consciousness of consciousness. The animal mind is only conscious of the objective universe.

Knowledge is the sphere of the material or fact-discerning mind. Truth is the domain of the spiritually endowed intellect that is conscious of knowing God. Knowledge is demonstrable; truth is experienced. Knowledge is a possession of the mind; truth an experience of the soul, the progressing self. Knowledge is a function of the nonspiritual level; truth is a phase of the mind-spirit level of the universes. The eye of the material mind perceives a world of factual knowledge; the eye of the spiritualized intellect discerns a world of true values. These two views, synchronized and harmonized, reveal the world of reality, wherein wisdom interprets the phenomena of the universe in terms of progressive personal experience.

Error (evil) is the penalty of imperfection. The qualities of imperfection or facts of misadaptation are disclosed on the material level by critical observation and by scientific analysis; on the moral level, by human experience. The presence of evil constitutes proof of the inaccuracies of mind and the immaturity of the evolving self. Evil is, therefore, also a measure of imperfection in universe interpretation. The possibility of making mistakes is inherent in the acquisition of wisdom, the scheme of progressing from the partial and temporal to the complete and eternal, from the relative and imperfect to the final and perfected. Error is the shadow of relative incompleteness which must of necessity fall across man's ascending universe path to Paradise perfection. Error (evil) is not an actual universe quality; it is simply the observation of a relativity in the relatedness of the imperfection of the incomplete finite to the ascending levels of the Supreme and Ultimate.

Although Jesus told all this to the lad in language best suited to his comprehension, at the end of the discussion Ganid was heavy of eye and was soon lost in slumber. They rose early the next morning to go aboard the boat bound for Lasea on the island of Crete. But before they embarked, the lad had still further questions to ask about evil, to which Jesus replied:

Evil is a relativity concept. It arises out of the observation of the imperfections which appear in the shadow cast by a finite universe of things and beings as such a cosmos obscures the living light of the universal expression of the eternal realities of the Infinite One.

Potential evil is inherent in the necessary incompleteness of the revelation of God as a time-space-limited expression of infinity and eternity. The fact of the partial in the presence of the complete constitutes relativity of reality, creates necessity for intellectual choosing, and establishes value levels of spirit recognition and response. The incomplete and finite concept of the Infinite which is held by the temporal and limited creature mind is, in and of itself, *potential evil.* But the augmenting error of unjustified deficiency in reasonable spiritual rectification of these originally inherent intellectual disharmonies and spiritual insufficiencies, is equivalent to the realization of *actual evil.*

All static, dead, concepts are potentially evil. The finite shadow of relative and living truth is continually moving. Static concepts invariably retard science, politics, society, and religion. Static concepts may represent a certain knowledge, but they are deficient in wisdom and devoid of truth. But do not permit the concept of relativity so to mislead you that you fail to recognize the co-ordination of the universe under the guidance of the cosmic mind, and its stabilized control by the energy and spirit of the Supreme.

Crete was their next stop. The travelers had but one purpose in going to Crete, and that was to play, to walk about over the island, and to climb the mountains. The Cretans of that time did not enjoy an enviable reputation among the surrounding peoples. Nevertheless, Jesus and Ganid won many souls to higher levels of thinking and living and thus laid the foundation for the quick reception of the later gospel teachings when the first preachers from Jerusalem arrived. Jesus loved these Cretans, notwithstanding the harsh words that Paul later spoke concerning them when he subsequently sent Titus to the island to reorganize their churches.

On the mountainside in Crete Jesus had his first long talk with Gonod regarding religion. And the father was much impressed, saying, "No wonder the boy believes everything you tell him, but I never knew they had such a religion even in Jerusalem, much less in Damascus." It was during the island sojourn that Gonod first proposed to Jesus that he go back to India with them, and Ganid was delighted with the thought that Jesus might consent to such an arrangement.

One day when Ganid asked Jesus why he had not devoted himself to the work of a public teacher, he said, "My son, everything must await the coming of its time. You are born into the world, but no amount of anxiety and no manifestation of impatience will help you to grow up. You must, in all such matters, wait upon time. Time alone will ripen the green fruit upon the tree. Season follows season and sundown follows sunrise only with the passing of time. I am now on the way to Rome with you and your father, and that is sufficient for today. My tomorrow is wholly in the hands of my Father in heaven." And then he told Ganid the story of Moses and the forty years of watchful waiting and continued preparation.

One thing happened on a visit to Fair Havens which Ganid never forgot; the memory of this episode always caused him to wish he might do something to change the caste system of his native India. A drunken degenerate was attacking a slave girl on the public highway. When Jesus saw the plight of the girl, he rushed forward and drew the maiden away from the assault of the madman. While the frightened child clung to him, he held the infuriated man at a safe distance by his powerful extended right arm until the poor fellow had exhausted himself beating the air with his angry blows. Ganid felt a strong impulse to help Jesus handle the affair, but his father forbade him. Though they could not speak the girl's language, she could understand their act of mercy and gave token of her heartfelt appreciation as they all three escorted her home. This was probably as near a personal encounter with his fellows as Jesus ever had throughout his entire life in the flesh. But he had a difficult task that evening trying to explain to Ganid why he did not smite the drunken man. Ganid thought this man should have been struck at least as many times as he had struck the girl.

While they were up in the mountains, Jesus had a long talk with a young man who was fearful and downcast. Failing to derive comfort and courage from association with his fellows, this youth had sought the solitude of the hills; he had grown up with a feeling of helplessness and inferiority. These natural tendencies had been augmented by numerous difficult circumstances that the lad had encountered as he grew up, notably, the loss of his father when he was twelve years of age.

As they met, Jesus said, "Greetings, my friend! Why so downcast on such a beautiful day? If something has happened to distress you, perhaps I can in some manner assist you. At any rate it affords me real pleasure to proffer my services."

The young man was disinclined to talk, and so Jesus made a second approach to his soul, saying, "I understand you come up in these hills to get away from folks; so, of course, you do not want to talk with me, but I would like to know whether you are familiar with these hills; do you know the direction of the trails? And, perchance, could you inform me as to the best route to Phenix?"

Now this youth was very familiar with these mountains, and he really became much interested in telling Jesus the way to Phenix, so much so that he marked out all the trails on the ground and fully explained every detail. But he was startled and made curious when Jesus, after saying good-bye and making as if he were taking leave, suddenly turned to him, saying, "I well know you wish to be left alone with your disconsolation; but it would be neither kind nor fair for me to receive such generous help from you as to how best to find my way to Phenix and then unthinkingly to go away from you without making the least effort to answer your appealing request for help and guidance regarding the best route to the goal of destiny which you seek in your heart while you tarry here on the mountainside. As you so well know the trails to Phenix, having traversed them many times, so do I well know the way to the city of your disappointed hopes and thwarted ambitions. And since you have asked me for help, I will not disappoint you."

The youth was almost overcome, but he managed to stammer out, "But..., I did not ask you for anything...."

And Jesus, laying a gentle hand on his shoulder, said, "No, son, not with words but with longing looks did you appeal to my heart. My boy, to one who loves his fellows there is an eloquent appeal for help in your countenance of discouragement and despair. Sit down with me while I tell you of the service trails and happiness highways which lead from the sorrows of self to the joys of loving activities in the brotherhood of men and in the service of the God of heaven."

By this time the young man very much desired to talk with Jesus, and he knelt at his feet imploring Jesus to help him, to show him the way of escape from his world of personal sorrow and defeat.

Said Jesus, "My friend, arise! Stand up like a man! You may be surrounded with small enemies and be retarded by many obstacles, but the big things and the real things of this world and the universe are on your side. The sun rises every morning to salute you just as it does the most powerful and prosperous man on earth. Look, you have a strong body and powerful muscles. Your physical equipment is better than the average. Of course, it is just about useless while you sit out here on the mountainside and grieve over your misfortunes, real and fancied. But you could do great things with your body if you would hasten off to where great things are waiting to be done. You are trying to run away from your unhappy self, but it cannot be done. You and your problems of living are real; you cannot escape them as long as you live. But look again, your mind is clear and capable. Your strong body has an intelligent mind to direct it. Set your mind at work to solve its problems; teach your intellect to work for you; refuse longer to be dominated by fear like an unthinking animal. Your mind should be your courageous ally in the solution of your life problems rather than your being, as you have been, its abject fear-slave and the bondservant of depression and defeat. But most valuable of all, your potential of real achievement is the spirit which lives within you, and which will stimulate and inspire your mind to control itself and activate the body if you will release it from the fetters of fear and thus enable your spiritual nature to begin your deliverance from the evils of inaction by the power-presence of living faith. And then, forthwith, will this faith vanquish fear of men by the compelling presence of that new and all-dominating *love of your fellows* which will so soon fill your soul to overflowing because of the consciousness which has been born in your heart that you are a child of God.

"This day, my son, you are to be reborn, re-established as a man of faith, courage, and devoted service to man, for God's sake. And when you become so readjusted to life within yourself, you become likewise readjusted to the universe; you have been born again — born of the spirit — and henceforth will your whole life become one of victorious accomplishment. Trouble will invigorate you; disappointment will spur you on; difficulties will challenge you; and obstacles will stimulate you. Arise, young man! Say farewell to the life of cringing fear and fleeing cowardice. Hasten back to duty and live your life in the flesh as a son of God, a mortal dedicated to the ennobling service of man on earth and destined to the superb and eternal service of God in eternity."

And this youth, Fortune, subsequently became the leader of the Christians in Crete and the close associate of Titus in his labors for the uplift of the Cretan believers.

The travelers were truly rested and refreshed when they made ready about noon one day to sail for Carthage in northern Africa, stopping for two days at Cyrene. It was here that Jesus and Ganid gave first aid to a lad named Rufus, who had been injured by the breakdown of a loaded oxcart. They carried him home to his mother, and his father, Simon, little dreamed that the man whose cross he subsequently bore by orders of a Roman soldier was the stranger who once befriended his son.

Most of the time en route to Carthage Jesus talked with his fellow travelers about things social, political, and commercial; hardly a word was said about religion. For the first time Gonod and Ganid discovered that Jesus was a good storyteller, and they kept him busy telling tales about his early life in Galilee. They also learned that he was reared in Galilee and not in either Jerusalem or Damascus.

When Ganid inquired what one could do to make friends, having noticed that the majority of persons whom they chanced to meet were attracted to Jesus, his teacher said, "Become interested in your fellows; learn how to love them and watch for the opportunity to do something for them which you are sure they want done," and then he quoted the olden Jewish proverb — "A man who would have friends must show himself friendly."

At Carthage Jesus had a long and memorable talk with a Mithraic priest about immortality, about time and eternity. This Persian had been educated at Alexandria, and he really desired to learn from Jesus. Put into the words of today, in substance Jesus said in answer to his many questions:

Time is the stream of flowing temporal events perceived by creature consciousness. Time is a name given to the succession-arrangement whereby events are recognized and segregated. The universe of space is a time-related phenomenon as it is viewed from any interior position outside of the fixed abode of Paradise. The motion of time is only revealed in relation to something which does not move in space as a time phenomenon. In the universe of universes Paradise and its Deities transcend both time and space. On the inhabited worlds, human personality (indwelt and oriented by the Paradise Father's spirit) is the only physically related reality that can transcend the material sequence of temporal events.

Animals do not sense time as does man, and even to man, because of his sectional and circumscribed view, time appears as a succession of events; but as man ascends, as he progresses inward, the enlarging view of this event procession is such that it is discerned more and more in its wholeness. That which formerly appeared as a succession of events then will be viewed as a whole and perfectly related cycle; in this way will circular simultaneity increasingly displace the onetime consciousness of the linear sequence of events.

There are seven different conceptions of space as it is conditioned by time. Space is measured by time, not time by space. The confusion of the scientist grows out of failure to recognize the reality of space. Space is not merely an intellectual concept of the variation in relatedness of universe objects. Space is not empty, and the only thing man knows which can even partially transcend space is mind. Mind can function independently of the concept of the space-relatedness of material objects. Space is relatively and comparatively finite to all beings of creature status. The nearer consciousness approaches the awareness of seven cosmic dimensions, the more does the concept of potential space approach ultimacy. But the space potential is truly ultimate only on the absolute level.

It must be apparent that universal reality has an expanding and always relative meaning on the ascending and perfecting levels of the cosmos. Ultimately, surviving mortals achieve identity in a seven-dimensional universe.

The time-space concept of a mind of material origin is destined to undergo successive enlargements as the conscious and conceiving personality ascends the levels of the universes. When man attains the mind intervening between the material and the spiritual planes of existence, his ideas of time-space will be enormously expanded both as to quality of perception and quantity of experience. The enlarging cosmic conceptions of an advancing spirit personality are due to augmentations of both depth of insight and scope of consciousness. And as personality passes on, upward and inward, to the transcendental levels of Deity-likeness, the time-space concept will increasingly approximate the timeless and spaceless concepts of the Absolutes. Relatively, and in accordance with transcendental attainment, these concepts of the absolute level are to be envisioned by the children of ultimate destiny.

The first stop on the way to Italy was at the island of Malta. Here Jesus had a long talk with a downhearted and discouraged young man named Claudus. This fellow had contemplated taking his life, but when he had finished talking with the scribe of Damascus, he said, "I will face life like a man; I am through playing the coward. I will go back to my people and begin all over again." Shortly he became an enthusiastic preacher of the Cynics, and still later on he joined hands with Peter in proclaiming Christianity in Rome and Naples, and after the death of Peter he went on to Spain preaching the gospel. But he never knew that the man who inspired him in Malta was the Jesus whom he subsequently proclaimed the world's Deliverer.

At Syracuse they spent a full week. The notable event of their stop here was the rehabilitation of Ezra, the backslidden Jew, who kept the tavern where Jesus and his companions stopped. Ezra was charmed by Jesus' approach and asked him to help him come back to the faith of Israel. He expressed his hopelessness by saying, "I want to be a true son of Abraham, but I cannot find God."

Said Jesus, "If you truly want to find God, that desire is in itself evidence that you have already found Him. Your trouble is not that you cannot find God, for the Father has already found you; your trouble is simply that you do not know God. Have you not read in the Prophet Jeremiah, `You shall seek me and find me when you shall search for me with all your heart'? And again, does not this same prophet say: `And I will give you a heart to know me, that I am the Lord, and you shall belong to my people, and I will be your God'? And have you not also read in the Scriptures where it says: 'He looks down upon men, and if any will say: I have sinned and perverted that which was right, and it profited me not, then will God deliver that man's soul from darkness, and he shall see the light'"?

And Ezra found God and to the satisfaction of his soul. Later, this Jew, in association with a well-to-do Greek proselyte, built the first Christian church in Syracuse.

At Messina they stopped for only one day, but that was long enough to change the life of a small boy, a fruit vendor, of whom Jesus bought fruit and in turn fed with the bread of life. The lad never forgot the words of Jesus and the kindly look which went with them when, placing his hand on the boy's shoulder, he said, "Farewell, my lad, be of good courage as you grow up to manhood and after you have fed the body learn how also to feed the soul. And my Father in heaven will be with you and go before you." The lad became a devotee of the Mithraic religion and later on turned to the Christian faith.

At last they reached Naples and felt they were not far from their destination, Rome. Gonod had much business to transact in Naples, and aside from the time Jesus was required as interpreter, he and Ganid spent their leisure visiting and exploring the city. Ganid was becoming adept at sighting those who appeared to be in need. They found abundant poverty in this city and distributed much alms. But Ganid never understood the meaning of Jesus' words when, after he had given a coin to a street beggar, he refused to pause and speak comfortingly to the man. Said Jesus, "Why waste words upon one who cannot perceive the meaning of what you say? The spirit of the Father cannot teach and save one who has no capacity for sonship." What Jesus meant was that the man was not of normal mind; that he lacked the ability to respond to spirit leading.

There was no outstanding experience in Naples; Jesus and the young man thoroughly canvassed the city and spread good cheer with many smiles upon hundreds of men, women, and children.

From here they went by way of Capua to Rome, making a stop of three days at Capua. By the Appian Way they journeyed on beside their pack animals toward Rome, all three being anxious to see this mistress of empire and the greatest city in all the world.

THE WORLD'S RELIGIONS

DURING THE Alexandrian sojourn of Jesus, Gonod, and Ganid, the young man spent much of his time and no small sum of his father's money making a collection of the teachings of the world's religions about God and His relations with mortal man. Ganid employed more than threescore learned translators in the making of this abstract of the religious doctrines of the world concerning the Deities. And it should be made plain in this record that all these teachings portraying monotheism were largely derived, directly or indirectly, from the preachments of the missionaries of Machiventa Melchizedek, who went forth from their Salem headquarters to spread the doctrine of one God - the Most High - to the ends of the earth.

There is presented herewith an abstract of Ganid's manuscript, which he prepared at Alexandria and Rome, and which was preserved in India for hundreds of years after his death. He collected this material under ten heads, as follows:

CYNICISM

The residual teachings of the disciples of Melchizedek, excepting those which persisted in the Jewish religion, were best preserved in the doctrines of the Cynics. Ganid's selection embraced the following:

"God is supreme; he is the Most High of heaven and earth. God is the perfected circle of eternity, and he rules the universe of universes. He is the sole maker of the heavens and the earth. When he decrees a thing, that thing is. Our God is one God, and he is compassionate and merciful. Everything that is high, holy, true, and beautiful is like our God. The Most High is the light of heaven and earth; he is the God of the east, the west, the north, and the south.

"Even if the earth should pass away, the resplendent face of the Supreme would abide in majesty and glory. The Most High is the first and the last, the beginning and the end of everything. There is but this one God, and his name is Truth.

God is self-existent, and he is devoid of all anger and enmity; he is immortal and infinite. Our God is omnipotent and bounteous. While he has many manifestations, we worship only God himself. God knows all — our secrets and our proclamations; he also knows what each of us deserves. His might is equal to all things.

"God is a peace giver and a faithful protector of all who fear and trust him. He gives salvation to all who serve him. All creation exists in the power of the Most High. His divine love springs forth from the holiness of his power, and affection is born of the might of his greatness. The Most High has decreed the union of body and soul and has endowed man with his own spirit. What man does must come to an end, but what the Creator does goes on forever. We gain knowledge from the experience of man, but we derive wisdom from the contemplation of the Most High.

"God pours rain upon the earth, he causes the sun to shine upon the sprouting grain, and he gives us the abundant harvest of the good things of this life and eternal salvation in the world to come. Our God enjoys great authority; his name is Excellent and his nature is unfathomable. When you are sick, it is the Most High who heals you. God is full of goodness toward all mankind; we have no friend like the Most High. His mercy fills all places and his goodness encompasses all souls. The Most High is changeless ; and he is our helper in every time of need. Wherever you turn to pray, there is the face of the Most High and the open ear of our God. You may hide yourself from men, but not from God. God is not a great distance from us; he is omnipresent. God fills all places and lives in the heart of the man who fears his holy name. Creation is in the Creator and the Creator in his creation. We search for the Most High and then find him in our hearts. You go in quest of a dear friend, and then you discover him within your soul.

"The man who knows God looks upon all men as equal; they are his brethren. Those who are selfish, those who ignore their brothers in the flesh, have only weariness as their reward. Those who love their fellows and who have pure hearts shall see God. God never forgets sincerity. He will guide the honest of heart into the truth, for God is truth.

"In your lives overthrow error and overcome evil by the love of the living truth. In all your relations with men do good for evil. The Lord God is merciful and loving; he is forgiving. Let us love God, for he first loved us. By God's love and through his mercy we shall be saved. Poor men and rich men are brothers. God is their Father. The evil you would not have done you, do not to others.

"At all times call upon his name, and as you believe in his name, so shall your prayer be heard. What a great honor it is to worship the Most High! All the worlds and the universes worship the Most High. And with all your prayers give thanks — ascend to worship. Prayerful worship shuns evil and forbids sin. At all times let us praise the name of the Most High. The man who takes shelter in the Most High conceals his defects from the universe. When you stand before God with a clean heart, you become fearless of all creation. The Most High is like a loving father and mother; he really loves us, his children on earth. Our God will forgive us and guide our footsteps into the ways of salvation. He will take us by the hand and lead us to himself. God saves those who trust him; he does not compel man to serve his name.

"If the faith of the Most High has entered your heart, then shall you abide free from fear throughout all the days of your life. Fret not yourself because of the prosperity of the ungodly; fear not those who plot evil; let the soul turn away from sin and put your whole trust in the God of salvation. The weary soul of the wandering mortal finds eternal rest in the arms of the Most High; the wise man hungers for the divine embrace; the earth child longs for the security of the arms of the Universal Father. The noble man seeks for that high estate wherein the soul of the mortal blends with the spirit of the Supreme. God is just: What fruit we receive not from our plantings in this world we shall receive in the next."

JUDAISM

The Kenites of Palestine salvaged much of the teaching of Melchizedek, and from these records, as preserved and modified by the Jews, Jesus and Ganid made the following selection:

"In the beginning God created the heavens and the earth and all things therein. And, behold, all he created was very good. The Lord, he is God; there is none beside him in heaven above or upon the earth beneath. Therefore shall you love the Lord your God with all your heart and with all your soul and with all your might. The earth shall be full of the knowledge of the Lord as the waters cover the sea. The heavens declare the glory of God, and the firmament shows his handiwork. Day after day utters speech; night after night shows knowledge. There is no speech or language where their voice is not heard. The Lord's work is great, and in wisdom has he made all things; the greatness of the Lord is unsearchable. He knows the number of the stars; he calls them all by their names.

"The power of the Lord is great and his understanding infinite. Says the Lord: `As the heavens are higher than the earth, so are my ways higher than your ways, and my thoughts higher than your thoughts.' God reveals the deep and secret things because the light dwells with him. The Lord is merciful and gracious; he is long-suffering and abundant in goodness and truth. The Lord is good and upright; the meek will he guide in judgment. Taste and see that the Lord is good! Blessed is the man who trusts God. God is our refuge and strength, a very present help in trouble.

"The mercy of the Lord is from everlasting to everlasting upon those who fear him and his righteousness even to our children's children. The Lord is gracious and full of compassion. The Lord is good to all, and his tender mercies are over all his creation; he heals the brokenhearted and binds up their wounds. Whither shall

I go from God's spirit? Whither shall I flee from the divine presence? Thus says the High and Lofty One who inhabits eternity, whose name is Holy: `I dwell in the high and holy place; also with him who is of a contrite heart and a humble spirit!' None can hide himself from our God, for he fills heaven and earth. Let the heavens be glad and let the earth rejoice. Let all nations say: The Lord reigns! Give thanks to God, for his mercy endures forever.

"The heavens declare God's righteousness, and all the people have seen his glory. It is God who has made us, and not we ourselves; we are his people, the sheep of his pasture. His mercy is everlasting, and his truth endures to all generations. Our God is governor among the nations. Let the earth be filled with his glory! O that men would praise the Lord for his goodness and for his wonderful gifts to the children of men!

"God has made man a little less than divine and has crowned him with love and mercy. The Lord knows the way of the righteous, but the way of the ungodly shall perish. The fear of the Lord is the beginning of wisdom; the knowledge of the Supreme is understanding. Says the Almighty God: `Walk before me and be perfect.' Forget not that pride goes before destruction and a haughty spirit before a fall. He who rules his own spirit is mightier than he who takes a city. Says the Lord God, the Holy One: `In returning to your spiritual rest shall you be saved; in quietness and confidence shall be your strength.' They who wait upon the Lord shall renew their strength; they shall mount up with wings like eagles. They shall run and not be weary; they shall walk and not be faint. The Lord shall give you rest from your fear. Says the Lord: `Fear not, for I am with you. Be not dismayed, for I am your God. I will strengthen you; I will help you; yes, I will uphold you with the right hand of my righteousness.'

"God is our Father; the Lord is our redeemer. God has created the universal hosts, and he preserves them all. His righteousness is like the mountains and his judgment like the great deep. He causes us to drink of the river of his pleasures, and in his light we shall see light. It is good to give thanks to the Lord and to sing praises to the Most High; to show forth loving-kindness in the morning and the divine faithfulness every night. God's kingdom is an everlasting kingdom, and his dominion endures throughout all generations. The Lord is my shepherd; I shall not want. He makes me to lie down in green pastures; he leads me beside still waters. He restores my soul. He leads me in the paths of righteousness. Yes, even though I walk through the valley of the shadow of death, I will fear no evil, for God is with me. Surely goodness and mercy shall follow me all the days of my life, and I shall dwell in the house of the Lord forever.

"Yahweh is the God of my salvation; therefore in the divine name will I put my trust. I will trust in the Lord with all my heart; I will lean not upon my own understanding. In all my ways I will acknowledge him, and he shall direct my paths. The Lord is faithful; he keeps his word with those who serve him; the just shall live by his faith. If you do not well, it is because sin lies at the door; men reap the evil they plough and the sin they sow. Fret not yourself because of evildoers. If you regard iniquity in your heart, the Lord will not hear you; if you sin against God, you also wrong your own soul. God will bring every man's work to judgment with every secret thing, whether it be good or evil. As a man thinks in his heart, so is he.

"The Lord is near all who call upon him in sincerity and in truth. Weeping may endure for a night, but joy comes in the morning. A merry heart does good like a medicine. No good thing will God withhold from those who walk uprightly. Fear God and keep his commandments, for this is the whole duty of man. Thus says the Lord who created the heavens and who formed the earth: `There is no God beside me, a just God and a savior. Look to me and be saved, all the ends of the earth. If you seek me, you shall find me if you search for me with all your heart.' The meek shall inherit the earth and shall delight themselves in the abundance of peace. Whoever sows iniquity shall reap calamity; they who sow the wind shall reap the whirlwind.

"`Come now, let us reason together,' says the Lord, `Though your sins be as scarlet, they shall be as white as snow. Though they be red like crimson, they shall be as wool.' But there is no peace for the wicked; it is your own sins which have withheld the good things from you. God is the health of my countenance and the joy of my soul. The eternal God is my strength; he is our dwelling place, and underneath are the everlasting arms. The Lord is near to those who are brokenhearted; he saves all who have a childlike spirit. Many are the afflictions of the righteous man, but the Lord delivers him out of them all. Commit your way to the Lord — trust him — and he will bring it to pass. He who dwells in the secret place of the Most High shall abide under the shadow of the Almighty.

"Love your neighbor as yourself; bear a grudge against no man. Whatsoever you hate do to no man. Love your brother, for the Lord has said: `I will love my children freely.' The path of the just is as a shining light which shines more and more until the perfect day. They who are wise shall shine as the brightness of the firmament and they who turn many to righteousness as the stars forever and ever. Let the wicked forsake his evil way and the unrighteous man his rebellious thoughts. Says the Lord: `Let them return to me, and I will have mercy on them; I will abundantly pardon.'

"Says God, the creator of heaven and earth: `Great peace have they who love my law. My commandments are: You shall love me with all your heart; you shall have no gods before me; you shall not take my name in vain; remember the Sabbath day to keep it holy; honor your father and mother; you shall not kill; you shall not commit adultery; you shall not steal; you shall not bear false witness; you shall not covet.'

"And to all who love the Lord supremely and their neighbors like themselves, the God of heaven says: `I will ransom you from the grave; I will redeem you from death. I will be merciful to your children, as well as just. Have I not said of my creatures on earth, you are the sons and daughters of the living God? And have I not loved you with an everlasting love? Have I not called you to become like me and to dwell forever with me in Paradise?'"

BUDDHISM

Ganid was shocked to discover how near Buddhism came to being a great and beautiful religion without God, without a personal and universal Deity. However, he did find some record of certain earlier beliefs which reflected something of the influence of the teachings of the Melchizedek missionaries who continued their work in India even to the times of Buddha. Jesus and Ganid collected the following statements from the Buddhist literature:

"Out of a pure heart shall gladness spring forth to the Infinite; all my being shall be at peace with this supermortal rejoicing. My soul is filled with content, and my heart overflows with the bliss of peaceful trust. I have no fear; I am free from anxiety. I dwell in security, and my enemies cannot alarm me. I am satisfied with the fruits of my confidence. I have found the approach to the Immortal easy of access. I pray for faith to sustain me on the long journey; I know that faith from beyond will not fail me. I know my brethren will prosper if they become imbued with the faith of the Immortal, even the faith that creates modesty, uprightness, wisdom, courage, knowledge, and perseverance. Let us forsake sorrow and disown fear. By faith let us lay hold upon true righteousness and genuine manliness. Let us learn to meditate on justice and mercy. Faith is man's true wealth; it is the endowment of virtue and glory.

"Unrighteousness is contemptible; sin is despicable. Evil is degrading, whether held in thought or wrought out in deeds. Pain and sorrow follow in the path of evil as the dust follows the wind. Happiness and peace of mind follow pure thinking and virtuous living as the shadow follows the substance of material things. Evil is the fruit of wrongly directed thinking. It is evil to see sin where there is no sin; to see no sin where there is sin. Evil is the path of false doctrines. Those who avoid evil by seeing things as they are gain joy by thus embracing the truth. Make an end of your misery by loathing sin. When you look up to the Noble One, turn away from sin with a whole heart. Make no apology for evil; make no excuse for sin. By your efforts to make amends for past sins you acquire strength to resist future tendencies thereto. Restraint is born of repentance. Leave no fault unconfessed to the Noble One.

"Cheerfulness and gladness are the rewards of deeds well done and to the glory of the Immortal. No man can rob you of the liberty of your own mind. When the faith of your religion has emancipated your heart, when the mind, like a mountain, is settled and immovable, then shall the peace of the soul flow tranquilly like a river of waters. Those who are sure of salvation are forever free from lust, envy, hatred, and the delusions of wealth. While faith is the energy of the better life, nevertheless, must you work out your own salvation with perseverance. If you would be certain of your final salvation, then make sure that you sincerely seek to fulfill all righteousness. Cultivate the assurance of the heart which springs from within and thus come to enjoy the ecstasy of eternal salvation.

"No religionist may hope to attain the enlightenment of immortal wisdom who persists in being slothful, indolent, feeble, idle, shameless, and selfish. But whoso is thoughtful, prudent, reflective, fervent, and earnest — even while he yet lives on earth — may attain the supreme enlightenment of the peace and liberty of divine wisdom. Remember, every act shall receive its reward. Evil results in sorrow and sin ends in pain. Joy and happiness are the outcome of a good life. Even the evildoer enjoys a season of grace before the time of the full ripening of his evil deeds, but inevitably there must come the full harvest of evil-doing. Let no man think lightly of sin, saying in his heart: `The penalty of wrongdoing shall not come near me.' What you do shall be done to you, in the judgment of wisdom. Injustice done to your fellows shall come back upon you. The creature cannot escape the destiny of his deeds.

"The fool has said in his heart, `Evil shall not overtake me'; but safety is found only when the soul craves reproof and the mind seeks wisdom. The wise man is a noble soul who is friendly in the midst of his enemies, tranquil among the turbulent, and generous among the grasping. Love of self is like weeds in a goodly field. Selfishness leads to grief; perpetual care kills. The tamed mind yields happiness. He is the greatest of warriors who overcomes and subdues himself. Restraint in all things is good. He alone is a superior person who esteems virtue and is observant of his duty. Let not anger and hate master you. Speak harshly of no one. Contentment is the greatest wealth. What is given wisely is well saved. Do not to others those things you would not wish done to you. Pay good for evil; overcome evil with the good.

"A righteous soul is more to be desired than the sovereignty of all the earth. Immortality is the goal of sincerity; death, the end of thoughtless living. Those who are earnest die not; the thoughtless are dead already. Blessed are they who have insight into the deathless state. Those who torture the living will hardly find happiness after death. The unselfish go to heaven, where they rejoice in the bliss of infinite liberality and continue to increase in noble generosity. Every mortal who thinks righteously, speaks nobly, and acts unselfishly shall not only enjoy virtue here during this brief life but shall also, after the dissolution of the body, continue to enjoy the delights of heaven."

HINDUISM

The missionaries of Melchizedek carried the teachings of the one God with them wherever they journeyed. Much of this monotheistic doctrine, together with other and previous concepts, became embodied in the subsequent teachings of Hinduism. Jesus and Ganid made the following excerpts:

"He is the great God, in every way supreme. He is the Lord who encompasses all things. He is the creator and controller of the universe of universes. God is one God; he is alone and by himself; he is the only one. And this one God is our Maker and the last destiny of the soul. The Supreme One is brilliant beyond description; he is the Light of Lights. Every heart and every world is illuminated by this divine light. God is our protector — he stands by the side of his creatures — and those who learn to know him become immortal. God is the great source of energy; he is the Great Soul. He exercises universal lordship over all. This one God is loving, glorious, and adorable. Our God is supreme in power and abides in the supreme abode. This true Person is eternal and divine; he is the primal Lord of heaven. All the prophets have hailed him, and he has revealed himself to us. We worship him. O Supreme Person, source of beings, Lord of creation, and ruler of the universe, reveal to us, your creatures, the power whereby you abide immanent! God has made the sun and the stars; he is bright, pure, and self-existent. His eternal knowledge is divinely wise. The Eternal is unpenetrated by evil. Inasmuch as the universe sprang from God, he does rule it appropriately. He is the cause of creation, and hence are all things established in him.

"God is the sure refuge of every good man when in need; the Immortal One cares for all mankind. God's salvation is strong and his kindness is gracious. He is a loving protector, a blessed defender. Says the Lord: `I dwell within their own souls as a lamp of wisdom. I am the splendor of the splendid and the goodness of the good. Where two or three gather together, there am I also.' The creature cannot escape the presence of the Creator. The Lord even counts the ceaseless winking of every mortal's eyes; and we worship this divine Being as our inseparable companion. He is all-prevailing, bountiful, omnipresent, and infinitely kind. The Lord is our ruler, shelter, and supreme controller, and his primeval spirit dwells within the mortal soul. The Eternal Witness to vice and virtue dwells within man's heart. Let us long meditate on the adorable and divine Vivifier; let his spirit fully direct our thoughts. From this unreal world lead us to the real! From darkness lead us to the light! From death guide us to immortality!

"With our hearts purged of all hate, let us worship the Eternal. Our God is the Lord of prayer; he hears the cry of his children. Let all men submit their wills to him, the Resolute. Let us delight in the liberality of the Lord of prayer. Make prayer your inmost friend and worship your soul's support. `If you will but worship me in love,' says the Eternal, `I will give you the wisdom to attain me, for my worship is the virtue common to all creatures.' God is the illuminator of the gloomy and the power of those who are faint. Since God is our strong friend, we have no more fear. We praise the name of the never-conquered Conqueror. We worship him because he is man's faithful and eternal helper. God is our sure leader and unfailing guide. He is the great parent of heaven and earth, possessed of unlimited energy and infinite wisdom. His splendor is sublime and his beauty divine. He is the supreme refuge of the universe and the changeless guardian of everlasting law. Our God is the Lord of life and the Comforter of all men; he is the lover of mankind and the helper of those who are distressed. He is our life giver and the Good Shepherd of the human flocks. God is our father, brother, and friend. And we long to know this God in our inner being.

"We have learned to win faith by the yearning of our hearts. We have attained wisdom by the restraint of our senses, and by wisdom we have experienced peace in the Supreme. He who is full of faith worships truly when his inner self is intent upon God. Our God wears the heavens as a mantle; he also inhabits the other six wide-spreading universes. He is supreme over all and in all. We crave forgiveness from the Lord for all of our trespasses against our fellows; and we would release our friend from the wrong he has done us. Our spirit loathes all evil; therefore, O Lord, free us from all taint of sin. We pray to God as a comforter, protector, and savior — one who loves us.

"The spirit of the Universe Keeper enters the soul of the simple creature. That man is wise who worships the One God. Those who strive for perfection must indeed know the Lord Supreme. He never fears who knows the blissful security of the Supreme, for the Supreme says to those who serve him, `Fear not, for I am with you.' The God of providence is our Father. God is truth. And it is the desire of God that his creatures should understand him — come fully to know the truth. Truth is eternal; it sustains the universe. Our supreme desire shall be union with the Supreme. The Great Controller is the generator of all things — all evolves from him. And this is the sum of duty: Let no man do to another what would be repugnant to himself; cherish no malice, smite not him who smites you, conquer anger with mercy, and vanquish hate by benevolence. And all this we should do because God is a kind friend and a gracious father who remits all our earthly offenses.

"God is our Father, the earth our mother, and the universe our birthplace. Without God the soul is a prisoner; to know God releases the soul. By meditation on God, by union with him, there comes deliverance from the illusions of evil and ultimate salvation from all material fetters. When man shall roll up space as a piece of leather, then will come the end of evil because man has found God. O God, save us from the threefold ruin of hell — lust, wrath, and avarice! O soul, gird yourself for the spirit struggle of immortality! When the end of mortal life comes, hesitate not to forsake this body for a more fit and beautiful form and to awake in the realms of the Supreme and Immortal, where there is no fear, sorrow, hunger, thirst, or death. To know God is to cut the cords of death. The God-knowing soul rises in the universe like the cream appears on top of the milk. We worship God, the all-worker, the Great Soul, who is ever seated in the heart of his creatures. And they who know that God is enthroned in the human heart are destined to become like him — immortal. Evil must be left behind in this world, but virtue follows the soul to heaven.

"It is only the wicked who say: The universe has neither truth nor a ruler; it was only designed for our lusts. Such souls are deluded by the smallness of their intellects. They thus abandon themselves to the enjoyment of their lusts and deprive their souls of the joys of virtue and the pleasures of righteousness. What can be greater than to experience salvation from sin? The man who has seen the Supreme is immortal. Man's friends of the flesh cannot survive death; virtue alone walks by man's side as he journeys ever onward toward the gladsome and sunlit fields of Paradise."

ZOROASTRIANISM

Zoroaster was himself directly in contact with the descendants of the earlier Melchizedek missionaries, and their doctrine of the one God became a central teaching in the religion which he founded in Persia. Aside from Judaism, no religion of that day contained more of these Salem teachings. From the records of this religion Ganid made the following excerpts:

"All things come from, and belong to, the One God — all-wise, good, righteous, holy, resplendent, and glorious . This, our God, is the source of all luminosity. He is the Creator, the God of all good purposes, and the protector of the justice of the universe. The wise course in life is to act in consonance with the spirit of truth. God is all-seeing, and he beholds both the evil deeds of the wicked and the good works of the righteous; our God observes all things with a flashing eye. His touch is the touch of healing. The Lord is an all-powerful benefactor. God stretches out his beneficent hand to both the righteous and the wicked. God established the world and ordained the rewards for good and for evil. The all-wise God has promised immortality to the pious souls who think purely and act righteously. As you supremely desire, so shall you be. The light of the sun is as wisdom to those who discern God in the universe.

"Praise God by seeking the pleasure of the Wise One. Worship the God of light by joyfully walking in the paths ordained by his revealed religion. There is but one Supreme God, the Lord of Lights. We worship him who made the waters, plants, animals, the earth, and the heavens. Our God is Lord, most beneficent. We worship the most beauteous, the bountiful Immortal, endowed with eternal light. God is farthest from us and at the same time nearest to us in that he dwells within our souls. Our God is the divine and holiest Spirit of Paradise, and yet he is more friendly to man than the most friendly of all creatures. God is most helpful to us in this greatest of all businesses, the knowing of himself. God is our most adorable and righteous friend; he is our wisdom, life, and vigor of soul and body. Through our good thinking the wise Creator will enable us to do his will, thereby attaining the realization of all that is divinely perfect.

"Lord, teach us how to live this life in the flesh while preparing for the next life of the spirit. Speak to us, Lord, and we will do your bidding. Teach us the good paths, and we will go right. Grant us that we may attain union with you. We know that the religion is right which leads to union with righteousness. God is our wise nature, best thought, and righteous act. May God grant us unity with the divine spirit and immortality in himself!

"This religion of the Wise One cleanses the believer from every evil thought and sinful deed. I bow before the God of heaven in repentance if I have offended in thought, word, or act - intentionally or unintentionally - and I offer prayers for mercy and praise for forgiveness. I know when I make confession, if I purpose not to do again the evil thing, that sin will be removed from my soul. I know that forgiveness takes away the bonds of sin. Those who do evil shall receive punishment, but those who follow truth shall enjoy the bliss of an eternal salvation. Through grace lay hold upon us and minister saving power to our souls. We claim mercy because we aspire to attain perfection; we would be like God."

SUDUANISM (JAINISM)

The third group of religious believers who preserved the doctrine of one God in India - the survival of the Melchizedek teaching - were known in those days as the Suduanists. Latterly these believers have become known as followers of Jainism. They taught:

"The Lord of Heaven is supreme. Those who commit sin will not ascend on high, but those who walk in the paths of righteousness shall find a place in heaven. We are assured of the life hereafter if we know truth. The soul of man may ascend to the highest heaven, there to develop its true spiritual nature, to attain perfection. The estate of heaven delivers man from the bondage of sin and introduces him to the final beatitudes; the righteous man has already experienced an end of sin and all its associated miseries. Self is man's invincible foe, and self is manifested as man's four greatest passions: anger, pride, deceit, and greed. Man's greatest victory is the conquest of himself. When man looks to God for forgiveness, and when he makes bold to enjoy such liberty, he is thereby delivered from fear. Man should journey through life treating his fellow creatures as he would like to be treated."

SHINTO

Only recently had the manuscripts of this Far-Eastern religion been lodged in the Alexandrian library. It was the one world religion of which Ganid had never heard. This belief also contained remnants of the earlier Melchizedek teachings as is shown by the following abstracts:

"Says the Lord: `You are all recipients of my divine power; all men enjoy my ministry of mercy. I derive great pleasure in the multiplication of righteous men throughout the land. In both the beauties of nature and the virtues of men does the

Prince of Heaven seek to reveal himself and to show forth his righteous nature. Since the olden people did not know my name, I manifested myself by being born into the world as a visible existence and endured such abasement even that man should not forget my name. I am the maker of heaven and earth; the sun and the moon and all the stars obey my will. I am the ruler of all creatures on land and in the four seas. Although I am great and supreme, still I have regard for the prayer of the poorest man. If any creature will worship me, I will hear his prayer and grant the desire of his heart.'

"Every time man yields to anxiety, he takes one step away from the leading of the spirit of his heart.' Pride obscures God. If you would obtain heavenly help, put away your pride; every hair of pride shuts off saving light, as it were, by a great cloud. If you are not right on the inside, it is useless to pray for that which is on the outside. `If I hear your prayers, it is because you come before me with a clean heart, free from falsehood and hypocrisy, with a soul which reflects truth like a mirror. If you would gain immortality, forsake the world and come to me.'"

TAOISM

The messengers of Melchizedek penetrated far into China, and the doctrine of one God became a part of the earlier teachings of several Chinese religions; the one persisting the longest and containing most of the monotheistic truth was Taoism, and Ganid collected the following from the teachings of its founder:

"How pure and tranquil is the Supreme One and yet how powerful and mighty, how deep and unfathomable! This God of heaven is the honored ancestor of all things. If you know the Eternal, you are enlightened and wise. If you know not the Eternal, then does ignorance manifest itself as evil, and thus do the passions of sin arise. This wondrous Being existed before the heavens and the earth were. He is truly spiritual; he stands alone and changes not. He is indeed the world's mother, and all creation moves around him. This Great One imparts himself to men and thereby enables them to excel and to survive. Even if one has but a little knowledge, he can still walk in the ways of the Supreme; he can conform to the will of heaven.

"All good works of true service come from the Supreme. All things depend on the Great Source for life. The Great Supreme seeks no credit for his bestowals. He is supreme in power, yet he remains hidden from our gaze. He unceasingly transmutes his attributes while perfecting his creatures. The heavenly Reason is slow and patient in his designs but sure of his accomplishments. The Supreme overspreads the universe and sustains it all. How great and mighty are his overflowing influence and drawing power! True goodness is like water in that it blesses everything and harms nothing. And like water, true goodness seeks the lowest places, even those levels which others avoid, and that is because it is akin to the Supreme. The Supreme creates all things, in nature nourishing them and in spirit perfecting them. And it is a mystery how the Supreme fosters, protects, and perfects the creature without compelling him. He guides and directs, but without self-assertion. He ministers progression, but without domination.

"The wise man universalizes his heart. A little knowledge is a dangerous thing. Those who aspire to greatness must learn to humble themselves. In creation the Supreme became the world's mother. To know one's mother is to recognize one's sonship. He is a wise man who regards all parts from the point of view of the whole. Relate yourself to every man as if you were in his place. Recompense injury with kindness. If you love people, they will draw near you — you will have no difficulty in winning them.

"The Great Supreme is all-pervading; he is on the left hand and on the right; he supports all creation and indwells all true beings. You cannot find the Supreme, neither can you go to a place where he is not. If a man recognizes the evil of his ways and repents of sin from the heart, then may he seek forgiveness; he may escape the penalty; he may change calamity into blessing. The Supreme is the secure refuge for all creation; he is the guardian and savior of mankind. If you seek for him daily, you shall find him. Since he can forgive sins, he is indeed most precious to all men. Always remember that God does not reward man for what he does but for what he is; therefore should you extend help to your fellows without the thought of rewards. Do good without thought of benefit to the self.

"They who know the laws of the Eternal are wise. Ignorance of the divine law is misery and disaster. They who know the laws of God are liberal minded. If you know the Eternal, even though your body perish, your soul shall survive in spirit service. You are truly wise when you recognize your insignificance. If you abide in the light of the Eternal, you shall enjoy the enlightenment of the Supreme. Those who dedicate their persons to the service of the Supreme are joyous in this pursuit of the Eternal. When man dies, the spirit begins to wing its long flight on the great home journey."

CONFUCIANISM

Even the least God-recognizing of the world's great religions acknowledged the monotheism of the Melchizedek missionaries and their persistent successors. Ganid's summary of Confucianism was:

"What Heaven appoints is without error. Truth is real and divine. Everything originates in Heaven, and the Great Heaven makes no mistakes. Heaven has appointed many subordinates to assist in the instruction and uplifting of the inferior creatures. Great, very great, is the One God who rules man from on high. God is majestic in power and awful in judgment. But this Great God has conferred a moral sense even on many inferior people. Heaven's bounty never stops. Benevolence is Heaven's choicest gift to men. Heaven has bestowed its nobility upon the soul of man; the virtues of man are the fruit of this endowment of Heaven's nobility.

The Great Heaven is all-discerning and goes with man in all his doings. And we do well when we call the Great Heaven our Father and our Mother. If we are thus servants of our divine ancestors, then may we in confidence pray to Heaven. At all times and in everything let us stand in awe of the majesty of Heaven. We acknowledge, O God, the Most High and sovereign Potentate, that judgment rests with you, and that all mercy proceeds from the divine heart.

"God is with us; therefore we have no fear in our hearts. If there be found any virtue in me, it is the manifestation of Heaven who abides with me. But this Heaven within me often makes hard demands on my faith. If God is with me, I have determined to have no doubt in my heart. Faith must be very near the truth of things, and I do not see how a man can live without this good faith. Good and evil do not befall men without cause. Heaven deals with man's soul in accordance with its purpose. When you find yourself in the wrong, do not hesitate to confess your error and be quick to make amends.

"A wise man is occupied with the search for truth, not in seeking for a mere living. To attain the perfection of Heaven is the goal of man. The superior man is given to self-adjustment, and he is free from anxiety and fear. God is with you; have no doubt in your heart. Every good deed has its recompense. The superior man murmurs not against Heaven nor holds a grudge against men. What you do not like when done to yourself, do not to others. Let compassion be a part of all punishment; in every way endeavor to make punishment a blessing. Such is the way of Great Heaven. While all creatures must die and return to the earth, the spirit of the noble man goes forth to be displayed on high and to ascend to the glorious light of final brightness."

"OUR RELIGION"

After the arduous labor of effecting this compilation of the teachings of the world religions concerning the Paradise Father, Ganid set himself to the task of formulating what he deemed to be a summary of the belief he had arrived at regarding God as a result of Jesus' teaching. This young man was in the habit of referring to such beliefs as "our religion." This was his record:

"The Lord our God is one Lord, and you should love him with all your mind and heart while you do your very best to love all his children as you love yourself. This one God is our heavenly Father, in whom all things consist, and who dwells, by his spirit, in every sincere human soul. And we who are the children of God should learn how to commit the keeping of our souls to him as to a faithful Creator. With our heavenly Father all things are possible. Since he is the Creator, having made all things and all beings, it could not be otherwise. Though we cannot see God, we can know him. And by daily living the will of the Father in heaven, we can reveal him to our fellow men.

"The divine riches of God's character must be infinitely deep and eternally wise. We cannot search out God by knowledge, but we can know him in our hearts by personal experience. While his justice may be past finding out, his mercy may be received by the humblest being on earth. While the Father fills the universe, he also lives in our hearts. The mind of man is human, mortal, but the spirit of man is divine, immortal. God is not only all-powerful but also all-wise. If our earth parents, being of evil tendency, know how to love their children and bestow good gifts on them, how much more must the good Father in heaven know how wisely to love his children on earth and to bestow suitable blessings upon them.

"The Father in heaven will not suffer a single child on earth to perish if that child has a desire to find the Father and truly longs to be like him. Our Father even loves the wicked and is always kind to the ungrateful. If more human beings could only know about the goodness of God, they would certainly be led to repent of their evil ways and forsake all known sin. All good things come down from the Father of light, in whom there is no variableness neither shadow of changing. The spirit of the true God is in man's heart. He intends that all men and women should be brothers and sisters. When mortals begin to feel after God, that is evidence that God has found them, and that they are in quest of knowledge about him. We live in God and God dwells in us.

"I will no longer be satisfied to believe that God is the Father of all my people; I will henceforth believe that he is also *my* Father. Always will I try to worship God with the help of the Spirit of Truth, which is my helper when I have become really God-knowing. But first of all I am going to practice worshiping God by learning how to do the will of God on earth; that is, I am going to do my best to treat each of my fellow mortals just as I think God would like to have him treated. And when we live this sort of a life in the flesh, we may ask many things of God, and he will give us the desire of our hearts that we may be the better prepared to serve our fellows. And all of this loving service of the children of God enlarges our capacity to receive and experience the joys of heaven, the high pleasures of the ministry of the spirit of heaven.

"I will every day thank God for his unspeakable gifts; I will praise him for his wonderful works to the children of men. To me he is the Almighty, the Creator, the Power, and the Mercy, but best of all, he is my spirit Father, and as his earth child I am sometime going forth to see him. And my tutor has said that by searching for him I shall become like him. By faith in God I have attained peace with him. This new religion of ours is very full of joy, and it generates an enduring happiness. I am confident that I shall be faithful even to death, and that I will surely receive the crown of eternal life.

"I am learning to prove all things and adhere to that which is good. Whatsoever I would that men should do to me, that I will do to my fellows. By this new faith I know that man may become the son of God, but it sometimes terrifies me when I stop to think that all men are my brothers, but it must be true. I do not see how I can rejoice in the fatherhood of God while I refuse to accept the brotherhood of man. Whosoever calls upon the name of the Lord shall be saved. If that is true, then all men must be my brothers.

"Henceforth will I do my good deeds in secret; I will also pray most when by myself. I will judge not that I may not be unfair to my fellows. I am going to learn to love my enemies; I have not truly mastered this practice of being Godlike. Though I see God in these other religions, I find him in `our religion' as being more beautiful, loving, merciful, personal, and positive. But most of all, this great and glorious Being is my spiritual Father; I am his child. And by no other means than my honest desire to be like him, I am eventually to find him and eternally to serve him. At last I have a religion with a God, a marvelous God, and he is a God of eternal salvation."

THE SOJOURN AT ROME

SINCE GONOD carried greetings from the princes of India to Tiberius, the Roman ruler, on the third day after their arrival in Rome the two Indians and Jesus appeared before him. The melancholy emperor was unusually cheerful on this day and chatted long with the trio. And when they had gone from his presence, the emperor, referring to Jesus, remarked to the aide standing on his right, "If I had that fellow's kingly bearing and gracious manner, I would be a real emperor, would I not?"

While at Rome, Ganid had regular hours for study and for visiting places of interest about the city. His father had much business to transact, and desiring that his son grow up to become a worthy successor in the management of his vast commercial interests, he thought the time had come to introduce the boy to the business world. There were many citizens of India in Rome, and often one of Gonod's own employees would accompany him as interpreter so that Jesus would have whole days to himself; this gave him time in which to become thoroughly acquainted with this city of two million inhabitants. He was frequently to be found in the forum, the center of political, legal, and business life. He often went up to the Capitolium and pondered the bondage of ignorance in which these Romans were held as he beheld this magnificent temple dedicated to Jupiter, Juno, and Minerva. He also spent much time on Palatine hill, on where were located the emperor's residence, the temple of Apollo, and the Greek and Latin libraries.

At this time the Roman Empire included all of southern Europe, Asia Minor, Syria, Egypt, and northwest Africa; and its inhabitants embraced the citizens of every country of the Eastern Hemisphere. His desire to study and mingle with this cosmopolitan aggregation of Earth-born mortals was the chief reason why Jesus had consented to make this journey.

Jesus learned much about men while in Rome, but the most valuable of all the manifold experiences of his six months' sojourn in that city was his contact with, and influence upon, the religious leaders of the empire's capital. Before the end of the first week in Rome Jesus had sought out, and had made the acquaintance of, the worthwhile leaders of the Cynics, the Stoics, and the mystery cults, in particular the Mithraic group. Whether or not it was apparent to Jesus that the Jews were going to reject his mission, he most certainly foresaw that his messengers were presently coming to Rome to proclaim the kingdom of heaven; and he therefore set about, in the most amazing manner, to prepare the way for the better and more certain reception of their message. He selected five of the leading Stoics, eleven of the Cynics, and sixteen of the mystery-cult leaders and spent much of his spare time for almost six months in intimate association with these religious teachers. And this was his method of instruction: Never once did he attack their errors or even mention the flaws in their teachings. In each case he would select the truth in what they taught and then proceed so to embellish and illuminate this truth in their minds that in a very short time this enhancement of the truth effectively crowded out the associated error; and thus were these Jesus-taught men and women prepared for the subsequent recognition of additional and similar truths in the teachings of the early Christian missionaries. It was this early acceptance of the teachings of the gospel preachers which gave that powerful impetus to the rapid spread of Christianity in Rome and from there throughout the empire.

The significance of this remarkable doing can the better be understood when we record the fact that, out of this group of thirty-two Jesus-taught religious leaders in Rome, only two were unfruitful; the thirty became pivotal individuals in the establishment of Christianity in Rome, and certain of them also aided in turning the chief Mithraic temple into the first Christian church of that city. We who view human activities from behind the scenes and in the light of more than nineteen centuries of time and universe education, have learned to recognize just three factors of paramount value in the early setting of the stage for the rapid spread of Christianity throughout Europe, and they are:

1. The choosing and holding of Simon Peter as an apostle.
2. The talk in Jerusalem with Stephen, whose death led to the winning of Saul of Tarsus.
3. The preliminary preparation of these thirty Romans for the subsequent leadership of the new religion in Rome and throughout the empire.

Through all their experiences, neither Stephen nor the thirty chosen ones ever realized that they had once talked with the man whose name became the subject of their religious teaching. Jesus' work in behalf of the original thirty-two was entirely personal. In his labors for these individuals the scribe of Damascus never met more than three of them at one time, seldom more than two, while most often he taught them singly. And he could do this great work of religious training because *these men and women were not tradition bound*; they were not victims of a settled preconception as to all future religious developments.

Many were the times in the years so soon to follow that Peter, Paul, and the other Christian teachers in Rome heard about this scribe of Damascus who had preceded them, and who had so obviously (and as they supposed unwittingly) prepared the way for their coming with the new gospel. Though Paul never really surmised the identity of this scribe of Damascus, he did, a short time before his death, because of the similarity of personal descriptions, reach the conclusion that the "tentmaker of Antioch" was also the "scribe of Damascus." On one occasion, while preaching in Rome, Simon Peter, on listening to a description of the Damascus scribe, surmised that this individual might have been Jesus but quickly dismissed the idea, knowing full well (so he thought) that the Master had never been in Rome.

It was with Angamon, the leader of the Stoics, that Jesus had an all-night talk early during his sojourn in Rome. This man subsequently became a great friend of Paul and proved to be one of the strong supporters of the Christian church at Rome. In substance, and restated in modern phraseology, Jesus taught Angamon:

The standard of true values must be looked for in the spiritual world and on divine levels of eternal reality. To an ascending mortal all lower and material standards must be recognized as transient, partial, and inferior. The scientist, as such, is limited to the discovery of the relatedness of material facts. Technically, he has no right to assert that he is either materialist or idealist, for in so doing he has assumed to forsake the attitude of a true scientist since any and all such assertions of attitude are the very essence of philosophy.

Unless the moral insight and the spiritual attainment of mankind are proportionately augmented, the unlimited advancement of a purely materialistic culture may eventually become a menace to civilization. A purely materialistic science harbors within itself the potential seed of the destruction of all scientific striving, for this very attitude presages the ultimate collapse of a civilization which has abandoned its sense of moral values and has repudiated its spiritual goal of attainment.

The materialistic scientist and the extreme idealist are destined always to be at loggerheads. This is not true of those scientists and idealists who are in possession of a common standard of high moral values and spiritual test levels. In every age scientists and religionists must recognize that they are on trial before the bar of human need. They must eschew all warfare between themselves while they strive valiantly to justify their continued survival by enhanced devotion to the service of human progress. If the so-called science or religion of any age is false, then must it either purify its activities or pass away before the emergence of a material science or spiritual religion of a truer and more worthy order.

Mardus was the acknowledged leader of the Cynics of Rome, and he became a great friend of the scribe of Damascus. Day after day he conversed with Jesus, and night upon night he listened to his supernal teaching. Among the more important discussions with Mardus was the one designed to answer this sincere Cynic's question about good and evil. In substance, and in twentieth-century phraseology, Jesus said:

My brother, good and evil are merely words symbolizing relative levels of human comprehension of the observable universe. If you are ethically lazy and socially indifferent, you can take as your standard of good the current social usages. If you are spiritually indolent and morally unprogressive, you may take as your standards of good the religious practices and traditions of your contemporaries. But the soul that survives time and emerges into eternity must make a living and personal choice between good and evil as they are determined by the true values of the spiritual standards established by the divine spirit which the Father in heaven has sent to dwell within the heart of man. This indwelling spirit, the Father Fragment, is the standard of personality survival.

Goodness, like truth, is always relative and unfailingly evil-contrasted. It is the perception of these qualities of goodness and truth that enables the evolving souls of men and women to make those personal decisions of choice which are essential to eternal survival.

The spiritually blind individual who logically follows scientific dictation, social usage, and religious dogma stands in grave danger of sacrificing his moral freedom and losing his spiritual liberty. Such a soul is destined to become an intellectual parrot, a social automaton, and a slave to religious authority.

Goodness is always growing toward new levels of the increasing liberty of moral self-realization and spiritual personality attainment - the discovery of, and identification with, the indwelling Father Fragment. An experience is good when it heightens the appreciation of beauty, augments the moral will, enhances the discernment of truth, enlarges the capacity to love and serve one's fellows, exalts the spiritual ideals, and unifies the supreme human motives of time with the eternal plans of the indwelling Mystery Monitor, all of which lead directly to an increased desire to do the Father's will, thereby fostering the divine passion to find God and to be more like Him.

As you ascend the universe scale of creature development, you will find increasing goodness and diminishing evil in perfect accordance with your capacity for goodness-experience and truth-discernment. The ability to entertain error or experience evil will not be fully lost until the ascending human soul achieves final spirit levels.

Goodness is living, relative, always progressing, invariably a personal experience, and everlastingly correlated with the discernment of truth and beauty. Goodness is found in the recognition of the positive truth-values of the spiritual level, which must, in human experience, be contrasted with the negative counterpart, the shadows of potential evil.

Until you attain Paradise levels, goodness will always be more of a quest than a possession, more of a goal than an experience of attainment. But even as you hunger and thirst for righteousness, you experience increasing satisfaction in the partial attainment of goodness. The presence of goodness and evil in the world is in itself positive proof of the existence and reality of man's moral will, the personality, which thus identifies these values and is also able to choose between them.

By the time of the attainment of Paradise the ascending mortal's capacity for identifying the self with true spirit values has become so enlarged as to result in the attainment of the perfection of the possession of the light of life. Such a perfected spirit personality becomes so wholly, divinely, and spiritually unified with the positive and supreme qualities of goodness, beauty, and truth that there remains no possibility that such a righteous spirit would cast any negative shadow of potential evil when exposed to the searching luminosity of the divine light of the infinite Rulers of Paradise. In all such spirit personalities, goodness is no longer partial, contrastive, and comparative; it has become divinely complete and spiritually replete; it approaches the purity and perfection of the Supreme.

The *possibility* of evil is necessary to moral choosing, but not the actuality thereof. A shadow is only relatively real. Actual evil is not necessary as a personal experience. Potential evil acts equally well as a decision stimulus in the realms of moral progress on the lower levels of spiritual development. Evil becomes a reality of personal experience only when a moral mind makes evil its choice.

Nabon was a Greek Jew and foremost among the leaders of the chief mystery cult in Rome, the Mithraic. While this high priest of Mithraism held many conferences with the Damascus scribe, he was most permanently influenced by their discussion of truth and faith one evening. Nabon had thought to make a convert of Jesus and had even suggested that he return to Palestine as a Mithraic teacher. He little realized that Jesus was preparing him to become one of the early converts to the gospel of the kingdom. Restated in modern phraseology, the substance of Jesus' teaching was:

Truth cannot be defined with words, only by living. Truth is always more than knowledge. Knowledge pertains to things observed, but truth transcends such purely material levels in that it consorts with wisdom and embraces such imponderables as human experience, even spiritual and living realities. Knowledge originates in science; wisdom, in true philosophy; truth, in the religious experience of spiritual living. Knowledge deals with facts; wisdom, with relationships; truth, with reality values.

Man tends to crystallize science, formulate philosophy, and dogmatize truth because he is mentally lazy in adjusting to the progressive struggles of living, while he is also terribly afraid of the unknown. Natural man is slow to initiate changes in his habits of thinking and in his techniques of living.

Revealed truth, personally discovered truth, is the supreme delight of the human soul; it is the joint creation of the material mind and the indwelling spirit. The eternal salvation of this truth-discerning and beauty-loving soul is assured by that hunger and thirst for goodness which leads this mortal to develop a singleness of purpose to do the Father's will, to find God and to become like Him. There is never conflict between true knowledge and truth. There may be conflict between knowledge and human beliefs, beliefs colored with prejudice, distorted by fear, and dominated by the dread of facing new facts of material discovery or spiritual progress.

But truth can never become man's possession without the exercise of faith. This is true because man's thoughts, wisdom, ethics, and ideals will never rise higher than his faith, his sublime hope. And all such true faith is predicated on profound reflection, sincere self-criticism, and uncompromising moral consciousness. Faith is the inspiration of the spiritized creative imagination.

Faith acts to release the superhuman activities of the divine spark, the immortal germ, that lives within the mind of man, and which is the potential of eternal survival. Plants and animals survive in time by the technique of passing on from one generation to another identical particles of themselves. The human soul (personality) of man survives mortal death by identity association with this indwelling spark of divinity, which is immortal, and which functions to perpetuate the human personality upon a continuing and higher level of progressive universe existence. The concealed seed of the human soul is an immortal spirit. The second generation of the soul is the first of a succession of personality manifestations of spiritual and progressing existences, terminating only when this divine entity attains the source of its existence, the personal source of all existence, God, the Universal Father.

Human life continues, survives, because it has a universe function, the task of finding God. The faith-activated soul of mortals cannot stop short of the attainment of this goal of destiny; and when it does once achieve this divine goal, it can never end because it has become like God - eternal.

Spiritual evolution is an experience of the increasing and voluntary choice of goodness attended by an equal and progressive lessening of the possibility of evil. With the attainment of finality of choice for goodness and of completed capacity for truth appreciation, there comes into existence a perfection of beauty and holiness whose righteousness eternally inhibits the possibility of the emergence of even the concept of potential evil. Such a God-knowing soul casts no shadow of doubting evil when functioning on such a high spirit level of divine goodness.

The presence of the Paradise spirit in the mind of man constitutes the revelation promise and the faith pledge of an eternal existence of divine progression for every soul seeking to achieve identity with this immortal and indwelling spirit fragment of the Universal Father.

Universe progress is characterized by increasing personality freedom because it is associated with the progressive attainment of higher and higher levels of self-understanding and consequent voluntary self-restraint. The attainment of perfection of spiritual self-restraint equals completeness of universe freedom and personal liberty. Faith fosters and maintains man's soul in the midst of the confusion of his early orientation in such a vast universe, whereas prayer becomes the great unifier of the various inspirations of the creative imagination and the faith urges of a soul trying to identify itself with the spirit ideals of the indwelling and associated divine presence.

Nabon was greatly impressed by these words, as he was by each of his talks with Jesus. These truths continued to burn within his heart, and he was of great assistance to the later arriving preachers of Jesus' gospel.

J esus did not devote all his leisure while in Rome to this work of preparing men and women to become future disciples in the oncoming kingdom. He spent much time gaining an intimate knowledge of all races and classes of men who lived in this, the largest and most cosmopolitan city of the world. In each of these numerous human contacts Jesus had a double purpose: He desired to learn their reactions to the life they were living in the flesh, and he was also minded to say or do something to make that life richer and more worth while. His religious teachings during these weeks were no different than those which characterized his later life as teacher of the twelve and preacher to the multitudes.

Always the burden of his message was: the fact of the heavenly Father's love and the truth of His mercy, coupled with the good news that man is a faith-child of this same God of love. Jesus' usual technique of social contact was to draw people out and into talking with him by asking them questions. The interview would usually begin by his asking them questions and end by their asking him questions. He was equally adept in teaching by either asking or answering questions. As a rule, to those he taught the most, he said the least. Those who derived most benefit from his personal ministry were overburdened, anxious, and dejected mortals who gained much relief because of the opportunity to unburden their souls to a sympathetic and understanding listener, and he was all that and more. And when these maladjusted human beings had told Jesus about their troubles, always was he able to offer practical and immediately helpful suggestions looking toward the correction of their real difficulties, albeit he did not neglect to speak words of present comfort and immediate consolation. And invariably would he tell these distressed mortals about the love of God and impart the information, by various and sundry methods, that they were the children of this loving Father in heaven.

In this manner, during the sojourn in Rome, Jesus personally came into affectionate and uplifting contact with upward of five hundred mortals of the realm. He thus gained a knowledge of the different races of mankind which he could never have acquired in Jerusalem and hardly even in Alexandria. He always regarded this six months as one of the richest and most informative of any like period of his earth life.

As might have been expected, such a versatile and aggressive man could not thus function for six months in the world's metropolis without being approached by numerous persons who desired to secure his services in connection with some business or, more often, for some project of teaching, social reform, or religious movement. More than a dozen such proffers were made, and he utilized each one as an opportunity for imparting some thought of spiritual ennoblement by well-chosen words or by some obliging service. Jesus was very fond of doing things, even little things, for all sorts of people.

He talked with a Roman senator on politics and statesmanship, and this one contact with Jesus made such an impression on this legislator that he spent the rest of his life vainly trying to induce his colleagues to change the course of the ruling policy from the idea of the government supporting and feeding the people to that of the people supporting the government. Jesus spent one evening with a wealthy slaveholder, talked about man as a child of God, and the next day this man, Claudius, gave freedom to one hundred and seventeen slaves. He visited at dinner with a Greek physician, telling him that his patients had minds and souls as well as bodies, and thus led this able doctor to attempt a more far-reaching ministry to his fellow men. He talked with all sorts of people in every walk of life. The only place in Rome he did not visit was the public baths. He refused to accompany his friends to the baths because of the sex promiscuity that prevailed in these moral cesspools.

To a Roman soldier, as they walked along the Tiber, he said, "Be brave of heart as well as of hand. Dare to do justice and be big enough to show mercy. Compel your lower nature to obey your higher nature as you obey your superiors. Revere goodness and exalt truth. Choose the beautiful in place of the ugly. Love your fellows and reach out for God with a whole heart, for God is your Father in heaven."

To the speaker at the forum he said, "Your eloquence is pleasing, your logic is admirable, your voice is pleasant, but your teaching is hardly true. If you could only enjoy the inspiring satisfaction of knowing God as your spiritual Father, then you might employ your powers of speech to liberate your fellows from the bondage of darkness and from the slavery of ignorance." This was the Marcus who heard Peter preach in Rome and became his successor. When they crucified

Simon Peter, it was this man who defied the Roman persecutors and boldly continued to preach the new gospel.

Meeting a poor man who had been falsely accused, Jesus went with him before the magistrate and, having been granted special permission to appear in his
behalf, made a superb address before those assembled. Jesus said, "Justice makes
a nation great, and the greater a nation the more solicitous will it be to see that injustice shall not befall even its most humble citizen. Woe upon any nation when
only those who possess money and influence can secure ready justice before its
courts! It is the sacred duty of a magistrate to acquit the innocent as well as to punish the guilty. Upon the impartiality, fairness, and integrity of its courts the endur-
ance of a nation depends. Civil government is founded on justice, even as true religion is founded on mercy." The judge reopened the case, and when the evidence
had been sifted, he discharged the prisoner. Of all Jesus' activities during these
days of personal ministry, this came the nearest to being a public appearance.

A certain rich man, a Roman citizen and a Stoic, became greatly interested in
Jesus' teaching, having been introduced by Angamon. After many intimate conferences this wealthy citizen asked Jesus what he would do with wealth if he had it.

Jesus answered, "I would bestow material wealth for the enhancement of
material life, even as I would minister knowledge, wisdom, and spiritual service
for the enrichment of the intellectual life, the ennoblement of the social life, and
the advancement of the spiritual life. I would administer material wealth as a wise
and effective trustee of the resources of one generation for the benefit and ennoblement of the next and succeeding generations."

But the rich man was not fully satisfied with Jesus' answer. He made bold to
ask again, "But what do you think a man in my position should do with his wealth?
Should I keep it, or should I give it away?"

And when Jesus perceived that he really desired to know more of the truth
about his loyalty to God and his duty to men, he further answered, "My good
friend, I discern that you are a sincere seeker after wisdom and an honest lover of
truth; therefore am I minded to lay before you my view of the solution of your
problems having to do with the responsibilities of wealth. I do this because you
have *asked* for my counsel, and in giving you this advice, I am not concerned with
the wealth of any other rich man; I am offering advice only to you and for your personal guidance. If you honestly desire to regard your wealth as a trust, if you really
wish to become a wise and efficient steward of your accumulated wealth, then
would I counsel you to make the following analysis of the sources of your riches.
Ask yourself, and do your best to find the honest answer, whence came this wealth?
And as a help in the study of the sources of your great fortune, I would suggest that
you bear in mind the following ten different methods of amassing material wealth:

"1. Inherited wealth — riches derived from parents and other ancestors.

"2. Discovered wealth — riches derived from the uncultivated resources of mother earth.

"3. Trade wealth — riches obtained as a fair profit in the exchange and barter of material goods.

"4. Unfair wealth — riches derived from the unfair exploitation or the enslavement of one's fellows.

"5. Interest wealth — income derived from the fair and just earning possibilities of invested capital.

"6. Genius wealth — riches accruing from the rewards of the creative and inventive endowments of the human mind.

"7. Accidental wealth — riches derived from the generosity of one's fellows or taking origin in the circumstances of life.

"8. Stolen wealth — riches secured by unfairness, dishonesty, theft, or fraud.

"9. Trust funds — wealth lodged in your hands by your fellows for some specific use, now or in the future.

"10. Earned wealth — riches derived directly from your own personal labor, the fair and just reward of your own daily efforts of mind and body.

"And so, my friend, if you would be a faithful and just steward of your large fortune, before God and in service to men, you must approximately divide your wealth into these ten grand divisions, and then proceed to administer each portion in accordance with the wise and honest interpretation of the laws of justice, equity, fairness, and true efficiency; albeit, the God of heaven would not condemn you if sometimes you erred, in doubtful situations, on the side of merciful and unselfish regard for the distress of the suffering victims of the unfortunate circumstances of mortal life. When in honest doubt about the equity and justice of material situations, let your decisions favor those who are in need, favor those who suffer the misfortune of undeserved hardships."

After discussing these matters for several hours and in response to the rich man's request for further and more detailed instruction, Jesus went on to amplify his advice. In substance he said, "While I offer further suggestions concerning your attitude toward wealth, I would admonish you to receive my counsel as given only to you and for your personal guidance. I speak only for myself and to you as an inquiring friend. I adjure you not to become a dictator as to how other rich men shall regard their wealth. I would advise you:

"1. As steward of inherited wealth you should consider its sources. You are under moral obligation to represent the past generation in the honest transmittal of legitimate wealth to succeeding generations after subtracting a fair toll for the benefit of the present generation. But you are not obligated to perpetuate any dishonesty or injustice involved in the unfair accumulation of wealth by your ancestors. Any portion of your inherited wealth that turns out to have been derived through fraud or unfairness, you may disburse in accordance with your convictions of justice, generosity, and restitution. The remainder of your legitimate inherited wealth you may use in equity and transmit in security as the trustee of one generation for another. Wise discrimination and sound judgment should dictate your decisions regarding the bequest of riches to your successors.

"2. Everyone who enjoys wealth as a result of discovery should remember that one individual can live on earth but a short season and should, therefore, make adequate provision for the sharing of these discoveries in helpful ways by the largest possible number of his fellow men. While the discoverer should not be denied all reward for efforts of discovery, neither should he selfishly presume to lay claim to all of the advantages and blessings to be derived from the uncovering of nature's hoarded resources.

"3. As long as men choose to conduct the world's business by trade and barter, they are entitled to a fair and legitimate profit. Every tradesman deserves wages for his services; the merchant is entitled to his hire. The fairness of trade and the honest treatment accorded one's fellows in the organized business of the world create many different sorts of profit wealth, and all these sources of wealth must be judged by the highest principles of justice, honesty, and fairness. The honest trader should not hesitate to take the same profit that he would gladly accord his fellow trader in a similar transaction. While this sort of wealth is not identical with individually earned income when business dealings are conducted on a large scale, at the same time, such honestly accumulated wealth endows its possessor with a considerable equity as regards a voice in its subsequent distribution.

"4. No mortal who knows God and seeks to do the divine will can stoop to engage in the oppressions of wealth. No noble man will strive to accumulate riches and amass wealth-power by the enslavement or unfair exploitation of his brothers in the flesh. Riches are a moral curse and a spiritual stigma when they are derived from the sweat of oppressed mortal man. All such wealth should be restored to those who have thus been robbed or to their children and their children's children. An enduring civilization cannot be built upon the practice of defrauding the laborer of his hire.

"5. Honest wealth is entitled to interest. As long as men borrow and lend, that which is fair interest may be collected provided the capital lent was legitimate wealth. First cleanse your capital before you lay claim to the interest. Do not become so small and grasping that you would stoop to the practice of usury. Never permit yourself to be so selfish as to employ money-power to gain unfair advantage over your struggling fellows. Yield not to the temptation to take usury from your brother in financial distress.

"6. If you chance to secure wealth by flights of genius, if your riches are derived from the rewards of inventive endowment, do not lay claim to an unfair portion of such rewards. The genius owes something to both his ancestors and his progeny; likewise is he under obligation to the race, nation, and circumstances of his inventive discoveries; he should also remember that it was as man among men that he labored and wrought out his inventions. It would be equally unjust to deprive the genius of all his increment of wealth. And it will ever be impossible for men to establish rules and regulations applicable equally to all these problems of the equitable distribution of wealth. You must first recognize all men and women as your brothers and sisters, and if you honestly desire to do by them as you would have them do by you, the commonplace dictates of justice, honesty, and fairness will guide you in the just and impartial settlement of every recurring problem of economic rewards and social justice.

"7. Except for the just and legitimate fees earned in administration, no man should lay personal claim to that wealth which time and chance may cause to fall into his hands. Accidental riches should be regarded somewhat in the light of a trust to be expended for the benefit of one's social or economic group. The possessors of such wealth should be accorded the major voice in the determination of the wise and effective distribution of such unearned resources. Civilized man will not always look upon all that he controls as his personal and private possession.

"8. If any portion of your fortune has been knowingly derived from fraud; if aught of your wealth has been accumulated by dishonest practices or unfair methods; if your riches are the product of unjust dealings with your fellows, make haste to restore all these ill-gotten gains to the rightful owners. Make full amends and thus cleanse your fortune of all dishonest riches.

"9. The trusteeship of the wealth of one person for the benefit of others is a solemn and sacred responsibility. Do not hazard or jeopardize such a trust. Take for yourself of any trust only that which all honest men would allow.

"10. That part of your fortune which represents the earnings of your own mental and physical efforts, if your work has been done in fairness and equity, is truly your own. No man can gainsay your right to hold and use such wealth as you may see fit provided your exercise of this right does not work harm upon your fellows."

When Jesus had finished counseling him, this wealthy Roman arose from his couch and, in saying farewell for the night, delivered himself of this promise, "My good friend, I perceive you are a man of great wisdom and goodness, and tomorrow I will begin the administration of all my wealth in accordance with your counsel."

Here in Rome also occurred that touching incident in which the Creator of a universe spent several hours restoring a lost child to his anxious mother. This little boy had wandered away from his home, and Jesus found him crying in distress. He and Ganid were on their way to the libraries, but they devoted themselves to getting the child back home. Ganid never forgot Jesus' comment: "You know, Ganid, most human beings are like the lost child. They spend much of their time crying in fear and suffering in sorrow when, in very truth, they are but a short distance from safety and security, even as this child was only a little way from home. And all those who know the way of truth and enjoy the assurance of knowing God should esteem it a privilege, not a duty, to offer guidance to their fellows in their efforts to find the satisfactions of living. Did we not supremely enjoy this ministry of restoring the child to his mother? So do those who lead men to God experience the supreme satisfaction of human service."

And from that day forward, for the remainder of his natural life, Ganid was continually on the lookout for lost children whom he might restore to their homes.

There was the widow with five children whose husband had been accidentally killed. Jesus told Ganid about the loss of his own father by an accident, and they went repeatedly to comfort this mother and her children, while Ganid sought money from his father to provide food and clothing. They did not cease their efforts until they had found a position for the eldest boy so that he could help in the care of the family.

That night, as Gonod listened to the recital of these experiences, he said to Jesus, good-naturedly, "I propose to make a scholar or a businessman of my son, and now you start out to make a philosopher or philanthropist of him."

And Jesus smilingly replied, "Perhaps we will make him all four; then can he enjoy a fourfold satisfaction in life as his ear for the recognition of human melody will be able to recognize four tones instead of one."

Gonod responded, "I perceive that you really are a philosopher. You must write a book for future generations."

Jesus replied, "Not a book. My mission is to live a life in this generation and for all generations. I..." but he stopped, saying to Ganid, "My son, it is time to retire."

Jesus, Gonod, and Ganid made five trips away from Rome to points of interest in the surrounding territory. On their visit to the northern Italian lakes Jesus had the long talk with Ganid concerning the impossibility of teaching a man about God if the man does not desire to know God. They had casually met a thoughtless pagan while on their journey up to the lakes, and Ganid was surprised that Jesus did not follow out his usual practice of enlisting the man in conversation, which would naturally lead up to the discussion of spiritual questions. Ganid asked his teacher why he evinced so little interest in this pagan.

Jesus answered, "Ganid, the man was not hungry for truth. He was not dissatisfied with himself. He was not ready to ask for help, and the eyes of his mind were not open to receive light for the soul. That man was not ripe for the harvest of salvation; he must be allowed more time for the trials and difficulties of life to prepare him for the reception of wisdom and higher learning. Or, if we could have him live with us, we might by our lives show him the Father in heaven, and thus would he become so attracted by our lives as sons of God that he would be constrained to inquire about our Father. You cannot reveal God to those who do not seek for Him; you cannot lead unwilling souls into the joys of salvation. Man must become hungry for truth as a result of the experiences of living, or he must desire to know God as the result of contact with the lives of those who are acquainted with the divine Father before another human being can act as the means of leading such a fellow mortal to the Father in heaven. If we know God, our real business on earth is so to live as to permit the Father to reveal himself in our lives, and thus will all God-seeking persons see the Father and ask for our help in finding out more about the God who in this manner finds expression in our lives."

It was on the visit to Switzerland, up in the mountains, that Jesus had an all-day talk with both father and son about Buddhism. Many times Ganid had asked Jesus direct questions about Buddha, but he had always received more or less evasive replies. Now, in the presence of the son, the father asked Jesus a direct question about Buddha, and he received a direct reply. Said Gonod, "I would really like to know what you think of Buddha."

Jesus answered, "Your Buddha was much better than your Buddhism. Buddha was a great man, even a prophet to his people, but he was an orphan prophet; by that I mean that he early lost sight of his spiritual Father, the Father in heaven. His experience was tragic. He tried to live and teach as a messenger of God, but without God. Buddha guided his ship of salvation right up to the safe harbor, right up to the entrance to the haven of mortal salvation, and there, because of faulty charts of navigation, the good ship ran aground. There it has rested these many generations, motionless and almost hopelessly stranded. And thereon have many of your people remained all these years. They live within hailing distance of the safe waters of rest, but they refuse to enter because the noble craft of the good Buddha met the misfortune of grounding just outside the harbor. And the Buddhist peoples never will enter this harbor unless they abandon the philosophic craft of their prophet and seize upon his noble spirit. Had your people remained true to the spirit of Buddha, you would have long since entered your haven of spirit tranquillity, soul rest, and assurance of salvation.

"You see, Gonod, Buddha knew God in spirit but failed clearly to discover him in mind; the Jews discovered God in mind but largely failed to know him in spirit. Today, the Buddhists flounder about in a philosophy without God, while my people are piteously enslaved to the fear of a God without a saving philosophy of life and liberty. You have a philosophy without a God; the Jews have a God but are largely without a philosophy of living as related thereto. Buddha, failing to envision God as a spirit and as a Father, failed to provide in his teaching the moral energy and the spiritual driving power which a religion must possess if it is to change a race and exalt a nation."

Then exclaimed Ganid, "Teacher, let's you and I make a new religion, one good enough for India and big enough for Rome, and maybe we can trade it to the Jews for Yahweh."

Jesus said, "Ganid, religions are not made. The religions of men grow up over long periods of time, while the revelations of God flash upon earth in the lives of the men and women who reveal God to their fellows."

But they did not comprehend the meaning of these prophetic words.

That night after they had retired, Ganid could not sleep. He talked a long time with his father and finally said, "You know, father, I sometimes think Joshua is a prophet." And his father only sleepily replied, "My son, there are others...."

From this day, for the remainder of his natural life, Ganid continued to evolve a religion of his own. He was mightily moved in his own mind by Jesus' broadmindedness, fairness, and tolerance. In all their discussions of philosophy and religion this youth never experienced feelings of resentment or reactions of antagonism.

What a scene for the celestial intelligences to behold, this spectacle of the Indian lad proposing to the Creator of a universe that they make a new religion! And though the young man did not know it, they were making a new and everlasting religion right then and there, this new way of salvation, the revelation of God to man through, and in, Jesus. That which the lad wanted most to do he was unconsciously actually doing. And it was, and is, ever thus. That which the enlightened and reflective human imagination of spiritual teaching and leading wholeheartedly and unselfishly wants to do and be, becomes measurably creative in accordance with the degree of mortal dedication to the divine doing of the Father's will. When man goes in partnership with God, great things may, and do, happen.

THE RETURN FROM ROME

WHEN PREPARING to leave Rome, Jesus said good-bye to none of his friends. The scribe of Damascus appeared in Rome without announcement and disappeared in like manner. It was a full year before those who knew and loved him gave up hope of seeing him again. Before the end of the second year small groups of those who had known him found themselves drawn together by their common interest in his teachings and through mutual memory of their good times with him. And these small groups of Stoics, Cynics, and mystery cultists continued to hold these irregular and informal meetings right up to the time of the appearance in Rome of the first preachers of the Christian religion.

Gonod and Ganid had purchased so many things in Alexandria and Rome that they sent all their belongings on ahead by pack train to Tarentum, while the three travelers walked leisurely across Italy over the great Appian Way. On this journey they encountered all sorts of human beings. Many noble Roman citizens and Greek colonists lived along this road, but already the progeny of great numbers of *inferior* slaves were beginning to make their appearance.

One day while resting at lunch, about halfway to Tarentum, Ganid asked Jesus a direct question as to what he thought of India's caste system.

Jesus said, "Though human beings differ in many ways, the one from another, before God and in the spiritual world all mortals stand on an equal footing. There are only two groups of mortals in the eyes of God: those who desire to do His will and those who do not. As the universe looks upon an inhabited world, it likewise discerns two great classes: those who know God and those who do not. Those who cannot know God are reckoned among the animals of any given realm. Mankind can appropriately be divided into many classes in accordance with differing qualifications, as they may be viewed physically, mentally, socially, vocationally, or morally, but as these different classes of mortals appear before the judgment bar of God, they stand on an equal footing; God is truly no respecter of persons. Although you cannot escape the recognition of differential human abilities and endowments in matters intellectual, social, and moral, you should make no such distinctions in the spiritual family of men and women when assembled for worship in the presence of God."

A very interesting incident occurred one afternoon by the roadside as they neared Tarentum. They observed a rough and bullying youth brutally attacking a smaller lad. Jesus hastened to the assistance of the assaulted youth, and when he had rescued him, he tightly held on to the offender until the smaller lad had made his escape. The moment Jesus released the little bully, Ganid pounced upon the boy and began soundly to thrash him, and to Ganid's astonishment Jesus promptly interfered.

After he had restrained Ganid and permitted the frightened boy to escape, the young man, as soon as he got his breath, excitedly exclaimed, "I cannot understand you, Teacher. If mercy requires that you rescue the smaller lad, does not justice demand the punishment of the larger and offending youth?"

In answering, Jesus said, "Ganid, it is true, you do not understand. Mercy ministry is always the work of the individual, but justice punishment is the function of the social, governmental, or universe administrative groups. As an individual I am beholden to show mercy; I must go to the rescue of the assaulted lad, and in all consistency I may employ sufficient force to restrain the aggressor. And that is just what I did. I achieved the deliverance of the assaulted lad; that was the end of mercy ministry. Then I forcibly detained the aggressor a sufficient length of time to enable the weaker party to the dispute to make his escape, after which I withdrew from the affair. I did not proceed to sit in judgment on the aggressor, thus to pass upon his motive, to adjudicate all that entered into his attack upon his fellow, and then undertake to execute the punishment which my mind might dictate as just recompense for his wrongdoing. Ganid, mercy may be lavish, but justice is precise. Cannot you discern that no two persons are likely to agree as to the punishment that would satisfy the demands of justice? One would impose forty lashes, another twenty, while still another would advise solitary confinement as a just punishment. Can you not see that on this world such responsibilities had better rest upon the group or be administered by chosen representatives of the group? In the universe, judgment is vested in those who fully know the antecedents of all wrongdoing as well as its motivation. In civilized society and in an organized universe the administration of justice presupposes the passing of just sentence consequent upon fair judgment, and such prerogatives are vested in the juridical groups of the worlds and in the all-knowing administrators of the higher universes of all creation."

For days they talked about this problem of manifesting mercy and administering justice. And Ganid, at least to some extent, understood why Jesus would not engage in personal combat. But Ganid asked one last question, to which he never received a fully satisfactory answer; and that question was: "But, Teacher, if a stronger and ill-tempered creature should attack you and threaten to destroy you, what would you do? Would you make no effort to defend yourself?"

Although Jesus could not fully and satisfactorily answer the lad's question, inasmuch as he was not willing to disclose to him that he (Jesus) was living on earth as the exemplification of the Paradise Father's love to an onlooking universe, he did say this much, "Ganid, I can well understand how some of these problems perplex you, and I will endeavor to answer your question. First, in all attacks which might be made upon my person, I would determine whether or not the aggressor was a son of God, my brother in the flesh, and if I thought such a creature did not possess moral judgment and spiritual reason, I would unhesitatingly defend myself to the full capacity of my powers of resistance, regardless of consequences to the attacker. But I would not thus assault a fellow man of sonship status, even in self-defense. That is, I would not punish him in advance and without judgment for his assault upon me. I would by every possible artifice seek to prevent and dissuade him from making such an attack and to mitigate it in case of my failure to abort it. Ganid, I have absolute confidence in my heavenly Father's overcare; I am consecrated to doing the will of my Father in heaven. I do not believe that *real* harm can befall me; I do not believe that my lifework can really be jeopardized by anything my enemies might wish to visit upon me, and surely we have no violence to fear from our friends. I am absolutely assured that the entire universe is friendly to me. This all-powerful truth I insist on believing with a wholehearted trust in spite of all appearances to the contrary."

But Ganid was not fully satisfied. Many times they talked over these matters, and Jesus told him some of his boyhood experiences and also about Jacob the stonemason's son. On learning how Jacob had appointed himself to defend Jesus during their youthful days, Ganid said, "Oh, I begin to see! In the first place very seldom would any normal human being want to attack such a kindly person as you, and even if anyone should be so unthinking as to do such a thing, there is pretty sure to be near at hand some other mortal who will fly to your assistance, even as you always go to the rescue of any person you observe to be in distress. In my heart, Teacher, I agree with you, but in my head I still think that if I had been Jacob, I would have enjoyed punishing those rude fellows who presumed to attack you just because they thought you would not defend yourself. I presume you are fairly safe in your journey through life since you spend much of your time helping others and ministering to your fellows in distress. Most likely there will always be someone on hand to defend you."

And Jesus replied, "That test has not yet come, Ganid, and when it does, we will have to abide by the Father's will."

And that was about all the lad could get his teacher to say on this difficult subject of self-defense and nonresistance. On another occasion he did draw from Jesus the opinion that organized society had every right to employ force in the execution of its just mandates.

While tarrying at the ship landing, waiting for the boat to unload cargo, the travelers observed a man mistreating his wife. As was his custom, Jesus intervened in behalf of the person subjected to attack. He stepped up behind the irate husband and, tapping him gently on the shoulder, said, "My friend, may I speak with you in private for a moment?"

The angry man was nonplused by such an approach and, after a moment of embarrassing hesitation, stammered out, "Err... why ... yes, what do you want with me?"

When Jesus had led him to one side, he said, "My friend, I perceive that something terrible must have happened to you; I very much desire that you tell me what could happen to such a strong man to lead him to attack his wife, the mother of his children, and that right out here before all eyes. I am sure you must feel that you have some good reason for this assault. What did the woman do to deserve such treatment from her husband? As I look upon you, I think I discern in your face the love of justice if not the desire to show mercy. I venture to say that, if you found me out by the wayside, attacked by robbers, you would unhesitatingly rush to my rescue. I dare say you have done many such brave things in the course of your life. Now, my friend, tell me what is the matter? Did the woman do something wrong, or did you foolishly lose your head and thoughtlessly assault her?"

It was not so much what he said that touched this man's heart as the kindly look and the sympathetic smile which Jesus bestowed upon him at the conclusion of his remarks. Said the man, "I perceive you are a priest of the Cynics, and I am thankful you restrained me. My wife has done no great wrong; she is a good woman, but she irritates me by the manner in which she picks on me in public, and I lose my temper. I am sorry for my lack of self-control, and I promise to try to live up to my former pledge to one of your brothers who taught me the better way many years ago. I promise you."

And then, in bidding him farewell, Jesus said, "My brother, always remember that man has no rightful authority over woman unless the woman has willingly and voluntarily given him such authority. Your wife has engaged to go through life with you, to help you fight its battles, and to assume the far greater share of the burden of bearing and rearing your children; and in return for this special service it is only fair that she receive from you that special protection which man can give to woman as the partner who must carry, bear, and nurture the children. The loving care and consideration which a man is willing to bestow upon his wife and their children are the measure of that man's attainment of the higher levels of creative and spiritual self-consciousness. Do you not know that men and women are partners with God in that they co-operate to create beings who grow up to possess themselves of the potential of immortal souls? The Father in heaven treats the Spirit Mother of the children of the universe as one equal to Himself. It is Godlike to share your life and all that relates thereto on equal terms with the mother partner who so fully shares with you that divine experience of reproducing yourselves in the lives of your children. If you can only love your children as God loves you, you will love and cherish your wife as the Father in heaven honors and exalts the Infinite Spirit, the mother of all the spirit children of a vast universe."

As the three travelers went on board the boat, they looked back upon the scene of the teary-eyed couple standing in silent embrace. Having heard the latter half of Jesus' message to the man, Gonod was all day occupied with meditations thereon, and he resolved to reorganize his home when he returned to India.

The journey to Nicopolis was pleasant but slow as the wind was not favorable. The three spent many hours recounting their experiences in Rome and reminiscing about all that had happened to them since they first met in Jerusalem. Ganid was becoming imbued with the spirit of personal ministry. He began work on the steward of the ship, but on the second day, when he got into deep religious water, he called on Joshua to help him out.

They spent several days at Nicopolis, the city that Augustus had founded some fifty years before as the "city of victory" in commemoration of the battle of Actium, this site being the land whereon he had camped with his army before the battle. They lodged in the home of one Jeramy, a Greek proselyte of the Jewish faith, whom they had met on shipboard. The Apostle Paul spent all winter with the son of Jeramy in the same house in the course of his third missionary journey. From Nicopolis they sailed on the same boat for Corinth, the capital of the Roman province of Achaia.

By the time they reached Corinth, Ganid was becoming very much interested in the Jewish religion, and so it was not strange that, one day as they passed the synagogue and saw the people going in, he requested Jesus to take him to the service. That day they heard a learned rabbi discourse on the "Destiny of Israel," and after the service they met one Crispus, the chief ruler of this synagogue. Many times they went back to the synagogue services, but chiefly to meet Crispus. Ganid grew to be very fond of Crispus, his wife, and their family of five children. He much enjoyed observing how a Jew conducted his family life.

While Ganid studied family life, Jesus was teaching Crispus the better ways of religious living. Jesus held more than twenty sessions with this forward-looking Jew; and it is not surprising, years afterward, when Paul was preaching in this very synagogue, and when the Jews had rejected his message and had voted to forbid his further preaching in the synagogue, and when he then went to the gentiles, that Crispus with his entire family embraced the new religion, and that he became one of the chief supports of the Christian church which Paul subsequently organized at Corinth.

During the eighteen months Paul preached in Corinth, being later joined by Silas and Timothy, he met many others who had been taught by the "Jewish tutor of the son of an Indian merchant."

At Corinth they met people of every race hailing from three continents. Next to Alexandria and Rome, it was the most cosmopolitan city of the Mediterranean Empire. There was much to attract one's attention in this city, and Ganid never grew weary of visiting the citadel that stood almost two thousand feet above the sea. He also spent a great deal of his spare time about the synagogue and in the home of Crispus. He was at first shocked, and later on charmed, by the status of woman in the Jewish home; it was a revelation to this young Indian.

Jesus and Ganid were often guests in another Jewish home, that of Justus, a devout merchant, who lived alongside the synagogue. And many times, subsequently, when the Apostle Paul sojourned in this home, did he listen to the recounting of these visits with the Indian lad and his Jewish tutor, while both Paul and Justus wondered whatever became of such a wise and brilliant Hebrew teacher.

When in Rome, Ganid observed that Jesus refused to accompany them to the public baths. Several times afterward the young man sought to induce Jesus further to express himself in regard to the relations of the sexes. Though he would answer the lad's questions, he never seemed disposed to discuss these subjects at great length. One evening as they strolled about Corinth out near where the wall of the citadel ran down to the sea, they were accosted by two public women. Ganid had digested the idea, and rightly, that Jesus was a man of high ideals, and that he abhorred everything which partook of uncleanness or savored of evil; accordingly he spoke sharply to these women and rudely motioned them away.

When Jesus saw this, he said to Ganid, "You mean well, but you should not presume thus to speak to the children of God, even though they chance to be His erring children. Who are we that we should sit in judgment on these women? Do you happen to know all of the circumstances which led them to resort to such methods of obtaining a livelihood? Stop here with me while we talk about these matters." The courtesans were astonished at what he said even more than was Ganid.

As they stood there in the moonlight, Jesus went on to say, "There lives within every human mind a divine spirit, the gift of the Father in heaven. This good spirit ever strives to lead us to God, to help us to find God and to know God; but also within mortals there are many natural physical tendencies that the Creator put there to serve the well-being of the individual and the race. Now, oftentimes, men and women become confused in their efforts to understand themselves and to grapple with the manifold difficulties of making a living in a world so largely dominated by selfishness and sin.

"I perceive, Ganid, that neither of these women is willfully wicked. I can tell by their faces that they have experienced much sorrow; they have suffered much at the hands of an apparently cruel fate; they have not intentionally chosen this sort of life; they have, in discouragement bordering on despair, surrendered to the pressure of the hour and accepted this distasteful means of obtaining a livelihood as the best way out of a situation that to them appeared hopeless. Ganid, some people are really wicked at heart; they deliberately choose to do mean things, but, tell me, as you look into these now tear-stained faces, do you see anything bad or wicked?"

And as Jesus paused for his reply, Ganid's voice choked up as he stammered out his answer, "No, Teacher, I do not. And I apologize for my rudeness to them; I crave their forgiveness."

Jesus continued, "And I bespeak for them that they have forgiven you as I speak for my Father in heaven that He has forgiven them. Now all of you come with me to a friend's house where we will seek refreshment and plan for the new and better life ahead."

Up to this time the amazed women had not uttered a word; they looked at each other and silently followed as the men led the way.

Imagine the surprise of Justus' wife when, at this late hour, Jesus appeared with Ganid and these two strangers, saying, "You will forgive us for coming at this hour, but Ganid and I desire a bite to eat, and we would share it with these our new-found friends, who are also in need of nourishment; and besides all this, we come to you with the thought that you will be interested in counseling with us as to the best way to help these women get a new start in life. They can tell you their story, but I surmise they have had much trouble, and their very presence here in your house testifies how earnestly they crave to know good people, and how willingly they will embrace the opportunity to show all the world, and even the angels of heaven, what brave and noble women they can become."

When Martha, Justus' wife, had spread the food on the table, Jesus, taking unexpected leave of them, said, "As it is getting late, and since the young man's father will be awaiting us, we pray to be excused while we leave you here together, three women, the beloved children of the Most High. And I will pray for your spiritual guidance while you make plans for a new and better life on earth and eternal life in the great beyond."

Thus did Jesus and Ganid take leave of the women. So far the two courtesans had said nothing; likewise was Ganid speechless. And for a few moments so was Martha, but presently she rose to the occasion and did everything for these strangers that Jesus had hoped for. The elder of these two women died a short time thereafter, with bright hopes of eternal survival, and the younger woman worked at Justus' place of business and later became a lifelong member of the first Christian church in Corinth.

Several times in the home of Crispus, Jesus and Ganid met one Gaius, who subsequently became a loyal supporter of Paul. During these two months in Corinth they held intimate conversations with scores of worthwhile individuals, and as a result of all these apparently casual contacts more than half of the individuals so affected became members of the subsequent Christian community.

When Paul first went to Corinth, he had not intended to make a prolonged visit. But he did not know how well the Jewish tutor had prepared the soil for his planting. And further, he discovered that great interest had already been aroused by Aquila and Priscilla, Aquila being one of the Cynics with whom Jesus had come in contact when in Rome. This couple were Jewish refugees from Rome, and they quickly embraced Paul's teachings. He lived with them and worked with them, for they were also tentmakers. It was because of these circumstances that Paul prolonged his stay in Corinth.

Jesus and Ganid had many more interesting experiences in Corinth. They had close converse with a great number of persons who greatly profited by the instruction received from Jesus.

The miller he taught about grinding up the grains of truth in the mill of living experience so as to render the difficult things of divine life readily receivable by even the weak and feeble among one's fellow mortals. Said Jesus, "Give the milk of truth to those who are babes in spiritual perception. In your living and loving ministry serve spiritual food in attractive form and suited to the capacity of receptivity of each of your inquirers."

To the Roman centurion he said, "Render unto Caesar the things which are Caesar's and unto God the things which are God's. The sincere service of God and the loyal service of Caesar do not conflict unless Caesar should presume to arrogate to himself that homage which alone can be claimed by Deity. Loyalty to God, if you should come to know him, would render you all the more loyal and faithful in your devotion to a worthy emperor."

To the earnest leader of the Mithraic cult he said, "You do well to seek for a religion of eternal salvation, but you err to go in quest of such a glorious truth among man-made mysteries and human philosophies. Know you not that the mystery of eternal salvation dwells within your own soul? Do you not know that the God of heaven has sent his spirit to live within you, and that this spirit will lead all truth-loving and God-serving mortals out of this life and through the portals of death up to the eternal heights of light where God waits to receive His children?

And never forget. You who know God are the children of God if you truly yearn to be like Him."

To the Epicurean teacher he said, "You do well to choose the best and esteem the good, but are you wise when you fail to discern the greater things of mortal life which are embodied in the spirit realms derived from the realization of the presence of God in the human heart? The great thing in all human experience is the realization of knowing the God whose spirit lives within you and seeks to lead you forth on that long and almost endless journey of attaining the personal presence of our common Father, the God of all creation, the Lord of universes."

To the Greek contractor and builder he said: "My friend, as you build the material structures of men, grow a spiritual character in the similitude of the divine spirit within your soul. Do not let your achievement as a temporal builder outrun your attainment as a spiritual son of the kingdom of heaven. While you build the mansions of time for another, neglect not to secure your title to the mansions of eternity for yourself. Ever remember, there is a city whose foundations are righteousness and truth, and whose builder and maker is God."

To the Roman judge he said, "As you judge men, remember that you yourself will also some day come to judgment before the bar of the Rulers of a universe. Judge justly, even mercifully, even as you shall some day thus crave merciful consideration at the hands of the Supreme Arbiter. Judge as you would be judged under similar circumstances, thus being guided by the spirit of the law as well as by its letter. And even as you accord justice dominated by fairness in the light of the need of those who are brought before you, so shall you have the right to expect justice tempered by mercy when you sometime stand before the Judge of all the earth."

To the mistress of the Greek inn he said, "Minister your hospitality as one who entertains the children of the Most High. Elevate the drudgery of your daily toil to the high levels of a fine art through the increasing realization that you minister to God in the persons whom He indwells by His spirit which has descended to live within the hearts of men, thereby seeking to transform their minds and lead their souls to the knowledge of the Paradise Father of all these bestowed gifts of the divine spirit."

Jesus had many visits with a Chinese merchant. In saying good-bye, he admonished him, "Worship only God, who is your true spirit ancestor. Remember that the Father's spirit ever lives within you and always points your soul-direction heavenward. If you follow the unconscious leadings of this immortal spirit, you are certain to continue on in the uplifted way of finding God. And when you do attain the Father in heaven, it will be because by seeking Him you have become more and more like Him. And so farewell, Chang, but only for a season, for we shall meet again in the worlds of light where the Father of spirit souls has provided many delightful stopping-places for those who are Paradise-bound."

To the traveler from Britain he said, "My brother, I perceive you are seeking for truth, and I suggest that the spirit of the Father of all truth may chance to dwell within you. Did you ever sincerely endeavor to talk with the spirit of your own soul? Such a thing is indeed difficult and seldom yields consciousness of success; but every honest attempt of the material mind to communicate with its indwelling spirit meets with certain success, notwithstanding that the majority of all such magnificent human experiences must long remain as superconscious registrations in the souls of such God-knowing mortals."

To the runaway lad Jesus said, "Remember, there are two things you cannot run away from; God and yourself. Wherever you may go, you take with you yourself and the spirit of the Heavenly Father, which lives, within your heart. My son, stop trying to deceive yourself; settle down to the courageous practice of facing the facts of life; lay firm hold on the assurances of sonship with God and the certainty of eternal life, as I have instructed you. From this day on purpose to be a real man, a man determined to face life bravely and intelligently."

To the condemned criminal he said at the last hour, "My brother, you have fallen on evil times. You lost your way; you became entangled in the meshes of crime. From talking to you, I well know you did not plan to do the thing which is about to cost you your temporal life. But you did do this evil, and your fellows have adjudged you guilty; they have determined that you shall die. You or I may not deny the state this right of self-defense in the manner of its own choosing. There seems to be no way of humanly escaping the penalty of your wrongdoing. Your fellows must judge you by what you did, but there is a Judge to whom you may appeal for forgiveness, and who will judge you by your real motives and better intentions. You need not fear to meet the judgment of God if your repentance is genuine and your faith sincere. The fact that your error carries with it the death penalty imposed by man does not prejudice the chance of your soul to obtain justice and enjoy mercy before the heavenly courts."

Jesus enjoyed many intimate talks with a large number of hungry souls, too many to find a place in this record. The three travelers enjoyed their sojourn in Corinth. Excepting Athens, which was more renowned as an educational center, Corinth was the most important city in Greece during these Roman times, and their two months' stay in this thriving commercial center afforded opportunity for all three of them to gain much valuable experience. Their sojourn in this city was one of the most interesting of all their stops on the way back from Rome.

Gonod had many interests in Corinth, but finally his business was finished, and they prepared to sail for Athens. They traveled on a small boat which could be carried overland on a land track from one of Corinth's harbors to the other, a distance of ten miles.

★ ★ ★

They shortly arrived at the olden center of Greek science and learning, and Ganid was thrilled with the thought of being in Athens, of being in Greece, the cultural center of the onetime Alexandrian empire, which had extended its borders even to his own land of India. There was little business to transact; so Gonod spent most of his time with Jesus and Ganid, visiting the many points of interest and listening to the interesting discussions of the lad and his versatile teacher.

A great university still thrived in Athens, and the trio made frequent visits to its halls of learning. Jesus and Ganid had thoroughly discussed the teachings of Plato when they attended the lectures in the museum at Alexandria. They all enjoyed the art of Greece, examples of which were still to be found here and there about the city.

Both the father and the son greatly enjoyed the discussion on science that Jesus had at their inn one evening with a Greek philosopher.

After this pedant had talked for almost three hours, and when he had finished his discourse, Jesus, in terms of modern thought, said: Scientists may some day measure the energy, or force manifestations, of gravitation, light, and electricity, but these same scientists can never (scientifically) tell you what these universe phenomena *are*. Science deals with physical-energy activities; religion deals with eternal values. True philosophy grows out of the wisdom that does its best to correlate these quantitative and qualitative observations. There always exists the danger that the purely physical scientist may become afflicted with mathematical pride and statistical egotism, not to mention spiritual blindness.

Logic is valid in the material world, and mathematics is reliable when limited in its application to physical things; but neither is to be regarded as wholly dependable or infallible when applied to life problems. Life embraces phenomena which are not wholly material. Arithmetic says that, if one man could shear a sheep in ten minutes, ten men could shear it in one minute. That is sound mathematics, but it is not true, for the ten men could not so do it; they would get in one another's way so badly that the work would be greatly delayed.

Mathematics asserts that, if one person stands for a certain unit of intellectual and moral value, ten persons would stand for ten times this value. But in dealing with human personality it would be nearer the truth to say that such a personality association is a sum equal to the square of the number of personalities concerned in the equation rather than the simple arithmetical sum. A social group of human beings in coordinated working harmony stands for a force far greater than the simple sum of its parts.

Quantity may be identified as a *fact,* thus becoming a scientific uniformity. Quality, being a matter of mind interpretation, represents an estimate of *values,* and must, therefore, remain an experience of the individual. When both science and religion become less dogmatic and more tolerant of criticism, philosophy will then begin to achieve *unity* in the intelligent comprehension of the universe.

There is unity in the cosmic universe if you could only discern its workings in actuality. The real universe is friendly to every child of the eternal God. The real problem is; how can the finite mind of man achieve a logical, true, and corresponding unity of thought? This universe-knowing state of mind can be had only by conceiving that the quantitative fact and the qualitative value have a common causation in the Paradise Father. Such a conception of reality yields a broader insight into the purposeful unity of universe phenomena; it even reveals a spiritual goal of progressive personality achievement. And this is a concept of unity that can sense the unchanging background of a living universe of continually changing impersonal relations and evolving personal relationships.

Matter and spirit and the state intervening between them are three interrelated and interassociated levels of the true unity of the real universe. Regardless of how divergent the universe phenomena of fact and value may appear to be, they are, after all, unified in the Supreme.

Reality of material existence attaches to unrecognized energy as well as to visible matter. When the energies of the universe are so slowed down that they acquire the requisite degree of motion, then, under favorable conditions, these same energies become mass. And forget not, the mind that can alone perceive the presence of apparent realities is itself also real. And the fundamental cause of this universe of energy-mass, mind, and spirit, is eternal; it exists and consists in the nature and reactions of the Universal Father and his absolute co-ordinates.

They were all more than astounded at the words of Jesus, and when the Greek took leave of them, he said, "At last my eyes have beheld a Jew who thinks something besides racial superiority and talks something besides religion." And they retired for the night.

The sojourn in Athens was pleasant and profitable, but it was not particularly fruitful in its human contacts. Too many of the Athenians of that day were either intellectually proud of their reputation of another day or mentally stupid and ignorant, being the offspring of the *inferior* slaves of those earlier periods when there was glory in Greece and wisdom in the minds of its people. Even then, there were still many keen minds to be found among the citizens of Athens.

On leaving Athens, the travelers went by way of Troas to Ephesus, the capital of the Roman province of Asia. They made many trips out to the famous temple of Artemis of the Ephesians, about two miles from the city. Artemis was the most famous goddess of all Asia Minor and a perpetuation of the still earlier mother goddess of ancient Anatolian times. The crude idol exhibited in the enormous temple dedicated to her worship was reputed to have fallen from heaven. Not all of Ganid's early training to respect images as symbols of divinity had been eradicated, and he thought it best to purchase a little silver shrine in honor of this fertility goddess of Asia Minor. That night they talked at great length about the worship of things made with human hands.

On the third day of their stay they walked down by the river to observe the dredging of the harbor's mouth. At noon they talked with a young Phoenician who was homesick and much discouraged; but most of all he was envious of a certain young man who had received promotion over his head.

Jesus spoke comforting words to him and quoted the olden Hebrew proverb. "A man's gift makes room for him and brings him before great men."

Of all the large cities they visited on this tour of the Mediterranean, they here accomplished the least of value to the subsequent work of the Christian missionaries. Christianity secured its start in Ephesus largely through the efforts of Paul, who resided here more than two years, making tents for a living and conducting lectures on religion and philosophy each night in the main audience chamber of the school of Tyrannus.

There was a progressive thinker connected with this local school of philosophy, and Jesus had several profitable sessions with him. In the course of these talks Jesus had repeatedly used the word "soul." This learned Greek finally asked him what he meant by "soul."

Said Jesus, "The soul is the self-reflective, truth-discerning, and spirit-perceiving part of man which forever elevates the human being above the level of the animal world. Self-consciousness, in and of itself, is not the soul. Moral self-consciousness is true human self-realization and constitutes the foundation of the human soul, and the soul is that part of man that represents the potential survival value of human experience. Moral choice and spiritual attainment, the ability to know God and the urge to be like him, are the characteristics of the soul. The soul of man cannot exist apart from moral thinking and spiritual activity. A stagnant soul is a dying soul. But the soul of man is distinct from the divine spirit that dwells within the mind. The divine spirit arrives simultaneously with the first moral activity of the human mind, and that is the occasion of the birth of the soul.

"The saving or losing of a soul has to do with whether or not the moral consciousness attains survival status through eternal alliance with its associated immortal spirit endowment. Salvation is the spiritualization of the self-realization of the moral consciousness, which thereby becomes possessed of survival value. All forms of soul conflict consist in the lack of harmony between the moral, or spiritual, self-consciousness and the purely intellectual self-consciousness.

"The human soul, when matured, ennobled, and spiritualized, approaches the heavenly status in that it comes near to being an entity intervening between the material and the spiritual, the material self and the divine spirit. The evolving soul of a human being is difficult of description and more difficult of demonstration because it is not discoverable by the methods of either material investigation or spiritual proving. Material science cannot demonstrate the existence of a soul, neither can pure spirit-testing. Notwithstanding the failure of both material science and spiritual standards to discover the existence of the human soul, every morally conscious mortal *knows* of the existence of *his or her* soul as a *real* and actual personal experience."

Shortly the travelers set sail for Cyprus, stopping at Rhodes. They enjoyed the long water voyage and arrived at their island destination much rested in body and refreshed in spirit.

It was their plan to enjoy a period of real rest and play on this visit to Cyprus as their tour of the Mediterranean was drawing to a close. They landed at Paphos and at once began the assembly of supplies for their sojourn of several weeks in the nearby mountains. On the third day after their arrival they started for the hills with their well-loaded pack animals.

For two weeks the trio greatly enjoyed themselves, and then, without warning, young Ganid was suddenly taken grievously ill. For two weeks he suffered from a raging fever, oftentimes becoming delirious; both Jesus and Gonod were kept busy attending the sick boy. Jesus skillfully and tenderly cared for the lad, and the father was amazed by both the gentleness and adeptness manifested in all his ministry to the afflicted youth. They were far from human habitations, and the boy was too ill to be moved; so they prepared as best they could to nurse him back to health right there in the mountains.

During Ganid's convalescence of three weeks Jesus told him many interesting things about nature and her various moods. And what fun they had as they wandered over the mountains, the boy asking questions, Jesus answering them, and the father marveling at the whole performance.

The last week of their sojourn in the mountains Jesus and Ganid had a long talk on the functions of the human mind. After several hours of discussion the lad asked a question. "But, Teacher, what do you mean when you say that man experiences a higher form of self-consciousness than do the higher animals?"

And as restated in modern phraseology, Jesus answered: My son, I have already told you much about the mind of man and the divine spirit that lives therein, but now let me emphasize that self-consciousness is a *reality*. When any animal becomes self-conscious, it becomes a primitive man. Such an attainment results from a co-ordination of function between impersonal energy and spirit-conceiving mind, and it is this phenomenon which warrants the bestowal of an absolute focal point for the human personality, the spirit of the Father in heaven.

Ideas are not simply a record of sensations; ideas are sensations plus the reflective interpretations of the personal self; and the self is more than the sum of one's sensations. There begins to be something of an approach to unity in an evolving selfhood, and that unity is derived from the indwelling presence of a part of absolute unity which spiritually activates such a self-conscious animal-origin mind.

No mere animal could possess a time self-consciousness. Animals possess a physiological co-ordination of associated sensation-recognition and memory thereof, but none experience a meaningful recognition of sensation or exhibit a purposeful association of these combined physical experiences such as is manifested in the conclusions of intelligent and reflective human interpretations. And this fact of self-conscious existence, associated with the reality of his subsequent spiritual experience, constitutes man a potential son of the universe and foreshadows his eventual attainment of the Supreme Unity of the universe.

Neither is the human self merely the sum of the successive states of consciousness. Without the effective functioning of a consciousness sorter and associator there would not exist sufficient unity to warrant the designation of a selfhood. Such an un-unified mind could hardly attain conscious levels of human status. If the associations of consciousness were just an accident, the minds of all men would then exhibit the uncontrolled and random associations of certain phases of mental madness.

A human mind, built up solely out of the consciousness of physical sensations, could never attain spiritual levels; this kind of material mind would be utterly lacking in a sense of moral values and would be without a guiding sense of spiritual dominance which is so essential to achieving harmonious personality unity in time, and which is inseparable from personality survival in eternity.

The human mind early begins to manifest qualities that are supermaterial; the truly reflective human intellect is not altogether bound by the limits of time. That individuals so differ in their life performances indicates, not only the varying endowments of heredity and the different influences of the environment, but also the degree of unification with the indwelling spirit of the Father which has been achieved by the self, the measure of the identification of the one with the other.

The human mind does not well stand the conflict of double allegiance. It is a severe strain on the soul to undergo the experience of an effort to serve both good and evil. The supremely happy and efficiently unified mind is the one wholly dedicated to the doing of the will of the Father in heaven. Unresolved conflicts destroy unity and may terminate in mind disruption. But the survival character of a soul is not fostered by attempting to secure peace of mind at any price, by the surrender of noble aspirations, and by the compromise of spiritual ideals; rather is such peace attained by the stalwart assertion of the triumph of that which is true, and this victory is achieved in the overcoming of evil with the potent force of good.

The next day they departed for Salamis, where they embarked for Antioch on the Syrian coast.

A ntioch was the capital of the Roman province of Syria, and here the imperial governor had his residence. Antioch had half a million inhabitants; it was the third city of the empire in size and the first in wickedness and flagrant immorality.

Gonod had considerable business to transact; so Jesus and Ganid were much by themselves. They visited everything about this polyglot city except the grove of Daphne. Gonod and Ganid visited this notorious shrine of shame, but Jesus declined to accompany them. Such scenes were not so shocking to Indians, but they were repellent to an idealistic Hebrew.

Jesus became sober and reflective as he drew nearer Palestine and the end of their journey. He visited with few people in Antioch; he seldom went about in the city. After much questioning as to why his teacher manifested so little interest in Antioch, Ganid finally induced Jesus to say, "This city is not far from Palestine; maybe I shall come back here sometime."

Ganid had a very interesting experience in Antioch. This young man had proved himself an apt pupil and already had begun to make practical use of some of Jesus' teachings. There was a certain Indian connected with his father's business in Antioch who had become so unpleasant and disgruntled that his dismissal had been considered. When Ganid heard this, he betook himself to his father's place of business and held a long conference with his fellow countryman. This man felt he had been put at the wrong job. Ganid told him about the Father in heaven and in many ways expanded his views of religion. But of all that Ganid said, the quotation of a Hebrew proverb did the most good, and that word of wisdom was, "Whatsoever your hand finds to do, do that with all your might."

After preparing their luggage for the camel caravan, they passed on down to Sidon and thence over to Damascus, and after three days they made ready for the long trek across the desert sands.

The caravan trip across the desert was not a new experience for these much-traveled men. After Ganid had watched his teacher help with the loading of their twenty camels and observed him volunteer to drive their own animal, he exclaimed, "Teacher, is there anything that you cannot do?"

Jesus only smiled, saying, "The teacher surely is not without honor in the eyes of a diligent pupil." And so they set forth for the ancient city of Ur.

Jesus was much interested in the early history of Ur, the birthplace of Abraham, and he was equally fascinated with the ruins and traditions of Susa, so much so that Gonod and Ganid extended their stay in these parts three weeks in order to afford Jesus more time to conduct his investigations and also to provide the better opportunity to persuade him to go back to India with them.

It was at Ur that Ganid had a long talk with Jesus regarding the difference between knowledge, wisdom, and truth. And he was greatly charmed with the saying of the Hebrew wise man: "Wisdom is the principal thing; therefore get wisdom. With all your quest for knowledge, get understanding. Exalt wisdom and she will promote you. She will bring you to honor if you will but embrace her."

At last the day came for the separation. They were all brave, especially the lad, but it was a trying ordeal. They were tearful of eye but courageous of heart. In bidding his teacher farewell, Ganid said, "Farewell, Teacher, but not forever. When I come again to Damascus, I will look for you. I love you, for I think the Father in heaven must be something like you; at least I know you are much like what you have told me about Him. I will remember your teaching, but most of all, I will never forget you."

Said the father, "Farewell to a great teacher, one who has made us better and helped us to know God."

Jesus replied, "Peace be upon you, and may the blessing of the Father in heaven ever abide with you." And Jesus stood on the shore and watched as the small boat carried them out to their anchored ship. Thus the Master left his friends from India at Charax, never to see them again in this world; nor were they, in this world, ever to know that the man who later appeared as Jesus of Nazareth was this same friend they had just taken leave of, Joshua their teacher.

In India, Ganid grew up to become an influential man, a worthy successor of his eminent father, and he spread abroad many of the noble truths that he had learned from Jesus, his beloved teacher. Later on in life, when Ganid heard of the strange teacher in Palestine who terminated his career on a cross, though he recognized the similarity between the gospel of this Son of Man and the teachings of his Jewish tutor, it never occurred to him that these two were actually the same person.

Thus ended that chapter in the life of the Son of Man which might be termed: *The mission of Joshua the teacher.*

The Transition Years

URING THE Mediterranean journey Jesus had carefully studied the people he met and the countries through which he passed, and at about this time he reached his final decision as to the remainder of his life on earth. He had fully considered and now finally approved the plan which provided that he be born of Jewish parents in Palestine, and he therefore deliberately returned to Galilee to await the beginning of his lifework as a public teacher of truth; he began to lay plans for a public career in the land of his father Joseph's people, and he did this of his own free will.

Jesus had found out through personal and human experience that Palestine was the best place in the entire Roman world wherein to set forth the closing chapters, and to enact the final scenes, of his life on earth. For the first time he became fully satisfied with the program of openly manifesting his true nature and of revealing his divine identity among the Jews and gentiles of his native Palestine. He definitely decided to finish his life on earth and to complete his career of mortal existence in the same land in which he entered the human experience as a helpless babe. His Earth career began among the Jews in Palestine, and he chose to terminate his life in Palestine and among the Jews.

After taking leave of Gonod and Ganid at Charax (in December of A.D. 23), Jesus returned by way of Ur to Babylon, where he joined a desert caravan that was on its way to Damascus. From Damascus he went to Nazareth, stopping only a few hours at Capernaum, where he paused to call on Zebedee's family. There he met his brother James, who had sometime previously come over to work in his place in Zebedee's boatshop. After talking with James and Jude (who also chanced to be in Capernaum) and after turning over to his brother James the little house which John Zebedee had managed to buy, Jesus went on to Nazareth.

At the end of his Mediterranean journey Jesus had received sufficient money to meet his living expenses almost up to the time of the beginning of his public ministry. But aside from Zebedee of Capernaum and the people whom he met on this extraordinary trip, the world never knew that he made this journey. His family always believed that he spent this time in study at Alexandria. Jesus never confirmed these beliefs, neither did he make open denial of such misunderstandings.

During his stay of a few weeks at Nazareth, Jesus visited with his family and friends, spent some time at the repair shop with his brother Joseph, but devoted most of his attention to Mary and Ruth. Ruth was then nearly fifteen years old, and this was Jesus' first opportunity to have long talks with her since she had become a young woman.

Both Simon and Jude had for some time wanted to get married, but they had disliked to do this without Jesus' consent; accordingly they had postponed these events, hoping for their eldest brother's return. Though they all regarded James as the head of the family in most matters, when it came to getting married, they wanted the blessing of Jesus. So Simon and Jude were married at a double wedding in early March of this year, A.D. 24. All the older children were now married; only Ruth, the youngest, remained at home with Mary.

Jesus visited with the individual members of his family quite normally and naturally, but when they were all together, he had so little to say that they remarked about it among themselves. Mary especially was disconcerted by this unusually peculiar behavior of her first-born son.

About the time Jesus was preparing to leave Nazareth, the conductor of a large caravan that was passing through the city was taken violently ill, and Jesus, being a linguist, volunteered to take his place. Since this trip would necessitate his absence for a year, and inasmuch as all his brothers were married and his mother was living at home with Ruth, Jesus called a family conference at which he proposed that his mother and Ruth go to Capernaum to live in the home which he had so recently given to James. Accordingly, a few days after Jesus left with the caravan, Mary and Ruth moved to Capernaum, where they lived for the rest of Mary's life in the home that Jesus had provided. Joseph and his family moved into the old Nazareth home.

This, his thirtieth on Earth, was one of the more unusual years in the inner experience of the Son of Man; great progress was made in effecting working harmony between his human mind and the indwelling Mystery Monitor. The Father Fragment had been actively engaged in reorganizing the thinking and in rehearsing the mind for the great events that were in the not then distant future. The personality of Jesus was preparing for his great change in attitude toward the world. These were the in-between times, the transition stage of that being who began life as God appearing as man, and who was now making ready to complete his earth career as man appearing as God.

✷ ✷ ✷

It was the first of April, A.D. 24, when Jesus left Nazareth on the caravan trip to the Caspian Sea region. The caravan that Jesus joined as its conductor was going from Jerusalem by way of Damascus and Lake Urmia through Assyria, Media, and Parthia to the southeastern Caspian Sea region. It was a full year before he returned from this journey.

For Jesus this caravan trip was another adventure of exploration and personal ministry. He had an interesting experience with his caravan family; passengers, guards, and camel drivers. Scores of men, women, and children residing along the route followed by the caravan lived richer lives as a result of their contact with Jesus, to them, the extraordinary conductor of a commonplace caravan. Not all who enjoyed these occasions of his personal ministry profited thereby, but the vast majority of those who met and talked with him were made better for the remainder of their natural lives.

Of all his world travels this Caspian Sea trip carried Jesus nearest to the Orient and enabled him to gain a better understanding of the Far-Eastern peoples. He made intimate and personal contact with every one of the surviving races of Earth excepting the red. He equally enjoyed his personal ministry to each of these varied races and blended peoples, and all of them were receptive to the living truth that he brought them. The Europeans from the Far West and the Asiatics from the Far East alike gave attention to his words of hope and eternal life and were equally influenced by the life of loving service and spiritual ministry which he so graciously lived among them.

The caravan trip was successful in every way. This was a most interesting episode in the human life of Jesus, for he functioned during this year in an executive capacity, being responsible for the material entrusted to his charge and for the safe conduct of the travelers making up the caravan party. And he most faithfully, efficiently, and wisely discharged his multiple duties.

On the return from the Caspian region, Jesus gave up the direction of the caravan at Lake Urmia, where he tarried for slightly over two weeks. He returned as a passenger with a later caravan to Damascus, where the owners of the camels besought him to remain in their service. Declining this offer, he journeyed on with the caravan train to Capernaum, arriving the first of April, A.D. 25. No longer did he regard Nazareth as his home. Capernaum had become the home of Jesus, James, Mary, and Ruth. But Jesus never again lived with his family; when in Capernaum he made his home with the Zebedees.

On the way to the Caspian Sea, Jesus had stopped several days for rest and recuperation at the old Persian city of Urmia on the western shores of Lake Urmia. On the largest of a group of islands situated a short distance offshore near Urmia was located a large building, a lecture amphitheater, dedicated to the "spirit of religion." This structure was really a temple of the philosophy of religions.

This temple of religion had been built by a wealthy merchant citizen of Urmia and his three sons. This man was Cymboyton, and he numbered among his ancestors many diverse peoples.

The lectures and discussions in this school of religion began at ten o'clock every morning in the week. The afternoon sessions started at three o'clock, and the evening debates opened at eight o'clock. Cymboyton or one of his three sons always presided at these sessions of teaching, discussion, and debate. The founder of this unique school of religions lived and died without ever revealing his personal religious beliefs.

On several occasions Jesus participated in these discussions, and before he left Urmia, Cymboyton arranged with Jesus to sojourn with them for two weeks on his return trip and give twenty-four lectures on "The Brotherhood of Men," and to conduct twelve evening sessions of questions, discussions, and debates on his lectures in particular and on the brotherhood of men in general.

In accordance with this arrangement, Jesus stopped off on the return trip and delivered these lectures. This was the most systematic and formal of all the Master's teaching on Earth. Never before or after did he say so much on one subject as was contained in these lectures and discussions on the brotherhood of men. In reality these lectures were on the "Kingdom of God" and the "Kingdoms of Men."

More than thirty religions and religious cults were represented on the faculty of this temple of religious philosophy. These teachers were chosen, supported, and fully accredited by their respective religious groups. At this time there were about seventy-five teachers on the faculty, and they lived in cottages each accommodating about a dozen persons. Every new moon these groups were changed by the casting of lots. Intolerance, a contentious spirit, or any other disposition to interfere with the smooth running of the community would bring about the prompt and summary dismissal of the offending teacher. He would be unceremoniously dismissed, and his alternate in waiting would be immediately installed in his place.

These teachers of the various religions made a great effort to show how similar their religions were in regard to the fundamental things of this life and the next. There was but one doctrine which had to be accepted in order to gain a seat on this faculty; every teacher must represent a religion which recognized God, some sort of supreme Deity. There were five independent teachers on the faculty who did not represent any organized religion, and it was as such an independent teacher that Jesus appeared before them.

(When we first prepared the summary of Jesus' teachings at Urmia, there arose a disagreement between the seraphim of the churches and the seraphim of progress as to the wisdom of including these teachings in this Revelation. Conditions of the twenty-first century, prevailing in both religion and human governments, are so different from those prevailing in Jesus' day that it was indeed difficult to adapt the Master's teachings at Urmia to the problems of the kingdom of God and the kingdoms of men as these world functions are existent in the present century. We were never able to formulate a statement of the Master's teachings that was acceptable to both groups of these seraphim of planetary government. Finally, the Melchizedek chairman of the revelatory commission appointed a commission of three of our number to prepare our view of the Master's Urmia teachings as adapted to twenty- first century religious and political conditions on Earth. Accordingly, the three completed such an adaptation of Jesus' teachings, restating his pronouncements as they would apply them to present-day world conditions, and we now present these statements as they stand after having been edited by the Melchizedek chairman of the revelatory commission.]

On the subject of sovereignty, divine and human, Jesus taught: Brotherhood of men is founded on the fatherhood of God. The family of God is derived from the love of God; God is love. God the Father divinely loves his children, all of them.

The kingdom of heaven, the divine government, is founded on the fact of divine sovereignty; God is spirit. Since God is spirit, this kingdom is spiritual. The kingdom of heaven is neither material nor merely intellectual; it is a spiritual relationship between God and man.

If different religions recognize the spirit sovereignty of God the Father, then will all such religions remain at peace. Only when one religion assumes that it is in some way superior to all others, and that it possesses exclusive authority over other religions, will such a religion presume to be intolerant of other religions or dare to persecute other religious believers.

Religious peace; brotherhood, can never exist unless all religions are willing to completely divest themselves of all ecclesiastical authority and fully surrender all concept of spiritual sovereignty. God alone is spirit sovereign.

You cannot have equality among religions (religious liberty) without having religious wars unless all religions consent to the transfer of all religious sovereignty to some superhuman level, to God Himself.

The kingdom of heaven in the hearts of men will create religious unity (not necessarily uniformity) because any and all religious groups composed of such religious believers will be free from all notions of ecclesiastical authority; religious sovereignty.

God is spirit, and God gives a fragment of his spirit self to dwell in the heart of man. Spiritually, all men are equal. The kingdom of heaven is free from castes, classes, social levels, and economic groups. All are brothers and sisters.

But the moment you lose sight of the spirit sovereignty of God the Father, some one religion will begin to assert its superiority over other religions; and then, instead of peace on earth and good will among men, there will start dissensions, recriminations, even religious wars, at least wars among religionists.

Freewill beings who regard themselves as equals, unless they mutually acknowledge themselves as subject to some supersovereignty, some authority over and above themselves, sooner or later are tempted to try out their ability to gain power and authority over other persons and groups. The concept of equality never brings peace except in the mutual recognition of some overcontrolling influence of supersovereignty.

The Urmia religionists lived together in comparative peace and tranquillity because they had fully surrendered all their notions of religious sovereignty. Spiritually, they all believed in a sovereign God; socially, full and unchallengeable authority rested in their presiding head, Cymboyton. They well knew what would happen to any teacher who assumed to lord it over his fellow teachers. There can be no lasting religious peace on Earth until all religious groups freely surrender all their notions of divine favor, chosen people, and religious sovereignty. Only when God the Father becomes supreme will men and women become religious brothers and sisters and live together in religious peace on earth.

[While the Master's teaching concerning the sovereignty of God is a truth — only complicated by the subsequent appearance of the religion about him among the world's religions — his presentations concerning political sovereignty are vastly complicated by the political evolution of nation life during the last two thousand years. In the times of Jesus there were only two great world powers — the Roman Empire in the West and the Han Empire in the East — and these were widely separated by the Parthian kingdom and other intervening lands of the Caspian and Turkestan regions. We have, therefore, in the following presentation departed more widely from the substance of the Master's teachings at Urmia concerning political sovereignty, at the same time attempting to depict the import of such teachings as they are applicable to the peculiarly critical stage of the evolution of political sovereignty in the twenty-first century after Christ.]

War on Earth will never end so long as nations cling to the illusive notions of unlimited national sovereignty. There are only two levels of relative sovereignty on an inhabited world: the spiritual free will of the individual mortal and the collective sovereignty of mankind as a whole. Between the level of the individual human being and the level of the total of humankind, all groupings and associations are relative, transitory, and of value only in so far as they enhance the welfare, well-being, and progress of the individual and the planetary grand total — man and mankind.

Religious teachers must always remember that the spiritual sovereignty of God overrides all intervening and intermediate spiritual loyalties. Someday civil rulers will learn that the Most Highs rule in the kingdoms of men.

This rule of the Most Highs in the kingdoms of men is not for the especial benefit of any especially favored group of mortals. There is no such thing as a "chosen people." The rule of the Most Highs, the overcontrollers of political evolution, is a rule designed to foster the greatest good to the greatest number of *all* citizens of Earth and for the greatest length of time.

Sovereignty is power and it grows by organization. This growth of the organization of political power is good and proper, for it tends to encompass ever-widening segments of the total of mankind. But this same growth of political organizations creates a problem at every intervening stage between the initial and natural organization of political power - the family - and the final consummation of political growth - the government of all mankind, by all mankind, and for all mankind.

Starting out with parental power in the family group, political sovereignty evolves by organization as families overlap into consanguineous clans which become united, for various reasons, into tribal units - superconsanguineous political groupings. And then, by trade, commerce, and conquest, tribes become unified as a nation, while nations themselves sometimes become unified by empire.

As sovereignty passes from smaller groups to larger groups, wars are lessened. That is, minor wars between smaller nations are lessened, but the potential for greater wars is increased as the nations wielding sovereignty become larger and larger. Presently, when all the world has been explored and occupied, when nations are few, strong, and powerful, when these great and supposedly sovereign nations come to touch borders, when only oceans separate them, then is the stage set for major wars, world-wide conflicts. So-called sovereign nations cannot rub elbows without generating conflicts and eventuating wars.

The difficulty in the evolution of political sovereignty from the family to all mankind, lies in the inertia-resistance exhibited on all intervening levels. Families have, on occasion, defied their clan, while clans and tribes have often been subversive of the sovereignty of the territorial state. Each new and forward evolution of political sovereignty is (and has always been) embarrassed and hampered by the "scaffolding stages" of the previous developments in political organization. And this is true because human loyalties, once mobilized, are hard to change. The same loyalty that makes possible the evolution of the tribe, makes difficult the evolution of the supertribe - the territorial state. And the same loyalty (patriotism) which makes possible the evolution of the territorial state, vastly complicates the evolutionary development of the government of all mankind.

Political sovereignty is created out of the surrender of self-determinism, first by the individual within the family and then by the families and clans in relation to the tribe and larger groupings. This progressive transfer of self-determination from the smaller to ever larger political organizations has generally proceeded unabated in the East since the establishment of the Ming and the Mogul dynasties. In the West it obtained for more than a thousand years right on down to the end of

World War I, when an unfortunate retrograde movement temporarily reversed this normal trend by re-establishing the submerged political sovereignty of numerous small groups in Europe.

Earth will not enjoy lasting peace until the so-called sovereign nations intelligently and fully surrender their sovereign powers into the hands of the brotherhood of men - mankind government. Internationalism - Leagues of Nations — can never bring permanent peace to mankind. Worldwide confederations of nations may effectively prevent minor wars and acceptably control the smaller nations, but they will not prevent world wars nor control the three, four, or five most powerful governments. In the face of real conflicts, one of these world powers will withdraw from the League and declare war. You cannot prevent nations going to war as long as they remain infected with the delusional virus of national sovereignty. Internationalism is a step in the right direction. An international police force will prevent many minor wars, but it will not be effective in preventing major wars, conflicts between the great military governments of earth.

As the number of truly sovereign nations (great powers) decreases, so do both opportunity and need for mankind government increase. When there are only a few really sovereign (great) powers, either they must embark on the life and death struggle for national (imperial) supremacy, or else, by voluntary surrender of certain prerogatives of sovereignty, they must create the essential nucleus of supernational power which will serve as the beginning of the real sovereignty of all mankind.

Peace will not come to Earth until every so-called sovereign nation surrenders its power to make war into the hands of a representative government of all mankind. Political sovereignty is innate with the peoples of the world. When all the peoples of Earth create a world government, they have the right and the power to make such a government SOVEREIGN; and when such a representative or democratic world power controls the world's land, air, and naval forces, peace on earth and good will among men can prevail; but not until then.

To use an important nineteenth- and twentieth-century illustration: The fifty states of the American Federal Union have long enjoyed peace. They have no more wars among themselves. They have surrendered their sovereignty to the federal government, and through the arbitrament of war, they have abandoned all claims to the delusions of self-determination. While each state regulates its internal affairs, it is not concerned with foreign relations, tariffs, immigration, military affairs, or interstate commerce. Neither do the individual states concern themselves with matters of citizenship. The fifty states suffer the ravages of war only when the federal government's sovereignty is in some way jeopardized.

These fifty states, having abandoned the twin sophistries of sovereignty and self-determination, enjoy interstate peace and tranquillity. So will the nations of Earth begin to enjoy peace when they freely surrender their respective sovereignties into the hands of a global government; the sovereignty of the brotherhood of men. In this world state the small nations will be as powerful as the great, even as the small state of Rhode Island has its two senators in the American Congress just the same as the populous state of California or the large state of Alaska.

The limited (state) sovereignty of these fifty states was created by men and for men. The superstate (national) sovereignty of the American Federal Union was created by the original thirteen of these states for their own benefit and for the benefit of their citizens. Sometime the supernational sovereignty of the planetary government of mankind will be similarly created by nations for their own benefit and for the benefit of all humanity.

Citizens are not born for the benefit of governments; governments are organizations created and devised for the benefit of men and women. There can be no end to the evolution of political sovereignty short of the appearance of the government of the sovereignty of all men. All other sovereignties are relative in value, intermediate in meaning, and subordinate in status.

With scientific progress, wars are going to become more and more devastating until they become almost racially suicidal. How many world wars must be fought and how many leagues of nations must fail before men will be willing to establish the government of mankind and begin to enjoy the blessings of permanent peace and thrive on the tranquillity of good will - world-wide good will - among men?

On the subjects of law, liberty, and sovereignty, Jesus taught those assembled: If one man craves freedom - liberty - he must remember that *all* others long for the same freedom. Groups of such liberty-loving mortals cannot live together in peace without becoming subservient to such laws, rules, and regulations as will grant each person the same degree of freedom while at the same time safeguarding an equal degree of freedom for all of his fellow mortals. If one man is to be absolutely free, then another must become an absolute slave. And the relative nature of freedom is true socially, economically, and politically. Freedom is the gift of civilization made possible by the enforcement of LAW.

Religion makes it spiritually possible to realize the brotherhood of men, but it will require mankind government to regulate the social, economic, and political problems associated with such a goal of human happiness and efficiency.

There shall be wars and rumors of wars; nation will rise against nation, just as long as the world's political sovereignty is divided up and unjustly held by a group of nation-states. England, Scotland, and Wales were always fighting each other until they gave up their respective sovereignties, reposing them in the United Kingdom.

Global wars will go on until the government of mankind is created. Global sovereignty will prevent global wars; nothing else can.

The fifty American free states live together in peace. There are among the citizens of these states all of the various nationalities and races that live in the near-continuously-warring nations of Europe. These Americans represent almost all the religions and religious sects and cults of the whole wide world, and yet here in North America they live together in peace. And all this is made possible because these fifty states have surrendered their sovereignty and have abandoned all notions of the supposed rights of self-determination.

It is not a question of armaments or disarmament. Neither does the question of conscription or voluntary military service enter into these problems of maintaining worldwide peace. If you take every form of modern mechanical armaments and all types of explosives away from strong nations, they will fight with fists, stones, and clubs as long as they cling to their delusions of the divine right of national sovereignty.

War is not man's great and terrible disease; war is a symptom, a result. The real disease is the virus of national sovereignty.

Earth nations have not possessed real sovereignty; they never have had a sovereignty that could protect them from the ravages and devastations of world wars. In the creation of the global government of mankind, the nations are not giving up sovereignty so much as they are actually creating a real, bona fide, and lasting world sovereignty which will henceforth be fully able to protect them from all war. Local affairs will be handled by local governments; national affairs, by national governments; international affairs will be administered by global government.

World peace cannot be maintained by treaties, diplomacy, foreign policies, alliances, balances of power, or any other type of makeshift juggling with the sovereignties of nationalism. World law must come into being and must be enforced by world government; the sovereignty of all mankind.

The individual will enjoy far more liberty under world government. Today, the citizens of the great powers are taxed, regulated, and controlled almost oppressively, and much of this present interference with individual liberties will vanish when the national governments are willing to trustee their sovereignty as regards international affairs into the hands of global government.

Under global government the national groups will be afforded a real opportunity to realize and enjoy the personal liberties of genuine democracy. The fallacy of self-determination will be ended. With global regulation of money and trade will come the new era of worldwide peace. Soon may a global language evolve, and there will be at least some hope of sometime having a global religion; or religions with a global viewpoint.

Collective security will never afford peace until the collectivity includes all mankind.

The political sovereignty of representative mankind government will bring lasting peace on earth, and the spiritual brotherhood of man will forever insure good will among all men. And there is no other way whereby peace on earth and good will among men can be realized.

After the death of Cymboyton, his sons encountered great difficulties in maintaining a peaceful faculty. The repercussions of Jesus' teachings would have been much greater if the later Christian teachers who joined the Urmia faculty had exhibited more wisdom and exercised more tolerance.

Cymboyton's eldest son had appealed to Abner at Philadelphia for help, but Abner's choice of teachers was most unfortunate in that they turned out to be unyielding and uncompromising. These teachers sought to make their religion dominant over the other beliefs. They never suspected that the oft-referred-to lectures of the caravan conductor had been delivered by Jesus himself.

As confusion increased in the faculty, the three brothers withdrew their financial support, and after five years the school closed. Later it was reopened as a Mithraic temple and eventually burned down in connection with one of their orgiastic celebrations.

When Jesus returned from the journey to the Caspian Sea, he knew that his world travels were about finished. He made only one more trip outside of Palestine, and that was into Syria. After a brief visit to Capernaum, he went to Nazareth, stopping over a few days to visit. In the middle of April he left Nazareth for Tyre. From there he journeyed on north, tarrying for a few days at Sidon, but his destination was Antioch.

This, his thirty-first on Earth, is the year of Jesus' solitary wanderings through Palestine and Syria. Throughout this year of travel he was known by various names in different parts of the country: the carpenter of Nazareth, the boatbuilder of Capernaum, the scribe of Damascus, and the teacher of Alexandria.

At Antioch the Son of Man lived for over two months, working, observing, studying, visiting, ministering, and all the while learning how man lives, how he thinks, feels, and reacts to the environment of human existence. For three weeks of this period he worked as a tentmaker. He remained longer in Antioch than at any other place he visited on this trip. Ten years later, when the Apostle Paul was preaching in Antioch and heard his followers speak of the doctrines of the *Damascus scribe,* he little knew that his pupils had heard the voice, and listened to the teachings, of the Master himself.

From Antioch Jesus journeyed south along the coast to Caesarea, where he tarried for a few weeks, continuing down the coast to Joppa. From Joppa he traveled inland to Jamnia, Ashdod, and Gaza. From Gaza he took the inland trail to Beersheba, where he remained for a week.

Jesus then started on his final tour, as a private individual, through the heart of Palestine, going from Beersheba in the south to Dan in the north. On this journey northward he stopped at Hebron, Bethlehem (where he saw his birthplace), Jerusalem (he did not visit Bethany), Beeroth, Lebonah, Sychar, Shechem, Samaria, Geba, En-Gannim, Endor, Madon; passing through Magdala and Capernaum, he journeyed on north; and passing east of the Waters of Merom, he went by Karahta to Dan, or Caesarea Philippi.

The indwelling Father Fragment now led Jesus to forsake the dwelling places of men and betake himself up to Mount Hermon that he might finish his work of mastering his human mind and complete the task of effecting his full consecration to the remainder of his lifework on earth.

This was one of those unusual and extraordinary epochs in the Master's life on Earth. Another and very similar one was the experience he passed through when alone in the hills near Pella just subsequent to his baptism. This period of isolation on Mount Hermon marked the termination of his purely human career, that is, the technical termination of the mortal bestowal, while the later isolation marked the beginning of the more divine phase of the bestowal. And Jesus lived alone with God for six weeks on the slopes of Mount Hermon.

After spending some time in the vicinity of Caesarea Philippi, Jesus made ready his supplies, and securing a beast of burden and a lad named Tiglath, he proceeded along the Damascus road to a village sometime known as Beit Jenn in the foothills of Mount Hermon. Here, near the middle of August, A.D. 25, he established his headquarters, and leaving his supplies in the custody of Tiglath, he ascended the lonely slopes of the mountain. Tiglath accompanied Jesus this first day up the mountain to a designated point about 6,000 feet above sea level, where they built a stone container in which Tiglath was to deposit food twice a week.

The first day, after he had left Tiglath, Jesus had ascended the mountain only a short way when he paused to pray. Among other things he asked his Father to send back the guardian seraphim to "be with Tiglath." He requested that he be permitted to go up to his last struggle with the realities of mortal existence alone. And his request was granted. He went into the great test with only his indwelling Father Fragment to guide and sustain him.

Jesus ate frugally while on the mountain; he abstained from all food only a day or two at a time. The superhuman beings who confronted him on this mountain, and with whom he wrestled in spirit, and whom he defeated in power, were *real;* they were his archenemies in the system of Satania, the rebels who had sown discord on this confused world. They were not phantasms of the imagination evolved out of the intellectual vagaries of a weakened and starving mortal who could not distinguish reality from the visions of a disordered mind.

Jesus spent the last three weeks of August and the first three weeks of September on Mount Hermon. During these weeks he finished the mortal task of achieving the circles of mind-understanding and personality-control. Throughout this period of communion with his heavenly Father the indwelling Mystery Monitor also completed the assigned services. The mortal goal of this earth creature was there attained. Only the final phase of mind and Monitor attunement remained to be consummated.

After more than five weeks of unbroken communion with his Paradise Father, Jesus became absolutely assured of his nature and of the certainty of his triumph over the material levels of time-space personality manifestation. He fully believed in, and did not hesitate to assert, the ascendancy of his divine nature over his human nature.

Near the end of the mountain sojourn Jesus asked his Father if he might be permitted to hold conference with his Satania enemies as the Son of Man, as Joshua ben Joseph. This request was granted. During the last week on Mount Hermon the great temptation, the universe trial, occurred. Satan (representing Lucifer) and the rebellious Planetary Prince, Caligastia, were present with Jesus and were made fully visible to him. And this "temptation," this final trial of human loyalty in the face of the misrepresentations of rebel personalities, had not to do with food, temple pinnacles, or presumptuous acts. It had not to do with the kingdoms of this world but with the sovereignty of a mighty and glorious universe. The symbolism of your records was intended for the backward ages of the world's childlike thought. And subsequent generations should understand what a great struggle the Son of Man passed through that eventful day on Mount Hermon.

To the many proposals and counterproposals of the emissaries of Lucifer, Jesus only made reply: "May the will of my Paradise Father prevail, and you, my rebellious son, may the Ancients of Days judge you divinely. I am your Creator-father; I can hardly judge you justly, and my mercy you have already spurned. I commit you to the adjudication of the Judges of a greater universe."

To all the Lucifer-suggested compromises and makeshifts, to all such specious proposals about the incarnation bestowal, Jesus only made reply, "The will of my Father in Paradise be done." And when the trying ordeal was finished, the detached guardian seraphim returned to Jesus' side and ministered to him.

On an afternoon in late summer, amid the trees and in the silence of nature, our Creator Son, Michael won the unquestioned sovereignty of his universe. On that day he completed the task set for Creator Sons to live to the full the incarnated life in the likeness of mortal flesh on the evolutionary worlds of time and space. The universe announcement of this momentous achievement was not made until the day of his baptism, months afterward, but it all really took place that day on the mountain. And when Jesus came down from his sojourn on Mount Hermon, the Lucifer rebellion in Satania and the secession on Earth by your Planetary Prince, Caligastia were virtually settled. Jesus had paid the last price required of him to attain the sovereignty of his universe, which in itself regulates the status of all rebels and determines that all such future upheavals (if they ever occur) may be dealt with summarily and effectively. Accordingly, it may be seen that the so-called "great temptation" of Jesus took place sometime before his baptism and not just after that event.

At the end of this sojourn on the mountain, as Jesus was making his descent, he met Tiglath coming up to the rendezvous with food. Turning him back, he said, "The period of rest is over; I must return to my Father's business." He was a silent and much changed man as they journeyed back to Dan, where he took leave of the lad, giving him the donkey. He then proceeded south by the same way he had come, to Capernaum.

It was now near the end of the summer, about the time of the Day of Atonement and the Feast of Tabernacles. Jesus had a family meeting in Capernaum over the Sabbath and the next day started for Jerusalem with John the son of Zebedee, going to the east of the lake and by Gerasa and on down the Jordan valley. While he visited some with his companion on the way, John noted a great change in Jesus.

Jesus and John stopped overnight at Bethany with Lazarus and his sisters, going early the next morning to Jerusalem. They spent almost three weeks in and around the city, at least John did. Many days John went into Jerusalem alone while Jesus walked about over the near-by hills and engaged in many seasons of spiritual communion with his Father in heaven.

Both of them were present at the solemn services of the Day of Atonement. John was much impressed by the ceremonies of this day of all days in the Jewish religious ritual, but Jesus remained a thoughtful and silent spectator. To the Son of Man this performance was pitiful and pathetic. He viewed it all as misrepresentative of the character and attributes of his Father in heaven. He looked upon the doings of this day as a travesty upon the facts of divine justice and the truths of infinite mercy. He burned to give vent to the declaration of the real truth about his Father's loving character and merciful conduct in the universe, but his faithful Monitor admonished him that his hour had not yet come. But that night, at Bethany, Jesus did drop numerous remarks which greatly disturbed John; and John never fully understood the real significance of what Jesus said in their hearing that evening.

Jesus planned to remain throughout the week of the Feast of Tabernacles with John. This feast was the annual holiday of all Palestine; it was the Jewish vacation time. Although Jesus did not participate in the merriment of the occasion, it was evident that he derived pleasure and experienced satisfaction as he beheld the lighthearted and joyous abandon of the young and the old.

In the midst of the week of celebration and ere the festivities were finished, Jesus took leave of John, saying that he desired to retire to the hills where he might the better commune with his Paradise Father. John would have gone with him, but Jesus insisted that he stay through the festivities, saying, "It is not required of you to bear the burden of the Son of Man; only the watchman must keep vigil while the city sleeps in peace." Jesus did not return to Jerusalem. After almost a week alone in the hills near Bethany, he departed for Capernaum. On the way home he spent a day and a night alone on the slopes of Gilboa, near where King Saul had taken his life; and when he arrived at Capernaum, he seemed more cheerful than when he had left John in Jerusalem.

The next morning Jesus went to the chest containing his personal effects, which had remained in Zebedee's workshop, put on his apron, and presented himself for work, saying, "It behooves me to keep busy while I wait for my hour to come." And he worked several months, until January of the following year, in the boatshop, by the side of his brother James. After this period of working with Jesus, no matter what doubts came up to becloud James's understanding of the lifework of the Son of Man, he never again really and wholly gave up his faith in the mission of Jesus.

During this final period of Jesus' work at the boatshop, he spent most of his time on the interior finishing of some of the larger craft. He took great pains with all his handiwork and seemed to experience the satisfaction of human achievement when he had completed a commendable piece of work. Though he wasted little time upon trifles, he was a painstaking workman when it came to the essentials of any given undertaking.

As time passed, rumors came to Capernaum of one John who was preaching while baptizing penitents in the Jordan, and John preached: "The kingdom of heaven is at hand; repent and be baptized." Jesus listened to these reports as John slowly worked his way up the Jordan valley from the ford of the river nearest to Jerusalem. But Jesus worked on, making boats, until John had journeyed up the river to a point near Pella in the month of January of the next year, A.D. 26, when he laid down his tools, declaring, "My hour has come," and presently presented himself to John for baptism.

But a great change had been coming over Jesus. Few of the people who had enjoyed his visits and ministrations as he had gone up and down in the land ever subsequently recognized in the public teacher the same person they had known and loved as a private individual in former years. And there was a reason for this failure of his early beneficiaries to recognize him in his later role of public and authoritative teacher. For long years this transformation of mind and spirit had been in progress, and it was finished during the eventful sojourn on Mount Hermon.

JOHN THE BAPTIST

JOHN THE Baptist was born March 25, 7 B.C., in accordance with the promise that Gabriel made to Elizabeth in June of the previous year. For five months Elizabeth kept secret Gabriel's visitation; and when she told her husband, Zacharias, he was greatly troubled and fully believed her narrative only after he had an unusual dream about six weeks before the birth of John. Excepting the visit of Gabriel to Elizabeth and the dream of Zacharias, there was nothing unusual or supernatural connected with the birth of John the Baptist.

On the eighth day John was circumcised according to the Jewish custom. He grew up as an ordinary child, day by day and year by year, in the small village known in those days as the City of Judah, about four miles west of Jerusalem.

The most eventful occurrence in John's early childhood was the visit, in company with his parents, to Jesus and the Nazareth family. This visit occurred in the month of June, 1 B.C., when he was a little over six years of age.

After their return from Nazareth John's parents began the systematic education of the lad. There was no synagogue school in this little village; however, as he was a priest, Zacharias was fairly well educated, and Elizabeth was far better educated than the average Judean woman; she was also of the priesthood, being a descendant of the "daughters of Aaron." Since John was an only child, they spent a great deal of time on his mental and spiritual training. Zacharias had only short periods of service at the temple in Jerusalem so that he devoted much of his time to teaching his son.

Zacharias and Elizabeth had a small farm on which they raised sheep. They hardly made a living on this land, but Zacharias received a regular allowance from the temple funds dedicated to the priesthood.

John had no school from which to graduate at the age of fourteen, but his parents had selected this as the appropriate year for him to take the formal Nazarite vow.

Accordingly, Zacharias and Elizabeth took their son to Engedi, down by the Dead Sea. This was the southern headquarters of the Nazarite brotherhood, and there the lad was duly and solemnly inducted into this order for life. After these ceremonies and the making of the vows to abstain from all intoxicating drinks, to let the hair grow, and to refrain from touching the dead, the family proceeded to Jerusalem, where, before the temple, John completed the making of the offerings which were required of those taking Nazarite vows.

John took the same life vows that had been administered to his illustrious predecessors, Samson and the prophet Samuel. A life Nazarite was looked upon as a sanctified and holy personality. The Jews regarded a Nazarite with almost the respect and veneration accorded the high priest, and this was not strange since Nazarites of lifelong consecration were the only persons, except high priests, who were ever permitted to enter the holy of holies in the temple.

John returned home from Jerusalem to tend his father's sheep and grew up to be a strong man with a noble character.

When sixteen years old, John, as a result of reading about Elijah, became greatly impressed with the prophet of Mount Carmel and decided to adopt his style of dress. From that day on John always wore a hairy garment with a leather girdle. At sixteen he was more than six feet tall and almost full-grown. With his flowing hair and peculiar mode of dress he was indeed a picturesque youth. And his parents expected great things of this their only son, a child of promise and a Nazarite for life.

After an illness of several months Zacharias died in July, A.D. 12, when John was just past eighteen years of age. This was a time of great embarrassment to John since the Nazarite vow forbade contact with the dead, even in one's own family. Although John had endeavored to comply with the restrictions of his vow regarding contamination by the dead, he doubted that he had been wholly obedient to the requirements of the Nazarite order; therefore, after his father's burial he went to Jerusalem, where, in the Nazarite corner of the women's court, he offered the sacrifices required for his cleansing.

In September of this year Elizabeth and John made a journey to Nazareth to visit Mary and Jesus. John had just about made up his mind to launch out in his lifework, but he was admonished, not only by Jesus' words but also by his example, to return home, take care of his mother, and await the "coming of the Father's hour." After bidding Jesus and Mary good-bye at the end of this enjoyable visit, John did not again see Jesus until the event of his baptism in the Jordan.

John and Elizabeth returned to their home and began to lay plans for the future. Since John refused to accept the priest's allowance due him from the temple funds, by the end of two years they had all but lost their home; so they decided to go south with the sheep herd. Accordingly, the summer that John was twenty years of age witnessed their removal to Hebron. In the so-called "wilderness of Judea" John tended his sheep along a brook that was tributary to a larger stream that entered the Dead Sea at Engedi. The Engedi colony included not only Nazarites of lifelong and time-period consecration but also numerous other ascetic herdsmen who congregated in this region with their herds and fraternized with the Nazarite brotherhood. They supported themselves by sheep raising and from gifts that wealthy Jews made to the order.

As time passed, John returned less often to Hebron, while he made more frequent visits to Engedi. He was so entirely different from the majority of the Nazarites that he found it very difficult fully to fraternize with the brotherhood. But he was very fond of Abner, the acknowledged leader and head of the Engedi colony.

Along the valley of this little brook John built no less than a dozen stone shelters and night corrals, consisting of piled-up stones, wherein he could watch over and safeguard his herds of sheep and goats. John's life as a shepherd afforded him a great deal of time for thought. He talked much with Ezda, an orphan lad of Beth-zur, whom he had in a way adopted, and who cared for the herds when he made trips to Hebron to see his mother and to sell sheep, as well as when he went down to Engedi for Sabbath services. John and the lad lived very simply, subsisting on mutton, goat's milk, wild honey, and the edible locusts of that region. Provisions brought from Hebron and Engedi from time to time supplemented this, their regular diet.

Elizabeth kept John posted about Palestinian and world affairs, and his conviction grew deeper and deeper that the time was fast approaching when the old order was to end; that he was to become the herald of the approach of a new age, "the kingdom of heaven." This rugged shepherd was very partial to the writings of the Prophet Daniel. He read a thousand times Daniel's description of the great image, which Zacharias had told him represented the history of the great kingdoms of the world, beginning with Babylon, then Persia, Greece, and finally Rome. John perceived that already was Rome composed of such polyglot peoples and races that it could never become a strongly cemented and firmly consolidated empire. He believed that Rome was even then divided, as Syria, Egypt, Palestine, and other provinces; and then he further read "in the days of these kings shall the God of heaven set up a kingdom which shall never be destroyed. And this kingdom shall not be left to other people but shall break in pieces and consume all these kingdoms, and it shall stand forever." "And there was given him dominion and glory and a kingdom that all peoples, nations, and languages should serve him. His dominion is an everlasting dominion, which shall not pass away, and his kingdom never shall be destroyed." "And the kingdom and dominion and the greatness of the kingdom under the whole heaven shall be given to the people of the saints of the Most High, whose kingdom is an everlasting kingdom, and all dominions shall serve and obey him."

John was never able completely to rise above the confusion produced by what he had heard from his parents concerning Jesus and by these passages which he read in the Scriptures. In Daniel he read: "I saw in the night visions, and, behold, one like the Son of Man came with the clouds of heaven, and there was given him dominion and glory and a kingdom." But these words of the prophet did not harmonize with what his parents had taught him. Neither did his talk with Jesus, at the time of his visit when he was eighteen years old, correspond with these statements of the Scriptures. Notwithstanding this confusion, throughout all of his perplexity his mother assured him that his distant cousin, Jesus of Nazareth, was the true Messiah, that he had come to sit on the throne of David, and that he (John) was to become his advance herald and chief support.

From all John heard of the vice and wickedness of Rome and the dissoluteness and moral barrenness of the empire, from what he knew of the evil doings of Herod Antipas and the governors of Judea, he was minded to believe that the end of the age was impending. It seemed to this rugged and noble child of nature that the world was ripe for the end of the age of man and the dawn of the new and divine age, the kingdom of heaven. The feeling grew in John's heart that he was to be the last of the old prophets and the first of the new. And he fairly vibrated with the mounting impulse to go forth and proclaim to all: "Repent! Get right with God! Get ready for the end; prepare yourselves for the appearance of the new and eternal order of earth affairs, the kingdom of heaven."

On August 17, A.D. 22, when John was twenty-eight years of age, his mother suddenly passed away. Elizabeth's friends, knowing of the Nazarite restrictions regarding contact with the dead, even in one's own family, made all arrangements for the burial of Elizabeth before sending for John. When he received word of the death of his mother, he directed Ezda to drive his herds to Engedi and started for Hebron.

On returning to Engedi from his mother's funeral, he presented his flocks to the brotherhood and for a season detached himself from the outside world while he fasted and prayed. John knew only of the old methods of approach to divinity; he knew only of the records of such as Elijah, Samuel, and Daniel. Elijah was his ideal of a prophet. Elijah was the first of the teachers of Israel to be regarded as a prophet, and John truly believed that he was to be the last of this long and illustrious line of the messengers of heaven.

For two and a half years John lived at Engedi, and he persuaded most of the brotherhood that "the end of the age was at hand"; that "the kingdom of heaven was about to appear." And all his early teaching was based upon the current Jewish idea and concept of the Messiah as the promised deliverer of the Jewish nation from the domination of their gentile rulers.

Throughout this period John read much in the sacred writings which he found at the Engedi home of the Nazarites. He was especially impressed by Isaiah and by Malachi, the last of the prophets up to that time. He read and reread the last five chapters of Isaiah, and he believed these prophecies. Then he would read in Malachi: "Behold, I will send you Elijah the prophet before the coming of the great and dreadful day of the Lord; and he shall turn the hearts of the fathers toward the children and the hearts of the children toward their fathers, lest I come and smite the earth with a curse." And it was only this promise of Malachi that Elijah would return that deterred John from going forth to preach about the coming kingdom and to exhort his fellow Jews to flee from the wrath to come. John was ripe for the proclamation of the message of the coming kingdom, but this expectation of the coming of Elijah held him back for more than two years. He knew he was not Elijah. What did Malachi mean? Was the prophecy literal or figurative? How could he know the truth? He finally dared to think that, since the first of the prophets was called Elijah, so the last should be known, eventually, by the same name. Nevertheless, he had doubts, doubts sufficient to prevent his ever calling himself Elijah.

It was the influence of Elijah that caused John to adopt his methods of direct and blunt assault upon the sins and vices of his contemporaries. He sought to dress like Elijah, and he endeavored to talk like Elijah; in every outward aspect he was like the olden prophet. He was just such a stalwart and picturesque child of nature, just such a fearless and daring preacher of righteousness. John was not illiterate, he did well know the Jewish sacred writings, but he was hardly cultured. He was a clear thinker, a powerful speaker, and a fiery denunciator. He was hardly an example to his age, but he was an eloquent rebuke.

At last he thought out the method of proclaiming the new age, the kingdom of God; he settled that he was to become the herald of the Messiah; he swept aside all doubts and departed from Engedi one day in March of A.D. 25 to begin his short but brilliant career as a public preacher.

In order to understand John's message, account should be taken of the status of the Jewish people at the time he appeared upon the stage of action. For almost one hundred years all Israel had been in a quandary; they were at a loss to explain their continuous subjugation to gentile overlords. Had not Moses taught that righteousness was always rewarded with prosperity and power? Were they not God's chosen people? Why was the throne of David desolate and vacant? In the light of the Mosaic doctrines and the precepts of the prophets the Jews found it difficult to explain their long-continued national desolation.

About one hundred years before the days of Jesus and John a new school of religious teachers arose in Palestine, the apocalyptists. These new teachers evolved a system of belief that accounted for the sufferings and humiliation of the Jews on the ground that they were paying the penalty for the nation's sins. They fell back onto the well-known reasons assigned to explain the Babylonian and other captivities of former times. But, so taught the apocalyptists, Israel should take heart; the days of their affliction were almost over; the discipline of God's chosen people was about finished; God's patience with the gentile foreigners was about exhausted. The end of Roman rule was synonymous with the end of the age and, in a certain sense, with the end of the world. These new teachers leaned heavily on the predictions of Daniel, and they consistently taught that creation was about to pass into its final stage; the kingdoms of this world were about to become the king- dom of God. To the Jewish mind of that day this was the meaning of that phrase - the kingdom of heaven - which runs throughout the teachings of both John and Jesus. To the Jews of Palestine the phrase "kingdom of heaven" had but one mean- ing: an absolutely righteous state in which God (the Messiah) would rule the na- tions of earth in perfection of power just as he ruled in heaven - "Your will be done on earth as in heaven."

In the days of John all Jews were expectantly asking, "How soon will the king- dom come?" There was a general feeling that the end of the rule of the gentile na- tions was drawing near. There was present throughout all Jewry a lively hope and a keen expectation that the consummation of the desire of the ages would occur during the lifetime of that generation.

While the Jews differed greatly in their estimates of the nature of the coming kingdom, they were alike in their belief that the event was impending, near at hand, even at the door. Many who read the Old Testament literally looked expect- antly for a new king in Palestine, for a regenerated Jewish nation delivered from its enemies and presided over by the successor of King David, the Messiah who would quickly be acknowledged as the rightful and righteous ruler of all the world.

Another, though smaller, group of devout Jews held a vastly different view of this kingdom of God. They taught that the coming kingdom was not of this world, that the world was approaching its certain end, and that "a new heaven and a new earth" were to usher in the establishment of the kingdom of God; that this king- dom was to be an everlasting dominion, that sin was to be ended, and that the citi- zens of the new kingdom were to become immortal in their enjoyment of this end- less bliss.

All were agreed that some drastic purging or purifying discipline would of ne- cessity precede the establishment of the new kingdom on earth. The literalists taught that a world-wide war would ensue which would destroy all unbelievers, while the faithful would sweep on to universal and eternal victory. The spiritists taught that the kingdom would be ushered in by the great judgment of God which would relegate the unrighteous to their well-deserved judgment of punishment and final destruction, at the same time elevating the believing saints of the chosen people to high seats of honor and authority with the Son of Man, who would rule over the redeemed nations in God's name. And this latter group even believed that many devout gentiles might be admitted to the fellowship of the new kingdom.

Some of the Jews held to the opinion that God might possibly establish this new kingdom by direct and divine intervention, but the vast majority believed that he would interpose some representative intermediary, the Messiah. And that was the only possible meaning the term Messiah could have had in the minds of the Jews of the generation of John and Jesus. *Messiah* could not possibly refer to one who merely taught God's will or proclaimed the necessity for righteous living. To all such holy persons the Jews gave the title of *prophet.* The Messiah was to be more than a prophet; the Messiah was to bring in the establishment of the new kingdom, the kingdom of God. No one who failed to do this could be the Messiah in the traditional Jewish sense.

Who would this Messiah be? Again the Jewish teachers differed. The older ones clung to the doctrine of the son of David. The newer taught that, since the new kingdom was a heavenly kingdom, the new ruler might also be a divine personality, one who had long sat at God's right hand in heaven. And strange as it may appear, those who thus conceived of the ruler of the new kingdom looked upon him not as a human Messiah, not as a mere *man,* but as "the Son of Man" - a Son of God - a heavenly Prince, long held in waiting thus to assume the rulership of the earth made new. Such was the religious background of the Jewish world when John went forth proclaiming: "Repent, for the kingdom of heaven is at hand!"

It becomes apparent, therefore, that John's announcement of the coming kingdom had not less than half a dozen different meanings in the minds of those who listened to his impassioned preaching. But no matter what significance they attached to the phrases which John employed, each of these various groups of Jewish-kingdom expectants was intrigued by the proclamations of this sincere, enthusiastic, rough-and-ready preacher of righteousness and repentance, who so solemnly exhorted his hearers to "flee from the wrath to come."

Early in the month of March, A.D. 25, John journeyed around the western coast of the Dead Sea and up the river Jordan to opposite Jericho, the ancient ford over which Joshua and the children of Israel passed when they first entered the promised land; and crossing over to the other side of the river, he established himself near the entrance to the ford and began to preach to the people who passed by on their way back and forth across the river. This was the most frequented of all the Jordan crossings.

It was apparent to all who heard John that he was more than a preacher. The great majority of those who listened to this strange man who had come up from the Judean wilderness went away believing that they had heard the voice of a prophet. No wonder the souls of these weary and expectant Jews were deeply stirred by such a phenomenon. Never in all Jewish history had the devout children of Abraham so longed for the "consolation of Israel" or more ardently anticipated "the restoration of the kingdom." Never in all Jewish history could John's message, "the kingdom of heaven is at hand," have made such a deep and universal appeal as at the very time he so mysteriously appeared on the bank of this southern crossing of the Jordan.

He came from the herdsmen, like Amos. He was dressed like Elijah of old, and he thundered his admonitions and poured forth his warnings in the "spirit and power of Elijah." It is not surprising that this strange preacher created a mighty stir throughout all Palestine as the travelers carried abroad the news of his preaching along the Jordan.

There was still another and a *new* feature about the work of this Nazarite preacher; he baptized every one of his believers in the Jordan "for the remission of sins." Although baptism was not a new ceremony among the Jews, they had never seen it employed as John now made use of it. It had long been the practice thus to baptize the gentile proselytes into the fellowship of the outer court of the temple, but never had the Jews themselves been asked to submit to the baptism of repentance. Only fifteen months intervened between the time John began to preach and baptize and his arrest and imprisonment at the instigation of Herod Antipas, but in this short time he baptized considerably over one hundred thousand penitents.

John preached four months at Bethany ford before starting north up the Jordan. Tens of thousands of listeners, some curious but many earnest and serious, came to hear him from all parts of Judea, Perea, and Samaria. Even a few came from Galilee.

In May of this year, while he still lingered at Bethany ford, the priests and Levites sent a delegation out to inquire of John whether he claimed to be the Messiah, and by whose authority he preached.

John answered these questioners by saying, "Go tell your masters that you have heard `the voice of one crying in the wilderness,' as spoken by the prophet, saying, `make ready the way of the Lord, make straight a highway for our God. Every valley shall be filled, and every mountain and hill shall be brought low; the uneven ground shall become a plain, while the rough places shall become a smooth valley; and all flesh shall see the salvation of God.'"

John was a heroic but tactless preacher. One day when he was preaching and baptizing on the west bank of the Jordan, a group of Pharisees and a number of Sadducees came forward and presented themselves for baptism. Before leading them down into the water, John, addressing them as a group said, "Who warned you to flee, as vipers before the fire, from the wrath to come? I will baptize you, but I warn you to bring forth fruit worthy of sincere repentance if you would receive the remission of your sins. Tell me not that Abraham is your father. I declare that

God is able of these twelve stones here before you to raise up worthy children for Abraham. And even now is the ax laid to the very roots of the trees. Every tree that brings not forth good fruit is destined to be cut down and cast into the fire." (The twelve stones to which he referred were the reputed memorial stones set up by Joshua to commemorate the crossing of the "twelve tribes" at this very point when they first entered the promised land.)

John conducted classes for his disciples, in the course of which he instructed them in the details of their new life and endeavored to answer their many questions. He counseled the teachers to instruct in the spirit as well as the letter of the law. He instructed the rich to feed the poor; to the tax gatherers he said, "Extort no more than that which is assigned you." To the soldiers he said, "Do no violence and exact nothing wrongfully. Be content with your wages." While he counseled all, "Make ready for the end of the age. The kingdom of heaven is at hand."

John still had confused ideas about the coming kingdom and its king. The longer he preached the more confused he became, but never did this intellectual uncertainty concerning the nature of the coming kingdom in the least lessen his conviction of the certainty of the kingdom's immediate appearance. In mind John might be confused, but in spirit never. He was in no doubt about the coming kingdom, but he was far from certain as to whether or not Jesus was to be the ruler of that kingdom. As long as John held to the idea of the restoration of the throne of David, the teachings of his parents that Jesus, born in the City of David, was to be the long-expected deliverer, seemed consistent; but at those times when he leaned more toward the doctrine of a spiritual kingdom and the end of the temporal age on earth, he was sorely in doubt as to the part Jesus would play in such events. Sometimes he questioned everything, but not for long. He really wished he might talk it all over with his cousin, but that was contrary to their expressed agreement.

As John journeyed north, he thought much about Jesus. He paused at more than a dozen places as he traveled up the Jordan. It was at Adam that he first made reference to "another one who is to come after me" in answer to the direct question which his disciples asked him, "Are you the Messiah?" And he went on to say, "There will come after me one who is greater than I, whose sandal straps I am not worthy to stoop down and unloose. I baptize you with water, but he will baptize you with the Holy Spirit. And his shovel is in his hand thoroughly to cleanse his threshing floor; he will gather the wheat into his garner, but the chaff will he burn up with the judgment fire."

In response to the questions of his disciples John continued to expand his teachings, from day to day adding more that was helpful and comforting compared with his early and cryptic message: "Repent and be baptized." By this time throngs were arriving from Galilee and the Decapolis. Scores of earnest believers lingered with their adored teacher day after day.

✮ ✮ ✮

By December of A.D. 25, when John reached the neighborhood of Pella in his journey up the Jordan, his fame had extended throughout all Palestine, and his work had become the chief topic of conversation in all the towns about the lake of Galilee. Jesus had spoken favorably of John's message, and this had caused many from Capernaum to join John's cult of repentance and baptism. James and John the fishermen sons of Zebedee had gone down in December, soon after the Baptist took up his preaching position near Pella, and had offered themselves for baptism. They went to see John once a week and brought back to Jesus fresh, firsthand reports of the evangelist's work.

Jesus' brothers James and Jude had talked about going down to John for baptism; and now that Jude had come over to Capernaum for the Sabbath services, both he and James, after listening to Jesus' discourse in the synagogue, decided to take counsel with him concerning their plans. This was on Saturday night, January 12, A.D. 26. Jesus requested that they postpone the discussion until the following day, when he would give them his answer. He slept very little that night, being in close communion with the Father in heaven. He had arranged to have noontime lunch with his brothers and to advise them concerning baptism by John. That Sunday morning Jesus was working as usual in the boatshop. James and Jude had arrived with the lunch and were waiting in the lumber room for him, as it was not yet time for the midday recess, and they knew that Jesus was very regular about such matters.

· Just before the noon rest, Jesus laid down his tools, removed his work apron, and merely announced to the three workmen in the room with him, "My hour has come." He went out to his brothers James and Jude, repeating, "My hour has come; let us go to John." And they started immediately for Pella, eating their lunch as they journeyed. This was on Sunday, January 13. They tarried for the night in the Jordan valley and arrived on the scene of John's baptizing about noon of the next day.

John had just begun baptizing the candidates for the day. Scores of repentants were standing in line awaiting their turn when Jesus and his two brothers took up their positions in this queue of earnest men and women who had become believers in John's preaching of the coming kingdom. John had been inquiring of Zebedee's sons about Jesus. He had heard of Jesus' remarks concerning his preaching, and he was day by day expecting to see him arrive on the scene, but he had not expected to greet him in the line of baptismal candidates.

Being engrossed with the details of rapidly baptizing such a large number of converts, John did not look up to see Jesus until the Son of Man stood in his immediate presence. When John recognized Jesus, the ceremonies were halted for a moment while he greeted his cousin in the flesh and asked, "But why do you come down into the water to greet me?"

And Jesus answered, "To be subject to your baptism."

John replied, "But I have need to be baptized by you. Why do you come to me?"

And Jesus whispered to John, "Bear with me now, for it becomes us to set this example for my brothers standing here with me, and that the people may know that my hour has come."

There was a tone of finality and authority in Jesus' voice. John was atremble with emotion as he made ready to baptize Jesus of Nazareth in the Jordan at noon on Monday, January 14, A.D. 26. Thus did John baptize Jesus and his two brothers James and Jude. And when John had baptized these three, he dismissed the others for the day, announcing that he would resume baptisms at noon the next day. As the people were departing, the four men still standing in the water heard a strange sound, and presently there appeared for a moment an apparition immediately over the head of Jesus, and they heard a voice saying, "This is my beloved Son in whom I am well pleased."

A great change came over the countenance of Jesus, and coming up out of the water in silence he took leave of them, going toward the hills to the east. And no man saw Jesus again for forty days.

John followed Jesus a sufficient distance to tell him the story of Gabriel's visit to his mother ere either had been born, as he had heard it so many times from his mother's lips. He allowed Jesus to continue on his way after he had said, "Now I know of a certainty that you are the Deliverer." But Jesus made no reply.

When John returned to his disciples (he now had some twenty-five or thirty who abode with him constantly), he found them in earnest conference, discussing what had just happened in connection with Jesus' baptism. They were all the more astonished when John now made known to them the story of the Gabriel visitation to Mary before Jesus was born, and also that Jesus spoke no word to him even after he had told him about this. There was no rain that evening, and this group of thirty or more talked long into the starlit night. They wondered where Jesus had gone, and when they would see him again.

After the experience of this day the preaching of John took on new and certain notes of proclamation concerning the coming kingdom and the expected Messiah. It was a tense time, these forty days of tarrying, waiting for the return of Jesus. But John continued to preach with great power, and his disciples began at about this time to preach to the overflowing throngs that gathered around John at the Jordan.

In the course of these forty days of waiting, many rumors spread about the countryside and even to Tiberias and Jerusalem. Thousands came over to see the new attraction in John's camp, the reputed Messiah, but Jesus was not to be seen.

When the disciples of John asserted that the strange man of God had gone to the hills, many doubted the entire story.

About three weeks after Jesus had left them, there arrived on the scene at Pella a new deputation from the priests and Pharisees at Jerusalem. They asked John directly if he was Elijah or the prophet that Moses promised; and when John said, "I am not," they made bold to ask, "Are you the Messiah?" and John answered, "I am not."

Then said these men from Jerusalem, "If you are not Elijah, nor the prophet, nor the Messiah, then why do you baptize the people and create all this stir?"

And John replied, "It should be for those who have heard me and received my baptism to say who I am, but I declare to you that, while I baptize with water, there has been among us one who will return to baptize you with the Holy Spirit."

These forty days were a difficult period for John and his disciples. What was to be the relation of John to Jesus? A hundred questions came up for discussion. Politics and selfish preferment began to make their appearance. Intense discussions grew up around the various ideas and concepts of the Messiah. Would he become a military leader and a Davidic king? Would he smite the Roman armies as Joshua had the Canaanites? Or would he come to establish a spiritual kingdom? John rather decided, with the minority, that Jesus had come to establish the kingdom of heaven, although he was not altogether clear in his own mind as to just what was to be embraced within this mission of the establishment of the kingdom of heaven.

These were strenuous days in John's experience, and he prayed for the return of Jesus. Some of John's disciples organized scouting parties to go in search of Jesus, but John forbade, saying, "Our times are in the hands of the God of heaven; He will direct His chosen Son."

It was early on the morning of Sabbath, February 23, that the company of John, engaged in eating their morning meal, looked up toward the north and beheld Jesus coming to them. As he approached them, John stood upon a large rock and, lifting up his sonorous voice, said, "Behold the Son of God, the deliverer of the world! This is he of whom I have said, `After me there will come one who is preferred before me because he was before me.' For this cause came I out of the wilderness to preach repentance and to baptize with water, proclaiming that the kingdom of heaven is at hand. And now comes one who shall baptize you with the Holy Spirit. And I beheld the divine spirit descending upon this man, and I heard the voice of God declare, `This is my beloved Son in whom I am well pleased.'"

Jesus bade them return to their food while he sat down to eat with John, his brothers James and Jude having returned to Capernaum.

Early in the morning of the next day he took leave of John and his disciples, going back to Galilee. He gave them no word as to when they would again see him. To John's inquiries about his own preaching and mission Jesus only said, "My Father will guide you now and in the future as He has in the past." And these two great men separated that morning on the banks of the Jordan, never again to greet each other in the flesh.

Since Jesus had gone north into Galilee, John felt led to retrace his steps southward. Accordingly, on Sunday morning, March 3, John and the remainder of his disciples began their journey south. About one quarter of John's immediate followers had meantime departed for Galilee in quest of Jesus. There was a sadness of confusion about John. He never again preached as he had before baptizing Jesus. He somehow felt that the responsibility of the coming kingdom was no longer on his shoulders. He felt that his work was almost finished; he was disconsolate and lonely. But he preached, baptized, and journeyed on southward.

Near the village of Adam, John tarried for several weeks, and it was here that he made the memorable attack upon Herod Antipas for unlawfully taking the wife of another man. By June of this year (A.D. 26) John was back at the Bethany ford of the Jordan, where he had begun his preaching of the coming kingdom more than a year previously. In the weeks following the baptism of Jesus the character of John's preaching gradually changed into a proclamation of mercy for the common people, while he denounced with renewed vehemence the corrupt political and religious rulers.

Herod Antipas, in whose territory John had been preaching, became alarmed lest he and his disciples should start a rebellion. Herod also resented John's public criticisms of his domestic affairs. In view of all this, Herod decided to put John in prison. Accordingly, very early in the morning of June 12, before the multitude arrived to hear the preaching and witness the baptizing, the agents of Herod placed John under arrest. As weeks passed and he was not released, his disciples scattered over all Palestine, many of them going into Galilee to join the followers of Jesus.

John had a lonely and somewhat bitter experience in prison. Few of his followers were permitted to see him. He longed to see Jesus but had to be content with hearing of his work through those of his followers who had become believers in the Son of Man. He was often tempted to doubt Jesus and his divine mission. If Jesus were the Messiah, why did he do nothing to deliver him from this unbearable imprisonment? For more than a year and a half this rugged man of God's outdoors languished in that despicable prison. And this experience was a great test of his faith in, and loyalty to, Jesus. Indeed, this whole experience was a great test of John's faith even in God. Many times was he tempted to doubt even the genuineness of his own mission and experience.

After he had been in prison several months, a group of his disciples came to him and, after reporting concerning the public activities of Jesus, said, "So you see, Teacher, that he who was with you at the upper Jordan prospers and receives all who come to him. He even feasts with publicans and sinners. You bore courageous witness to him, and yet he does nothing to effect your deliverance."

But John answered his friends, "This man can do nothing unless it has been given him by his Father in heaven. You well remember that I said, `I am not the Messiah, but I am one sent on before to prepare the way for him.' And that I did. He who has the bride is the bridegroom, but the friend of the bridegroom who stands near by and hears him rejoices greatly because of the bridegroom's voice. This, my joy, therefore is fulfilled. He must increase but I must decrease. I am of this earth and have declared my message. Jesus of Nazareth comes down to the earth from heaven and is above us all. The Son of Man has descended from God, and the words of God he will declare to you. For the Father in heaven gives not the spirit by measure to His own Son. The Father loves His Son and will presently put all things in the hands of this Son. He who believes in the Son has eternal life. And these words which I speak are true and abiding."

These disciples were amazed at John's pronouncement, so much so that they departed in silence. John was also much agitated, for he perceived that he had uttered a prophecy. Never again did he wholly doubt the mission and divinity of Jesus. But it was a sore disappointment to John that Jesus sent him no word, that he came not to see him, and that he exercised none of his great power to deliver him from prison. But Jesus knew all about this. He had great love for John, but being now cognizant of his divine nature and knowing fully the great things in preparation for John when he departed from this world and also knowing that John's work on earth was finished, he constrained himself not to interfere in the natural outworking of the great preacher-prophet's career.

This long suspense in prison was humanly unbearable. Just a few days before his death John again sent trusted messengers to Jesus, inquiring: "Is my work done? Why do I languish in prison? Are you truly the Messiah, or shall we look for another?"

And when these two disciples gave this message to Jesus, the Son of Man replied, "Go back to John and tell him that I have not forgotten but to suffer me also this, for it becomes us to fulfill all righteousness. Tell John what you have seen and heard; that the poor have good tidings preached to them, and, finally, tell the beloved herald of my earth mission that he shall be abundantly blessed in the age to come if he finds no occasion to doubt and stumble over me."

And this was the last word John received from Jesus. This message greatly comforted him and did much to stabilize his faith and prepare him for the tragic end of his life in the flesh which followed so soon upon the heels of this memorable occasion.

☆ ☆ ☆

As John was working in southern Perea when arrested, he was taken immediately to the prison of the fortress of Machaerus, where he was incarcerated until his execution. Herod ruled over Perea as well as Galilee, and he maintained residence at this time at both Julias and Machaerus in Perea. In Galilee the official residence had been moved from Sepphoris to the new capital at Tiberias.

Herod feared to release John lest he instigate rebellion. He feared to put him to death lest the multitude riot in the capital, for thousands of Pereans believed that John was a holy man, a prophet. Therefore Herod kept the Nazarite preacher in prison, not knowing what else to do with him. Several times John had been before Herod, but never would he agree either to leave the domains of Herod or to refrain from all public activities if he were released. And this new agitation concerning Jesus of Nazareth, which was steadily increasing, admonished Herod that it was no time to turn John loose. Besides, John was also a victim of the intense and bitter hatred of Herodias, Herod's unlawful wife.

On numerous occasions Herod talked with John about the kingdom of heaven, and while sometimes seriously impressed with his message, he was afraid to release him from prison.

Since much building was still going on at Tiberias, Herod spent considerable time at his Perean residences, and he was partial to the fortress of Machaerus. It was a matter of several years before all the public buildings and the official residence at Tiberias were fully completed.

In celebration of his birthday Herod made a great feast in the Machaerian palace for his chief officers and other men high in the councils of the government of Galilee and Perea. Since Herodias had failed to bring about John's death by direct appeal to Herod, she now set herself to the task of having John put to death by cunning planning.

In the course of the evening's festivities and entertainment, Herodias presented her daughter to dance before the banqueters. Herod was very much pleased with the damsel's performance and, calling her before him, said, "You are charming. I am much pleased with you. Ask me on this my birthday for whatever you desire, and I will give it to you, even to the half of my kingdom." And Herod did all this while well under the influence of his many wines.

The young lady drew aside and inquired of her mother what she should ask of Herod.

Herodias said, "Go to Herod and ask for the head of John the Baptist."

And the young woman, returning to the banquet table, said to Herod, "I request that you forthwith give me the head of John the Baptist on a platter."

Herod was filled with fear and sorrow, but because of his oath and because of all those who sat at meat with him, he would not deny the request. And Herod

Antipas sent a soldier, commanding him to bring the head of John. So was John that night beheaded in the prison, the soldier bringing the head of the prophet on a platter and presenting it to the young woman at the rear of the banquet hall. And the damsel gave the platter to her mother.

When John's disciples heard of this, they came to the prison for the body of John, and after laying it in a tomb, they went and told Jesus.

Baptism and the Forty Days

JESUS BEGAN his public work at the height of the popular interest in John's preaching and at a time when the Jewish people of Palestine were eagerly looking for the appearance of the Messiah. There was a great contrast between John and Jesus. John was an eager and earnest worker, but Jesus was a calm and happy laborer; only a few times in his entire life was he ever in a hurry. Jesus was a comforting consolation to the world and somewhat of an example; John was hardly a comfort or an example. He preached the kingdom of heaven but hardly entered into the happiness thereof. Though Jesus spoke of John as the greatest of the prophets of the old order, he also said that the least of those who saw the great light of the new way and entered thereby into the kingdom of heaven was indeed greater than John.

When John preached the coming kingdom, the burden of his message was, Repent! Flee from the wrath to come. When Jesus began to preach, there remained the exhortation to repentance, but such a message was always followed by the gospel, the good tidings of the joy and liberty of the new kingdom.

The Jews entertained many ideas about the expected deliverer, and each of these different schools of Messianic teaching was able to point to statements in the Hebrew scriptures as proof of their contentions. In a general way, the Jews regarded their national history as beginning with Abraham and culminating in the Messiah and the new age of the kingdom of God. In earlier times they had envisaged this deliverer as "the servant of the Lord," then as "the Son of Man," while latterly some even went so far as to refer to the Messiah as the "Son of God." But no matter whether he was called the "seed of Abraham" or "the son of David," all were agreed that he was to be the Messiah, the "anointed one." Thus did the concept evolve from the "servant of the Lord" to the "son of David," "Son of Man," and "Son of God."

In the days of John and Jesus the more learned Jews had developed an idea of the coming Messiah as the perfected and representative Israelite, combining in himself as the "servant of the Lord" the threefold office of prophet, priest, and king.

The Jews devoutly believed that, as Moses had delivered their fathers from Egyptian bondage by miraculous wonders, so would the coming Messiah deliver the Jewish people from Roman domination by even greater miracles of power and marvels of racial triumph. The rabbis had gathered together almost five hundred passages from the Scriptures which, notwithstanding their apparent contradictions, they averred were prophetic of the coming Messiah. And amidst all these details of time, technique, and function, they almost completely lost sight of the *personality* of the promised Messiah. They were looking for a restoration of Jewish national glory; Israel's temporal exaltation, rather than for the salvation of the world. It therefore becomes evident that Jesus of Nazareth could never satisfy this materialistic Messianic concept of the Jewish mind. Many of their reputed Messianic predictions, had they but viewed these prophetic utterances in a different light, would have very naturally prepared their minds for a recognition of Jesus as the terminator of one age and the inaugurator of a new and better dispensation of mercy and salvation for all nations.

The Jews had been brought up to believe in the doctrine of the *Shekinah*. But this reputed symbol of the Divine Presence was not to be seen in the temple. They believed that the coming of the Messiah would effect its restoration. They held confusing ideas about racial sin and the supposed evil nature of man. Some taught that Adam's sin had cursed the human race, and that the Messiah would remove this curse and restore man to divine favor. Others taught that God, in creating man, had put into his being both good and evil natures; that when He observed the outworking of this arrangement, He was greatly disappointed, and that "He repented that He had thus made man." And those who taught this believed that the Messiah was to come in order to redeem man from this inherent evil nature.

The majority of the Jews believed that they continued to languish under Roman rule because of their national sins and because of the halfhearted faith of the gentile proselytes. The Jewish nation had not wholeheartedly *repented;* therefore did the Messiah delay his coming. There was much talk about repentance; wherefore the mighty and immediate appeal of John's preaching, "Repent and be baptized, for the kingdom of heaven is at hand." And the kingdom of heaven could mean only one thing to any devout Jew: The coming of the Messiah.

There was one feature of the bestowal of Michael which was utterly foreign to the Jewish conception of the Messiah, and that was the *union* of the two natures, the human and the divine. The Jews had variously conceived of the Messiah as perfected human, superhuman, and even as divine, but they never entertained the concept of the *union* of the human and the divine. And this was the great stumbling block of Jesus' early disciples. They grasped the human concept of the Messiah as the son of David, as presented by the earlier prophets; as the Son of Man, the superhuman idea of Daniel and some of the later prophets; and even as the Son of God, as depicted by the author of the Book of Enoch and by certain of his contemporaries; but never had they for a single moment entertained the true concept of the union in one earth personality of the two natures, the human and the divine. The incarnation of the Creator in the form of the creature had not been revealed beforehand. It was revealed only in Jesus; your world knew nothing of such things until the Creator Son was made flesh and dwelt among the mortals of the realm.

Jesus was baptized at the very height of John's preaching when Palestine was aflame with the expectancy of his message; "the kingdom of God is at hand," when all Jewry was engaged in serious and solemn self-examination. The Jewish sense of racial solidarity was very profound. The Jews not only believed that the sins of the father might afflict his children, but they firmly believed that the sin of one individual might curse the nation. Accordingly, not all who submitted to John's baptism regarded themselves as being guilty of the specific sins which John denounced. Many devout souls were baptized by John for the good of Israel. They feared for some sin of ignorance on their part that might delay the coming of the Messiah. They felt themselves to belong to a guilty and sin-cursed nation, and they presented themselves for baptism that they might by so doing manifest fruits of race penitence. It is therefore evident that Jesus in no sense received John's baptism as a rite of repentance or for the remission of sins. In accepting baptism at the hands of John, Jesus was only following the example of many pious Israelites.

When Jesus of Nazareth went down into the Jordan to be baptized, he was a mortal of the realm who had attained the pinnacle of human evolutionary ascension in all matters related to the conquest of mind and to self-identification with the spirit. He stood in the Jordan that day a perfected mortal of the evolutionary worlds of time and space. Perfect synchrony and full communication had become established between the mortal mind of Jesus and the indwelling spirit Adjuster, the divine gift of his Father in Paradise. And just such an Adjuster indwells all normal beings living on Earth, as well as the other evolutionary worlds of his realm, since the ascension of Michael to the headship of his universe, except that Jesus' Adjuster had been previously prepared for this special mission by similarly indwelling another superhuman incarnated in the likeness of mortal flesh, Machiventa Melchizedek.

Ordinarily, when a mortal of the realm attains such high levels of personality perfection, there occur those preliminary phenomena of spiritual elevation which terminate in eventual fusion of the matured soul of the mortal with its associated divine Adjuster. And such a change was apparently due to take place in the personality experience of Jesus of Nazareth on that very day when he went down into the Jordan with his two brothers to be baptized by John. This ceremony was the final act of his purely human life on Earth, and many superhuman observers expected to witness the fusion of the Adjuster with its indwelt mind, but they were all destined to suffer disappointment. Something new and even greater occurred. As John laid his hands upon Jesus to baptize him, the indwelling Adjuster took final leave of the perfected human soul of Joshua ben Joseph. And in a few moments this divine entity returned from Divinington as a Personalized Adjuster and chief of his kind throughout the entire local universe of Michael's domain. Thus did Jesus observe his own former divine spirit descending on its return to him in personalized form. And he heard this same spirit of Paradise origin now speak, saying, "This is my beloved Son in whom I am well pleased."

And John, with Jesus' two brothers, also heard these words. John's disciples, standing by the water's edge, did not hear these words, neither did they see the apparition of the Personalized Adjuster. Only the eyes of Jesus beheld the Personalized Adjuster.

When the returned and now exalted Personalized Adjuster had thus spoken, all was silence. And while the four of them tarried in the water, Jesus, looking up to the near-by Adjuster, prayed, "My Father who reigns in heaven, hallowed be your name. Your kingdom come! Your will be done on earth, even as it is in heaven." When he had prayed, the "heavens were opened," and the Son of Man saw the vision, presented by the now Personalized Adjuster, of himself as a Son of God as he was before he came to earth in the likeness of mortal flesh, and as he would be when the incarnated life should be finished. Only Jesus saw this heavenly vision.

It was the voice of the Personalized Adjuster that John and Jesus heard, speaking in behalf of the Universal Father, for the Adjuster is of, and as, the Paradise Father. Throughout the remainder of Jesus' earth life this Personalized Adjuster was associated with him in all his labors; Jesus was in constant communion with this exalted Mystery Monitor.

When Jesus was baptized, he repented of no misdeeds; he made no confession of sin. His was the baptism of consecration to the performance of the will of the heavenly Father. At his baptism he heard the unmistakable call of his Father, the final summons to be about his Father's business, and he went away into private seclusion for forty days to think over these manifold problems. In thus retiring for a season from active personality contact with his earthly associates, Jesus, as he was and on Earth, was following the very procedure that obtains on the higher worlds whenever an ascending mortal fuses with the inner presence of the Universal Father.

This day of baptism ended the purely human life of Jesus. The divine Son has found his Father, the Universal Father has found His incarnated Son, and they speak the one to the other.

(Jesus was almost thirty-one and one-half years old when he was baptized. While Luke says that Jesus was baptized in the fifteenth year of the reign of Tiberius Caesar, which would be A.D. 29 since Augustus died in A.D. 14, it should be recalled that Tiberius was co-emperor with Augustus for two and one-half years before the death of Augustus, having had coins struck in his honor in October, A.D. 11. The fifteenth year of his actual rule was, therefore, this very year of A.D. 26, that of Jesus' baptism. And this was also the year that Pontius Pilate began his rule as governor of Judea.)

Jesus had endured the great temptation of his mortal bestowal before his baptism when he had been wet with the dews of Mount Hermon for six weeks. There on Mount Hermon, as an unaided mortal of the realm, he had met and defeated Caligastia, the Earth pretender, the fallen prince of this world, the betrayer of a sworn and sacred trust. That eventful day, on the universe records, Jesus of Nazareth had become the Planetary Prince of Earth. And this Prince of Earth, so soon to be proclaimed supreme Sovereign of his local creation, now went into forty days of retirement to formulate the plans and determine upon the technique of proclaiming the new kingdom of God in the hearts of men.

After his baptism he entered upon the forty days of adjusting himself to the changed relationships of the world and the universe occasioned by the personalization of his Father Fragment. During this isolation in the Perean hills he determined upon the policy to be pursued and the methods to be employed in the new and changed phase of earth life which he was about to inaugurate.

Jesus did not go into retirement for the purpose of fasting and for the affliction of his soul. He was not an ascetic, and he came forever to destroy all such notions regarding these misguided approaches to God. His reasons for seeking this retirement were entirely different from those that had actuated Moses and Elijah, and even John the Baptist. Jesus was then wholly self-conscious concerning his relation to the universe of his making and also to the universe of universes, supervised by the Paradise Father, his Father in heaven. He now fully recalled the bestowal charge and its instructions administered by his elder brother, Immanuel, ere he entered upon his Earth incarnation. He now clearly and fully comprehended all these far-flung relationships, and he desired to be away for a season of quiet meditation so that he could think out the plans and decide upon the procedures for the prosecution of his public labors in behalf of this world and for all other worlds in his local universe, for his other children not of this flock.

While wandering about in the hills, seeking a suitable shelter, Jesus encountered his universe chief executive, Gabriel, the Bright and Morning Star of

Michael's local creation. Gabriel now re-established personal communication with the Creator Son of the universe; they met directly for the first time since Michael took leave of his associates on Salvington when he went to Edentia preparatory to entering upon the Earth bestowal. Gabriel, by direction of Immanuel and on authority of the Ancients of Days, now laid before Jesus information indicating that his bestowal experience on Earth was practically finished so far as concerned the earning of the perfected sovereignty of his universe and the termination of the Lucifer rebellion. The former was achieved on the day of his baptism when the personalization of his Adjuster demonstrated the perfection and completion of his bestowal in the likeness of mortal flesh, and the latter was a fact of history on that day when he came down from Mount Hermon to join the waiting lad, Tiglath. Jesus was now informed, upon the highest authority of the local universe and the superuniverse, that his bestowal work was finished in so far as it affected his personal status in relation to sovereignty and rebellion. He had already had this assurance direct from Paradise in the baptismal vision and in the phenomenon of the personalization of his indwelling Mystery Monitor.

While he tarried on the mountain, talking with Gabriel, the Constellation Father of Edentia appeared to Jesus and Gabriel in person, saying: "The records are completed. The sovereignty of Michael number 611,121 over his universe of Nebadon rests in completion at the right hand of the Universal Father. I bring to you the bestowal release of Immanuel, your sponsor-brother for the Earth incarnation. You are at liberty now or at any subsequent time, in the manner of your own choosing, to terminate your incarnation bestowal, ascend to the right hand of your Father, receive your sovereignty, and assume your well-earned unconditional rulership of all Nebadon. I also testify to the completion of the records of the superuniverse, by authorization of the Ancients of Days, having to do with the termination of all sin-rebellion in your universe and endowing you with full and unlimited authority to deal with any and all such possible upheavals in the future. Technically, your work on Earth and in the flesh of the mortal creature is finished. Your course from now on is a matter of your own choosing."

When the Most High Father of Edentia had taken leave, Jesus held long converse with Gabriel regarding the welfare of the universe and, sending greetings to Immanuel, proffered his assurance that, in the work which he was about to undertake on Earth, he would be ever mindful of the counsel he had received in connection with the pre-bestowal charge administered on Salvington.

Throughout all of these forty days of isolation James and John the sons of Zebedee were engaged in searching for Jesus. Many times they were not far from his abiding place, but never did they find him.

Day by day, up in the hills, Jesus formulated the plans for the remainder of his Earth bestowal. He first decided not to teach contemporaneously with John. He planned to remain in comparative retirement until the work of John achieved its purpose, or until John was suddenly stopped by imprisonment. Jesus well knew that John's fearless and tactless preaching would presently arouse the fears and enmity of the civil rulers. In view of John's precarious situation, Jesus began definitely to plan his program of public labors in behalf of his people and the world, in behalf of every inhabited world throughout his vast universe. Michael's mortal bestowal was *on* Earth but *for* all worlds of Nebadon. He has sheep, "not of this flock."

The first thing Jesus did, after thinking through the general plan of coordinating his program with John's movement, was to review in his mind the instructions of Immanuel. Carefully he thought over the advice given him concerning his methods of labor, and that he was to leave no permanent writing on the planet. Never again did Jesus write on anything except sand. On his next visit to Nazareth, much to the sorrow of his brother Joseph, Jesus destroyed all of his writing that was preserved on the boards about the carpenter shop, and which hung upon the walls of the old home. And Jesus pondered well over Immanuel's advice pertaining to his economic, social, and political attitude toward the world as he should find it.

Jesus did not fast during this forty days' isolation. The longest period he went without food was his first two days in the hills when he was so engrossed with his thinking that he forgot all about eating. But on the third day he went in search of sustenance. Neither was he *tempted* during this time by any evil spirits or rebel personalities of station on this world or from any other world.

These forty days were the occasion of the final conference between the human and the divine minds, or rather the first real functioning of these two minds as now made one. The results of this momentous season of meditation demonstrated conclusively that the divine mind has triumphantly and spiritually dominated the human intellect. The mind of man has become the mind of God from this time on, and though the selfhood of the mind of man is ever present, always does this spiritualized human mind say, "Not my will but yours be done."

The transactions of this eventful time were not the fantastic visions of a starved and weakened mind, neither were they the confused and puerile symbolisms which afterward gained record as the "temptations of Jesus in the wilderness." Rather was this a season for thinking over the whole eventful and varied career of the Earth bestowal and for the careful laying of those plans for further ministry which would best serve this world while also contributing something to the betterment of all other rebellion-isolated spheres. Lucifer's rebellion had affected not only Earth, but other evolutionary world's entrusted to his care as well. Jesus thought over the whole span of human life on Earth, from the days of the first couple, Andon and Fonta, down through Adam's default, and on to the ministry of the Melchizedek of Salem.

Gabriel had reminded Jesus that there were two ways in which he might manifest himself to the world in case he should choose to tarry on Earth for a time.

And it was made clear to Jesus that his choice in this matter would have nothing to do with either his universe sovereignty or the termination of the Lucifer rebellion. These two ways of world ministry were:

1.   His own way — the way that might seem most pleasant and profitable from the standpoint of the immediate needs of this world and the present edification of his own universe.

2.   The Father's way — the exemplification of a farseeing ideal of creature life visualized by the high personalities of the Paradise administration of the universe of universes.

It was thus made clear to Jesus that there were two ways in which he could order the remainder of his earth life. Each of these ways had something to be said in its favor as it might be regarded in the light of the immediate situation. The Son of Man clearly saw that his choice between these two modes of conduct would have nothing to do with his reception of universe sovereignty; that was a matter already settled and sealed on the records of the universe of universes and only awaited his demand in person. But it was indicated to Jesus that it would afford his Paradise brother, Immanuel, great satisfaction if he, Jesus, should see fit to finish up his earth career of incarnation as he had so nobly begun it, always subject to the Father's will. On the third day of this isolation Jesus promised himself he would go back to the world to finish his earth career, and that in a situation involving any two ways he would always choose the Father's will. And he lived out the remainder of his earth life always true to that resolve. Even to the bitter end he invariably subordinated his sovereign will to that of his heavenly Father.

The forty days in the mountain wilderness were not a period of great temptation but rather the period of the Master's *great decisions.* During these days of lone communion with himself and his Father's immediate presence; the Personalized Adjuster (he no longer had a personal seraphic guardian), he arrived, one by one, at the great decisions which were to control his policies and conduct for the remainder of his earth career. Subsequently the tradition of a great temptation became attached to this period of isolation through confusion with the fragmentary narratives of the Mount Hermon struggles, and further because it was the custom to have all great prophets and human leaders begin their public careers by undergoing these supposed seasons of fasting and prayer. It had always been Jesus' practice, when facing any new or serious decisions, to withdraw for communion with his own spirit that he might seek to know the will of God.

In all this planning for the remainder of his earth life, Jesus was always torn in his human heart by two opposing courses of conduct :

1. He entertained a strong desire to win his people (and the whole world) to believe in him and to accept his new spiritual kingdom. And he well knew their ideas concerning the coming Messiah.

2. To live and work as he knew his Father would approve, to conduct his work in behalf of other worlds in need, and to continue, in the establishment of the kingdom, to reveal the Father and show forth his divine character of love.

Throughout these eventful days Jesus lived in an ancient rock cavern, a shelter in the side of the hills near a village sometime called Beit Adis. He drank from the small spring that came from the side of the hill near this rock shelter.

On the third day after beginning this conference with himself and his Personalized Adjuster, Jesus was presented with the vision of the assembled celestial hosts of Nebadon sent by their commanders to wait upon the will of their beloved Sovereign. This mighty host embraced twelve legions of seraphim and proportionate numbers of every order of universe intelligence. And the first great decision of Jesus' isolation had to do with whether or not he would make use of these mighty personalities in connection with the ensuing program of his public work on Earth.

Jesus decided that he would *not* utilize a single personality of this vast assemblage unless it should become evident that this was his *Father's will*. Notwithstanding this general decision, this vast host remained with him throughout the balance of his earth life, always in readiness to obey the least expression of their Sovereign's will. Although Jesus did not constantly behold these attendant personalities with his human eyes, his associated Personalized Adjuster did constantly behold, and could communicate with, all of them.

Before coming down from the forty days' retreat in the hills, Jesus assigned the immediate command of this attendant host of universe personalities to his recently Personalized Adjuster, and for more than four years of Earth time did these selected personalities from every division of universe intelligences obediently and respectfully function under the wise guidance of this exalted and experienced Personalized Mystery Monitor. In assuming command of this mighty assembly, the Adjuster, being a onetime part and essence of the Paradise Father, assured Jesus that in no case would these superhuman agencies be permitted to serve, or manifest themselves in connection with, or in behalf of, his earth career unless it should develop that the Father willed such intervention. Thus by one great decision Jesus voluntarily deprived himself of all superhuman co-operation in all matters having to do with the remainder of his mortal career unless the Father might independently choose to participate in some certain act or episode of the Son's earth labors.

In accepting this command of the universe hosts in attendance upon Christ Michael, the Personalized Adjuster took great pains to point out to Jesus that, while such an assembly of universe creatures could be limited in their *space* activities by the delegated authority of their Creator, such limitations were not operative in connection with their function in *time*. And this limitation was dependent on the fact that Adjusters are non-time beings when once they are personalized. Accordingly was Jesus admonished that, while the Adjuster's control of the living intelligences placed under his command would be complete and perfect as to all matters involving *space,* there could be no such perfect limitations imposed regarding *time.* Said the Adjuster, "I will, as you have directed, enjoin the employment of this attendant host of universe intelligences in any manner in connection with your earth career except in those cases where the Paradise Father directs me to release such agencies in order that His divine will of your choosing may be accomplished, and in those instances where you may engage in any choice or act of your divine-human will which shall only involve departures from the natural earth order as to *time*. In all such events I am powerless, and your creatures here assembled in perfection and unity of power are likewise helpless. If your united natures once entertain such desires, these mandates of your choice will be forthwith executed. Your wish in all such matters will constitute the abridgment of time, and the thing projected *is* existent. Under my command this constitutes the fullest possible limitation which can be imposed upon your potential sovereignty. In my self-consciousness time is nonexistent, and therefore I cannot limit your creatures in anything related thereto."

Thus did Jesus become apprised of the working out of his decision to go on living as a man among men. He had by a single decision excluded all of his attendant universe hosts of varied intelligences from participating in his ensuing public ministry except in such matters as concerned *time* only. It therefore becomes evident that any possible supernatural or supposedly superhuman accompaniments of Jesus' ministry pertained wholly to the elimination of time unless the Father in heaven specifically ruled otherwise. No miracle, ministry of mercy, or any other possible event occurring in connection with Jesus' remaining earth labors could possibly be of the nature or character of an act transcending the natural laws established and regularly working in the affairs of man as he lives on Earth *except* in this expressly stated matter of *time.* No limits, of course, could be placed upon the manifestations of "the Father's will." The elimination of time in connection with the expressed desire of this potential Sovereign of a universe could only be avoided by the direct and explicit act of the *will* of this God-man to the effect that time, as related to the act or event in question, *should not be shortened or eliminated.* In order to prevent the appearance of apparent *time miracles,* it was necessary for Jesus to remain constantly time conscious. Any lapse of time consciousness on his part, in connection with the entertainment of definite desire, was equivalent to the enactment of the thing conceived in the mind of this Creator Son, and without the intervention of time.

Through the supervising control of his associated and Personalized Adjuster it was possible for Michael perfectly to limit his personal earth activities with reference to space, but it was not possible for the Son of Man thus to limit his new earth status as potential Sovereign of Nebadon as regards *time*. And this was the actual status of Jesus of Nazareth as he went forth to begin his public ministry on Earth.

Having settled his policy concerning all personalities of all classes of his created intelligences, so far as this could be determined in view of the inherent potential of his new status of divinity, Jesus now turned his thoughts toward himself. What would he, now the fully self-conscious creator of all things and beings existent in this universe, do with these creator prerogatives in the recurring life situations which would immediately confront him when he returned to Galilee to resume his work among men? In fact, already, and right where he was in these lonely hills, had this problem forcibly presented itself in the matter of obtaining food. By the third day of his solitary meditations the human body grew hungry. Should he go in quest of food as any ordinary man would, or should he merely exercise his normal creative powers and produce suitable bodily nourishment ready at hand? And this great decision of the Master has been portrayed to you as a temptation, as a challenge by supposed enemies that he "command that these stones become loaves of bread."

Jesus thus settled upon another and consistent policy for the remainder of his earth labors. As far as his personal necessities were concerned, and in general even in his relations with other personalities, he now deliberately chose to pursue the path of normal earthly existence; he definitely decided against a policy which would transcend, violate, or outrage his own established natural laws. But he could not promise himself, as he had already been warned by his Personalized Adjuster, that these natural laws might not, in certain conceivable circumstances, be greatly *accelerated*. In principle, Jesus decided that his lifework should be organized and prosecuted in accordance with natural law and in harmony with the existing social organization. The Master thereby chose a program of living that was the equivalent of deciding against miracles and wonders. Again he decided in favor of "the Father's will"; again he surrendered everything into the hands of his Paradise Father.

Jesus' human nature dictated that the first duty was self-preservation; that is the normal attitude of the natural man on the worlds of time and space, and it is, therefore, a legitimate reaction of an Earth mortal. But Jesus was not concerned merely with this world and its creatures; he was living a life designed to instruct and inspire the manifold creatures of a far-flung universe.

Before his baptismal illumination he had lived in perfect submission to the will and guidance of his heavenly Father. He emphatically decided to continue on in just such implicit mortal dependence on the Father's will. He purposed to follow the unnatural course; he decided not to seek self-preservation. He chose to go on pursuing the policy of refusing to defend himself. He formulated his conclusions in the words of Scripture familiar to his human mind: "Man shall not live by bread alone but by every word that proceeds from the mouth of God." In reaching this conclusion in regard to the appetite of the physical nature as expressed in hunger for food, the Son of Man made his final declaration concerning all other urges of the flesh and the natural impulses of human nature.

His superhuman power he might possibly use for others, but for himself, never. And he pursued this policy consistently to the very end, when it was jeeringly said of him: "He saved others; himself he cannot save" - because he would not.

The Jews were expecting a Messiah who would do even greater wonders than Moses, who was reputed to have brought forth water from the rock in a desert place and to have fed their forefathers with manna in the wilderness. Jesus knew the sort of Messiah his compatriots expected, and he had all the powers and prerogatives to measure up to their most sanguine expectations, but he decided against such a magnificent program of power and glory. Jesus looked upon such a course of expected miracle working as a harking back to the olden days of ignorant magic and the degraded practices of the savage medicine men. Possibly, for the salvation of his creatures, he might accelerate natural law, but to transcend his own laws, either for the benefit of himself or the over awing of his fellow men, that he would not do. And the Master's decision was final.

Jesus sorrowed for his people; he fully understood how they had been led up to the expectation of the coming Messiah, the time when "the earth will yield its fruits ten thousandfold, and on one vine there will be a thousand branches, and each branch will produce a thousand clusters, and each cluster will produce a thousand grapes, and each grape will produce a gallon of wine." The Jews believed the Messiah would usher in an era of miraculous plenty. The Hebrews had long been nurtured on traditions of miracles and legends of wonders.

He was not a Messiah coming to multiply bread and wine. He came not to minister to temporal needs only; he came to reveal his Father in heaven to his children on earth, while he sought to lead his earth children to join him in a sincere effort so to live as to do the will of the Father in heaven.

In this decision Jesus of Nazareth portrayed to an onlooking universe the folly and sin of prostituting divine talents and God-given abilities for personal aggrandizement or for purely selfish gain and glorification. That was the sin of Lucifer and his minion, the fallen Planetary Prince, whom Jesus had so recently deposed.

This great decision of Jesus portrays dramatically the truth that selfish satisfaction and sensuous gratification, alone and of themselves, are not able to confer happiness upon evolving human beings. There are higher values in mortal existence - intellectual mastery and spiritual achievement - which far transcend the necessary gratification of man's purely physical appetites and urges. Man's natural endowment of talent and ability should be chiefly devoted to the development and ennoblement of his higher powers of mind and spirit.

Jesus thus revealed to the creatures of his universe the technique of the new and better way, the higher moral values of living and the deeper spiritual satisfactions of evolutionary human existence on the worlds of space.

Having made his decisions regarding such matters as food and physical ministration to the needs of his material body, the care of the health of himself and his associates, there remained yet other problems to solve. What would be his attitude when confronted by personal danger? He decided to exercise normal watchcare over his human safety and to take reasonable precaution to prevent the untimely termination of his career in the flesh but to refrain from all superhuman intervention when the crisis of his life in the flesh should come. As he was formulating this decision, Jesus was seated under the shade of a tree on an overhanging ledge of rock with a precipice right there before him. He fully realized that he could cast himself off the ledge and out into space, and that nothing could happen to harm him provided he would rescind his first great decision not to invoke the interposition of his celestial intelligences in the prosecution of his lifework on Earth, and provided he would abrogate his second decision concerning his attitude toward self-preservation.

Jesus knew his fellow countrymen were expecting a Messiah who would be above natural law. Well had he been taught that Scripture; "There shall no evil befall you, neither shall any plague come near your dwelling. For He shall give His angels charge over you, to keep you in all your ways. They shall bear you up in their hands lest you dash your foot against a stone." Would this sort of presumption, this defiance of his Father's laws of gravity, be justified in order to protect himself from possible harm or, perchance, to win the confidence of his mis-taught and distracted people? But such a course, however gratifying to the sign-seeking Jews, would be, not a revelation of his Father, but a questionable trifling with the established laws of the universe of universes.

Understanding all of this and knowing that the Master refused to work in defiance of his established laws of nature in so far as his personal conduct was concerned, you know of a certainty that he never walked on the water nor did anything else which was an outrage to his material order of administering the world; always, of course, bearing in mind that there had, as yet, been found no way whereby he could be wholly delivered from the lack of control over the element of time in connection with those matters put under the jurisdiction of the Personalized Adjuster.

Throughout his entire earth life Jesus was consistently loyal to this decision. No matter whether the Pharisees taunted him for a sign, or the watchers at Calvary dared him to come down from the cross, he steadfastly adhered to the decision of this hour on the hillside.

The next great problem with which this God-man wrestled and which he presently decided in accordance with the will of the Father in heaven, concerned the question as to whether or not any of his superhuman powers should be employed for the purpose of attracting the attention and winning the adherence of his fellow men. Should he in any manner lend his universe powers to the gratification of the Jewish hankering for the spectacular and the marvelous? He decided that he should not. He settled upon a policy of procedure that eliminated all such practices as the method of bringing his mission to the notice of men. And he consistently lived up to this great decision. Even when he permitted the manifestation of numerous time-shortening ministrations of mercy, he almost invariably admonished the recipients of his healing ministry to tell no man about the benefits they had received. And always did he refuse the taunting challenge of his enemies to "show us a sign" in proof and demonstration of his divinity.

Jesus very wisely foresaw that the working of miracles and the execution of wonders would call forth only outward allegiance by overawing the material mind; such performances would not reveal God nor save men. He refused to become a mere wonder-worker. He resolved to become occupied with but a single task, the establishment of the kingdom of heaven.

Throughout all this momentous dialogue of Jesus' communing with himself, there was present the human element of questioning and near-doubting, for Jesus was man as well as God. It was evident he would never be received by the Jews as the Messiah if he did not work wonders. Besides, if he would consent to do just one unnatural thing, the human mind would know of a certainty that it was in subservience to a truly divine mind. Would it be consistent with "the Father's will" for the divine mind to make this concession to the doubting nature of the human mind? Jesus decided that it would not and cited the presence of the Personalized Adjuster as sufficient proof of divinity in partnership with humanity.

Jesus had traveled much; he recalled Rome, Alexandria, and Damascus. He knew the methods of the world — how people gained their ends in politics and commerce by compromise and diplomacy. Would he utilize this knowledge in the furtherance of his mission on earth? He likewise decided against all compromise with the wisdom of the world and the influence of riches in the establishment of the kingdom. He again chose to depend exclusively on the Father's will.

Jesus was fully aware of the shortcuts open to one of his powers. He knew many ways in which the attention of the nation, and the whole world, could be immediately focused upon himself. Soon the Passover would be celebrated at Jerusalem; the city would be thronged with visitors. He could ascend the pinnacle of the temple and before the bewildered multitude walk out on the air; that would be the kind of a Messiah they were looking for. But he would subsequently disappoint them since he had not come to re-establish David's throne. And he knew the futility of the fallen former Prince of Earth's method of trying to get ahead of the natural, slow, and sure way of accomplishing the divine purpose. Again the Son of Man bowed obediently to the Father's way, the Father's will.

Jesus chose to establish the kingdom of heaven in the hearts of mankind by natural, ordinary, difficult, and trying methods, just such procedures as his earth children must subsequently follow in their work of enlarging and extending that heavenly kingdom. For well did the Son of Man know that it would be "through much tribulation that many of the children of all ages would enter into the kingdom." Jesus was now passing through the great test of civilized man, to have power and steadfastly refuse to use it for purely selfish or personal purposes.

In your consideration of the life and experience of the Son of Man, it should be ever borne in mind that the Son of God was incarnate in the mind of a first-century human being, not in the mind of a twentieth-century or other-century mortal. By this we mean to convey the idea that the human endowments of Jesus were of natural acquirement. He was the product of the hereditary and environmental factors of his time, plus the influence of his training and education. His humanity was genuine, natural, wholly derived from the antecedents of, and fostered by, the actual intellectual status and social and economic conditions of that day and generation. While in the experience of this God-man there was always the possibility that the divine mind would transcend the human intellect, nonetheless, when, and as, his human mind functioned, it did perform as would a true mortal mind under the conditions of the human environment of that day.

Jesus portrayed to all the worlds of his vast universe the folly of creating artificial situations for the purpose of exhibiting arbitrary authority or of indulging exceptional power for the purpose of enhancing moral values or accelerating spiritual progress. Jesus decided that he would not lend his mission on earth to a repetition of the disappointment of the reign of the Maccabees. He refused to prostitute his divine attributes for the purpose of acquiring unearned popularity or for gaining political prestige. He would not countenance the transmutation of divine and creative energy into national power or international prestige. Jesus of Nazareth refused to compromise with *evil*, much less to consort with sin. The Master triumphantly put loyalty to his Father's will above every other earthly and temporal consideration.

Having settled such questions of policy as pertained to his individual relations to natural law and spiritual power, he turned his attention to the choice of methods to be employed in the proclamation and establishment of the kingdom of God. John had already begun this work; how might Jesus continue the message? How should he take over John's mission? How should he organize his followers for effective effort and intelligent co-operation? Jesus was now reaching the final decision which would forbid that he further regard himself as the Jewish Messiah, at least as the Messiah was popularly conceived in that day.

The Jews envisaged a deliverer who would come in miraculous power to cast down Israel's enemies and establish the Jews as world rulers, free from want and oppression. Jesus knew that this hope would never be realized. He knew that the kingdom of heaven had to do with the overthrow of evil in the hearts of men, and that it was purely a matter of spiritual concern. He thought out the advisability of inaugurating the spiritual kingdom with a brilliant and dazzling display of power (and such a course would have been permissible and wholly within the jurisdiction of Michael), but he fully decided against such a plan. He would not compromise with the revolutionary techniques of Caligastia, the deposed Planetary Prince of Earth. He had won the world in potential by submission to the Father's will, and he proposed to finish his work as he had begun it, and as the Son of Man.

You can hardly imagine what would have happened on Earth had this God-man, now in potential possession of all power in heaven and on earth, once decided to unfurl the banner of sovereignty, to marshal his wonder-working battalions in militant array! But he would not compromise. He would not serve evil that the worship of God might presumably be derived therefrom. He would abide by the Father's will. He would proclaim to an onlooking universe, "You shall worship the Lord your God and Him only shall you serve."

As the days passed, with ever-increasing clearness Jesus perceived what kind of a truth-revealer he was to become. He discerned that God's way was not going to be the easy way. He began to realize that the cup of the remainder of his human experience might possibly be bitter, but he decided to drink it.

Even his human mind is saying good-bye to the throne of David. Step by step this human mind follows in the path of the divine. The human mind still asks questions but unfailingly accepts the divine answers as final rulings in this combined life of living as a man in the world while all the time submitting unqualifiedly to the doing of the Father's eternal and divine will.

Rome was mistress of the Western world. The Son of Man, now in isolation and achieving these momentous decisions, with the hosts of heaven at his command, represented the last chance of the Jews to attain world dominion; but this earthborn Jew, who possessed such tremendous wisdom and power, declined to use his universe endowments either for the aggrandizement of himself or for the enthronement of his people. He saw, as it were, "the kingdoms of this world," and he possessed the power to take them. The Most Highs of Edentia had resigned all these powers into his hands, but he did not want them. The kingdoms of earth were paltry things to interest the Creator and Ruler of a universe. He had only one objective, the further revelation of God to man, the establishment of the kingdom, the rule of the heavenly Father in the hearts of mankind.

The idea of battle, contention, and slaughter was repugnant to Jesus; he would have none of it. He would appear on earth as the Prince of Peace to reveal a God of love. Before his baptism he had again refused the offer of the Zealots to lead them in rebellion against the Roman oppressors. And now he made his final decision regarding those Scriptures that his mother had taught him, such as: "The Lord has said to me, `You are my Son; this day have I begotten you. Ask of me, and I will give you the heathen for your inheritance and the uttermost parts of the earth for your possession. You shall break them with a rod of iron; you shall dash them in pieces like a potter's vessel.'"

Jesus of Nazareth reached the conclusion that such utterances did not refer to him. At last, and finally, the human mind of the Son of Man made a clean sweep of all these Messianic difficulties and contradictions; Hebrew scriptures, parental training, chazan teaching, Jewish expectations, and human ambitious longings. Once and for all he decided upon his course. He would return to Galilee and quietly begin the proclamation of the kingdom and trust his Father (the Personalized Adjuster) to work out the details of procedure day by day.

By these decisions Jesus set a worthy example for every person on every world throughout a vast universe when he refused to apply material tests to prove spiritual problems, when he refused presumptuously to defy natural laws. And he set an inspiring example of universe loyalty and moral nobility when he refused to grasp temporal power as the prelude to spiritual glory.

If the Son of Man had any doubts about his mission and its nature when he went up in the hills after his baptism, he had none when he came back to his fellows following the forty days of isolation and decisions.

Jesus has formulated a program for the establishment of the Father's kingdom. He will not cater to the physical gratification of the people. He will not deal out bread to the multitudes as he has so recently seen it being done in Rome. He will not attract attention to himself by wonderworking, even though the Jews are expecting just that sort of a deliverer. Neither will he seek to win acceptance of a spiritual message by a show of political authority or temporal power.

In rejecting these methods of enhancing the coming kingdom in the eyes of the expectant Jews, Jesus made sure that these same Jews would certainly and finally reject all of his claims to authority and divinity. Knowing all this, Jesus long sought to prevent his early followers alluding to him as the Messiah.

Throughout his public ministry he was confronted with the necessity of dealing with three constantly recurring situations: the clamor to be fed, the insistence on miracles, and the final request that he allow his followers to make him king.

But Jesus never departed from the decisions that he made during these days of his isolation in the Perean hills.

On the last day of this memorable isolation, before starting down the mountain to join John and his disciples, the Son of Man made his final decision. And this decision he communicated to the Personalized Adjuster in these words, "And in all other matters, as in these now of decision-record, I pledge you I will be subject to the will of my Father."

And when he had thus spoken, he journeyed down the mountain. And his face shone with the glory of spiritual victory and moral achievement.

End Part One

Appendix A

Immanuel's Charge to Michael

"My Creator brother, I am about to witness your seventh and final universe bestowal. Most faithfully and perfectly have you executed the six previous commissions, and I entertain no thought but that you will be equally triumphant on this, your terminal sovereignty bestowal. Heretofore you have appeared on your bestowal spheres as a fully developed being of the order of your choosing. Now you are about to appear upon Earth, the disordered and disturbed planet of your choice, not as a fully developed mortal, but as a helpless babe. This, my comrade, will be a new and untried experience for you. You are about to pay the full price of bestowal and to experience the complete enlightenment of the incarnation of a Creator in the likeness of a creature.

"Throughout each of your former bestowals you have voluntarily chosen to subject yourself to the will of the three Paradise Deities and their divine interassociations. Of the seven phases of the will of the Supreme you have in your previous bestowals been subject to all but the personal will of your Paradise Father. Now that you have elected to be wholly subject to your Father's will throughout your seventh bestowal, I, as the personal representative of our Father, assume the unqualified jurisdiction of your universe for the time of your incarnation.

"In entering upon the Earth bestowal, you have voluntarily divested yourself of all extraplanetary support and special assistance such as might be rendered by any creature of your own creation. As your created sons of Nebadon are wholly dependent upon you for safe conduct throughout their universe careers, so now must you become wholly and unreservedly dependent upon your Paradise Father for safe conduct throughout the unrevealed vicissitudes of your ensuing mortal career. And when you shall have finished this bestowal experience, you will know in very truth the full meaning and the rich significance of that faith-trust which you so unvaryingly require all your creatures to master as a part of their intimate relationship with you as their local universe Creator and Father.

"Throughout your Earth bestowal you need be concerned with but one thing, the unbroken communion between you and your Paradise Father; and it will be by the perfection of such a relationship that the world of your bestowal, even all the universe of your creation, will behold a new and more understandable revelation of your Father and my Father, the Universal Father of all. Your concern, therefore, has only to do with your personal life on Earth. I will be fully and efficiently responsible for the security and unbroken administration of your universe from the moment of your voluntary relinquishment of authority until you return to us as Universe Sovereign, confirmed by Paradise, and receive back from my hands, not the vicegerent authority which you now surrender to me, but, instead, the supreme power over, and jurisdiction of, your universe.

Appendix A

"And that you may know with assurance that I am empowered to do all that I am now promising (knowing full well that I am the assurance of all Paradise for the faithful performance of my word), I announce to you that there has just been communicated to me a mandate of the Ancients of Days on Uversa which will prevent all spiritual jeopardy in Nebadon throughout the period of your voluntary bestowal. From the moment you surrender consciousness, upon the beginning of the mortal incarnation, until you return to us as supreme and unconditional sovereign of this universe of your own creation and organization, nothing of serious import can happen in all Nebadon. In this interim of your incarnation, I hold the orders of the Ancients of Days which unqualifiedly mandate the instantaneous and automatic extinction of any being guilty of rebellion or presuming to instigate insurrection in the universe of Nebadon while you are absent on this bestowal. My brother, in view of the authority of Paradise inherent in my presence and augmented by the judicial mandate of Uversa, your universe and all its loyal creatures will be secure during your bestowal. You may proceed upon your mission with but a single thought — the enhanced revelation of our Father to the intelligent beings of your universe.

"As in each of your previous bestowals, I would remind you that I am recipient of your universe jurisdiction as brother-trustee. I exercise all authority and wield all power in your name. I function as would our Paradise Father and in accordance with your explicit request that I thus act in your stead. And such being the fact, all this delegated authority is yours again to exercise at any moment you may see fit to requisition its return. Your bestowal is, throughout, wholly voluntary. As a mortal incarnate in the realm you are without celestial endowments, but all your relinquished power may be had at any time you may choose to reinvest yourself with universe authority. If you should choose to reinstate yourself in power and authority, remember, it will be wholly for *personal* reasons since I am the living and supreme pledge whose presence and promise guarantee the safe administration of your universe in accordance with your Father's will. Rebellion, such as has three times occurred in Nebadon, cannot occur during your absence from Salvington on this bestowal. For the period of the Earth bestowal the Ancients of Days have decreed that rebellion in Nebadon shall be invested with the automatic seed of its own annihilation.

"As long as you are absent on this final and extraordinary bestowal, I pledge (with Gabriel's co-operation) the faithful administration of your universe; and as I commission you to undertake this ministry of divine revelation and to undergo this experience of perfected human understanding, I act in behalf of my Father and your Father and offer you the following counsel, which should guide you in the living of your earth life as you become progressively self-conscious regarding the divine mission of your continued sojourn in the flesh:

Appendix A

"1. In accordance with the usages and in conformity with the technique of Sonarington — in compliance with the mandates of the Eternal Son of Paradise — I have provided in every way for your immediate entrance upon this mortal bestowal in harmony with the plans formulated by you and placed in my keeping by Gabriel. You will grow up on Earth as a child of the realm, complete your human education — all the while subject to the will of your Paradise Father — live your life on Earth as you have determined, terminate your planetary sojourn, and prepare for ascension to your Father to receive from him the supreme sovereignty of your universe.

"2. Apart from your earth mission and your universe revelation, but incidental to both, I counsel that you assume, after you are sufficiently self-conscious of your divine identity, the additional task of technically terminating the Lucifer rebellion in the system of Satania, and that you do all this as the *Son of Man;* thus, as a mortal creature of the realm, in weakness made powerful by faith-submission to the will of your Father, I suggest that you graciously achieve all you have repeatedly declined arbitrarily to accomplish by power and might when you were so endowed at the time of the inception of this sinful and unjustified rebellion. I would regard it as a fitting climax of your mortal bestowal if you should return to us as the Son of Man, Planetary Prince of Earth, as well as the Son of God, supreme sovereign of your universe. As a mortal man, the lowest type of intelligent creature in Nebadon, meet and adjudicate the blasphemous pretensions of Caligastia and Lucifer and, in your assumed humble estate, forever end the shameful misrepresentations of these fallen children of light. Having steadfastly declined to discredit these rebels through the exercise of your creator prerogatives, now it would be fitting that you should, in the likeness of the lowest creatures of your creation, wrest dominion from the hands of these fallen Sons; and so would your whole local universe in all fairness clearly and forever recognize the justice of your doing in the role of mortal flesh those things which mercy admonished you not to do by the power of arbitrary authority. And having thus by your bestowal established the possibility of the sovereignty of the Supreme in Nebadon, you will in effect have brought to a close the unadjudicated affairs of all preceding insurrections, notwithstanding the greater or lesser time lag involved in the realization of this achievement. By this act the pending dissensions of your universe will be in substance liquidated. And with the subsequent endowment of supreme sovereignty over your universe, similar challenges to your authority can never recur in any part of your great personal creation.

Appendix A

"3. When you have succeeded in terminating the Earth secession, as you undoubtedly will, I counsel you to accept from Gabriel the conference of the title of 'Planetary Prince of Earth' as the eternal recognition by your universe of your final bestowal experience; and that you further do any and all things, consistent with the purport of your bestowal, to atone for the sorrow and confusion brought upon Earth by the Caligastia betrayal and the subsequent Adamic default.

"4. In accordance with your request, Gabriel and all concerned will co-operate with you in the expressed desire to end your Earth bestowal with the pronouncement of a dispensational judgment of the realm, accompanied by the termination of an age, the resurrection of the sleeping mortal survivors, and the establishment of the dispensation of the bestowed Spirit of Truth.

"5. As concerns the planet of your bestowal and the immediate generation of men living thereon at the time of your mortal sojourn, I counsel you to function largely in the role of a teacher. Give attention, first, to the liberation and inspiration of man's spiritual nature. Next, illuminate the darkened human intellect, heal the souls of men, and emancipate their minds from age-old fears. And then, in accordance with your mortal wisdom, minister to the physical well-being and material comfort of your brothers in the flesh. Live the ideal religious life for the inspiration and edification of all your universe.

"6. On the planet of your bestowal, set rebellion-segregated man spiritually free. On Earth, make a further contribution to the sovereignty of the Supreme, thus extending the establishment of this sovereignty throughout the broad domains of your personal creation. In this, your material bestowal in the likeness of the flesh, you are about to experience the final enlightenment of a time-space Creator, the dual experience of working within the nature of man with the will of your Paradise Father. In your temporal life the will of the finite creature and the will of the infinite Creator are to become as one, even as they are also uniting in the evolving Deity of the Supreme Being. Pour out upon the planet of your bestowal the Spirit of Truth and thus make all normal mortals on that isolated sphere immediately and fully accessible to the ministry of the segregated presence of our Paradise Father, the Thought Adjusters of the realms.

"7. In all that you may perform on the world of your bestowal, bear constantly in mind that you are living a life for the instruction and edification of all your universe. You are *bestowing* this life of mortal incarnation upon Earth, but you are to *live* such a life for the spiritual inspiration of every human and superhuman intelligence that has lived, now exists, or may yet live on every inhabited world which has formed, now forms, or may yet form a part of the vast galaxy of your administrative domain. Your earth life in the likeness of mortal flesh shall not be so lived as to constitute an *example* for the mortals of Earth in the days of your earthly sojourn nor for any subsequent generation of human beings on Earth or on any other world. Rather shall your life in the flesh on Earth be the *inspiration* for all lives upon all Nebadon worlds throughout all generations in the ages to come.

"8. Your great mission to be realized and experienced in the mortal incarnation is embraced in your decision to live a life wholeheartedly motivated to do the will of your Paradise Father, thus to *reveal God,* your Father, in the flesh and especially to the creatures of the flesh. At the same time you will also *interpret,* with a new enhancement, our Father, to the supermortal beings of all Nebadon. Equally with this ministry of new revelation and augmented interpretation of the Paradise Father to the human and the superhuman type of mind, you will also so function as to make a new revelation of man to God. Exhibit in your one short life in the flesh, as it has never before been seen in all Nebadon, the transcendent possibilities attainable by a God-knowing human during the short career of mortal existence, and make a new and illuminating *interpretation* of man and the vicissitudes of his planetary life to all the superhuman intelligences of all Nebadon, and for all time. You are to go down to Earth in the likeness of mortal flesh, and living as a man in your day and generation, you will so function as to show your entire universe the ideal of perfected technique in the supreme engagement of the affairs of your vast creation: The achievement of God seeking man and finding him and the phenomenon of man seeking God and finding him; and doing all of this to mutual satisfaction and doing it during one short lifetime in the flesh.

"9. I caution you ever to bear in mind that, while in fact you are to become an ordinary human of the realm, in potential you will remain a Creator Son of the Paradise Father. Throughout this incarnation, although you will live and act as a Son of Man, the creative attributes of your personal divinity will follow you from Salvington to Earth. It will ever be within your power-of-will to terminate the incarnation at any moment subsequent to the arrival of your Thought Adjuster. Prior to the arrival and reception of the Adjuster I will vouch for your personality integrity. But subsequent to the arrival of your Adjuster and concomitant with your progressive recognition of the nature and import of your bestowal mission, you should refrain from the formulation of any superhuman will-to-attainment, achievement, or power in view of the fact that your creator prerogatives will remain associated with your mortal personality because of the inseparability of these attributes from your personal presence. But no superhuman repercussions will attend your earthly career apart from the will of the Paradise Father unless you should, by an act of conscious and deliberate will, make an undivided decision which would terminate in whole-personality choice.

"And now, my brother, in taking leave of you as you prepare to depart for Earth and after counseling you regarding the general conduct of your bestowal, allow me to present certain advices that have been arrived at in consultation with Gabriel, and which concern minor phases of your mortal life. We further suggest:

"1. That, in the pursuit of the ideal of your mortal earth life, you also give some attention to the realization and exemplification of some things practical and immediately helpful to your fellow mortals.

"2. As concerns family relationships, give precedence to the accepted customs of family life as you find them established in the day and generation of your bestowal. Live your family and community life in accordance with the practices of the people among whom you have elected to appear.

"3. In your relations to the social order we advise that you confine your efforts largely to spiritual regeneration and intellectual emancipation. Avoid all entanglements with the economic structure and the political commitments of your day. More especially devote yourself to living the ideal religious life on Earth.

"4. Under no circumstances and not even in the least detail, should you interfere with the normal and orderly progressive evolution of the Earth races. But this prohibition must not be interpreted as limiting your efforts to leave behind you on Earth an enduring and improved system of *positive religious ethics*. As a dispensational Son you are granted certain privileges pertaining to the advancement of the *spiritual* and *religious* status of the world peoples.

"5. As you may see fit, you are to identify yourself with existing religious and spiritual movements as they may be found on Earth but in every possible manner seek to avoid the formal establishment of an organized cult, a crystallized religion, or a segregated ethical grouping of mortal beings. Your life and teachings are to become the common heritage of all religions and all peoples.

"6. To the end that you may not unnecessarily contribute to the creation of subsequent stereotyped systems of Earth religious beliefs or other types of nonprogressive religious loyalties, we advise you still further: Leave no writings behind you on the planet. Refrain from all writing upon permanent materials; enjoin your associates to make no images or other likenesses of yourself in the flesh. See that nothing potentially idolatrous is left on the planet at the time of your departure.

"7. While you will live the normal and average social life of the planet, being a normal individual of the male sex, you will probably not enter the marriage relation, which relation would be wholly honorable and consistent with your bestowal; but I must remind you that one of the incarnation mandates of Sonarington forbids the leaving of human offspring behind on any planet by a bestowal Son of Paradise origin.

"8. In all other details of your oncoming bestowal we would commit you to the leading of the indwelling Adjuster, the teaching of the ever-present divine spirit of human guidance, and the reason-judgment of your expanding human mind of hereditary endowment. Such an association of creature and Creator attributes will enable you to live for us the perfect life of man on the planetary spheres, not necessarily perfect as regarded by any one man in any one generation on any one world (much less on Earth) but wholly and supremely replete as evaluated on the more highly perfected and perfecting worlds of your far-flung universe.

"And now, may your Father and my Father, who has ever sustained us in all past performances, guide and sustain you and be with you from the moment you leave us and achieve the surrender of your consciousness of personality, throughout your gradual return to recognition of your divine identity incarnate in human form, and then on through the whole of your bestowal experience on Earth until your deliverance from the flesh and your ascension to our Father's right hand of sovereignty. When I shall again see you on Salvington, we shall welcome your return to us as the supreme and unconditional sovereign of this universe of your own making, serving, and completed understanding.

"In your stead I now reign. I assume jurisdiction of all Nebadon as acting sovereign during the interim of your seventh and mortal bestowal on Earth. And to you, Gabriel, I commit the safekeeping of the Son of Man about-to-be until he shall presently and in power and glory be returned to me as the Son of Man and the Son of God. And, Gabriel, I am your sovereign until Michael thus returns."

CONTENTS

Part Two

Appendix B

Contents Part Two Cont.

Appendix B

CONTENTS

PART THREE

Give a Gift to Loved Ones, Friends, and Colleagues That Can Change Their Lives.

CHECK YOUR LEADING BOOKSTORE OR ORDER HERE

Yes I want additional copies of The Greatest Story Ever Revealed. Please send the following number of copies:

__ Part One @ $12.99 each
__ Part Two @ $16.99 each
__ Part Three @ $12.99 each
__ Boxed Set @ $39.99 each

Shipping and handling $4.00 for first book or set plus $2.00 for each additional book or set.

My check or Money Order for $_____ is enclosed.

Please charge my _Visa _MC _Discover _ AMEX Credit card.

Name _____

Organization _____

Address _____

City/State/Zip _____

Card#_____exp_____

Signature_____

Please make your check payable and mail to:
Hart_Burn Press
PO Box 99
Newton Jct, NH 03859-0099
Fax: 603-382-8794 Email: info@stevehartbooks.com

"The doctrines which flowed from the lips of Jesus himself are within the grasp of a child; but thousands of volumes have not yet explained the Platonisms engrafted on them."

-Thomas Jefferson